LIFE AFTER DEATH

A Guardsman's Tale

James Paul Watson

ISBN's:
Paperback: 978-1-80227-118-8
eBook: 978-1-80227-119-5
Hardback: 978-1-80227-120-1

Contents

Acknowledgments

I would like to thank my wife, Jayne, who has supported me throughout this journey and throughout my ongoing struggle with my own mental health. Without her, I would be truly lost.

Additionally, I would like to thank all of the veterans, soldiers and their families who have participated in this project. Many of these would like to remain nameless due to the stigma that is regrettably still associated with poor mental health, which is something that we must overcome.

Introduction

As a child, I was always fascinated by the concept of superheroes, the ongoing battle of good versus evil, superpowers, amazing gadgets, different personas, and secret identities! This concept transcended with me into adulthood and helped me mould my own persona as a soldier. As a soldier, my uniform was my armour and whilst in uniform, I would act and feel differently than how I would without it. This was evident in the late summer of 2003, when I was driving through London towards Wellington Barracks. It was the early hours of the morning when I witnessed a brawl across the street. I suddenly felt a tightness across my chest and began to become nauseous. I was having trouble focusing my vision whilst driving my car but was too afraid to stop. For the first time in my adult life, I was feeling genuine fear – this feeling was overwhelming; I was having a panic attack! I was 24 years old, a section commander in the British Army, an infantry man who had completed three operational tours of duty and a few months earlier I was leading my men to war in Iraq; now, I felt naked and vulnerable without them. I was afraid. Where was my uniform? Where was my armour?

It would be over a decade later until I experienced these horrendously painful feelings again and it was no coincidence that it happened at the same time as ISIS was invading parts of Iraq. However, along with the anxiety and panic attacks, I was now also experiencing bad dreams, nightmares, and flashbacks! I would experience heat and smells from blasts and would wake up disorientated and confused. It was June 2015; I was still a serving soldier, but at this point, not for much longer. I was due to be medically discharged in the August as the result of a spinal injury sustained in Afghanistan several years earlier. I was fortunate to be self-aware of the symptoms of Post-Traumatic Stress Disorder (PTSD), in myself and immediately sought help from the very institution that was accountable for them to begin with. However, I was left woefully and bitterly disappointed with the treatment that I would initially receive.

I had previously been trained and appointed as a Unit Welfare Officer and had witnessed how the early untreated symptoms of PTSD could quickly manifest out of control. I was very conscious of this, and I was determined for the sake of my family that this would not happen to me. Regrettably, I was mistaken. By the time I saw a military therapist, I had less than 6 weeks left of my 20 years' service to complete. I was transitioning to civilian life at a personal recovery unit, having recently undergone spinal surgery for the third time in three years. Despite this, I got the impression that there was no long-term plan, let alone any continuity with future mental health providers to treat my deteriorating mental health, or spinal injury for that matter. After two brief sessions with a therapist, I was informed that I was managing extremely well and that my training and experiences as a former Welfare Officer would sustain me in the future. Regrettably, this was not the case as, like most soldiers suffering with battlefield trauma, it takes a tremendous amount of courage to initially seek help. Additionally, to be told that I had the tools to manage my mental health myself would only further exacerbate my underlying trauma. In hindsight, the Army simply wanted me off their books. I was someone else's problem now.

For the following two years, I felt like a pressure cooker that could blow at any moment and was fearful as I didn't know what the trigger may be. I kept comforting myself, telling myself that I was in control as I couldn't understand why I was so angry all the time! Eventually, on the 22 May 2017, I inevitably blew! The trigger was the terror attack on the Ariana Grande concert at the Manchester Arena where 800 people were injured and 22 people, including children, died. I automatically felt responsible for this unspeakable act of terror on several irrational subconscious levels, but why?

Three months prior, I had taken my daughter to watch the 'Marvel Live' show at this very arena and had spoken to my wife afterwards about how concerned I was about the exiting policy of the spectators from the venue. I had explained to her that the way the spectators exited from the show towards the heavily confined exits established the perfect conditions for a terrorist attack. At the time, I thought that I was being paranoid as I almost had a panic attack myself whilst exiting the Manchester Arena. I secretly knew that I was still suffering with my own mental health but was too ashamed to admit it. After the attack, I didn't sleep for 3 days and I blamed myself for not doing something to prevent it. My subconscious was screaming "this attack was your fault; you are to blame." Later, to further vindicate personal blame, I would also irrationally conclude that I was solely responsible for this atrocity, as a consequence of my actions and decisions throughout the 2003 War in Iraq. I was suppressing guilt and trauma that had manifested into irrational thoughts to the point of almost self-loathing that was significantly linked to my military service.

I understand now that I was subconsciously punishing myself as a result of the trauma of warfare, not just from the 2003 War in Iraq but also from the liberation of Kosovo in 1999, and the genocide that I witnessed first-hand there. Only after seeking help was I then able to understand why I was feeling this way. As an Infantry soldier, I had been hardened to ignore pain and to suppress my emotions through behavioural training and conditioning, and this alone has long-term harmful effects. There are days when I still have trouble managing my PTSD, as part of the guilt that has haunted me for over 20 years still remains.

Soldiers have a strict code of military values and standards instilled into them and, as such, justify the horrors of war and their experiences through a righteous warranted lens, but once that lens is removed, how does one morally justify such actions? How does a veteran live with themselves if they are not just? This is the story of that lost generation, a generation that feels abandoned by society, rejected, along with our triumphs, struggles and ongoing psychological battles within ourselves. This is a personal account of how the modern soldier lives with warfare and the hidden scars that they, unfortunately, must carry with them every day; this is a Guardsman's tale!

Chapter 1.
Know the Boy – Understand the Man

'Pain is weakness! Emotions are weakness!' These are some of the phrases that were once screamed at British Army soldiers whilst they were participating in arduous training exercises such as 'bayonet fighting'. You are taught to block out your emotions, to fight through and go beyond what you believed was physically possible and to ignore pain. Then, if you cannot successfully achieve this level of emotional and physical numbness, you are unreservedly deemed as being weak and weeded out!

So, I ask the question - why is this type of training important and what (if any) are the lasting psychological effects? The answer is a simple one; the British Army requires its soldiers to act and feel like machines and this is achieved through behavioural psychological training. Warfare is a brutal and unforgiving environment where soldiers are required to kill other human beings without question, hesitation, or any conscious thought, for that matter. You are rigorously drilled to react, almost as if programmed. Yes, this made us, man for man, the best army in the world, but what was the psychological aftermath for not only those who went through this rigorous psychological training, but also those who had to implement it throughout two decades of persistent warfare?

The British Army tends to focus their training methods on lessons learned from the most recent wars or conflicts. In my case, my training was primarily derived from the brutal attrition battles that occurred in the Falklands War and also the counter-terrorist lessons learned from the troubles in Northern Ireland. My generation would use these lessons as a platform to prepare us for twenty years of constant deployments; in my case, I would be deployed on six operational tours of duty within a fourteen-year period that would ultimately see me injured in Afghanistan.

After being medically discharged from the British Army in 2015 as a result of a spinal injury, I gradually began to become actively involved within the injured veterans' community in Greater Manchester. It was mainly through my involvement with charities such as Help for Heroes, SSAFA and the Royal British Legion that I got the impression that this huge veterans' community was not being represented and was, subsequently, being silenced and ignored. Veterans would inform me of their struggles with their ongoing medical care from either their physical or mental injuries, and, more often, both. They would complain about their daily struggles due to the lack of support and continuation of the medical care that they were receiving; after all, let us not forget that these veterans' groups are funded by charities and not the Government that had sent them to war! This made me question what the Government and politicians actually did to support our veterans? Apart from publicly laying a wreath once a year at Remembrance, what do they actually do? Where is the support?

Initially, I found I almost resented this situation and chose to ignore their stories as this was not the post-military life and future that I had envisaged for my family and myself. The majority of these veterans had become extremely bitter and disillusioned over time due to their poor aftercare and, as such, had become to regret their service. I was still a proud soldier at this point, clinging onto the identity and purpose that the British Army had moulded me into throughout the past two decades. I refused to contemplate their outlook as I didn't want that same mindset to engulf me over time. Looking back, I knew that I had underlying mental health issues and I subconsciously acknowledged that once I let go of my military identity, let go of Colour Sergeant Watson, that I would face a new battle, not against a foreign army but one within myself. Therefore, I chose to ignore their screams for help and stood firm on the more palpable narrative that the Ministry of Defence is loyal to its soldiers and the veterans' community.

I had never been fascinated by politics and didn't particularly agree with either of the main national political parties. I had voted Labour in my early years, but as I grew older, got married, had started a family, and had a mortgage, my voting trends favoured more towards the Conservative Party. I was a swing voter who would vote on what I believed was best for the country at that particular time. In the veterans' community, I had heard the first-hand shocking stories concerning far too many veterans and their treatment and frequent failures when challenging the Government regarding their aftercare. Regardless of the political spectrum, the very institutions of both our local and national Government were failing our veterans and, as a result of this, the relationship between the two had become fragmented. Our veterans, my brethren, were failing because the political system didn't understand their needs and concerns; nor did they want to for that matter. Veteran suicide rates were going through the roof and our veterans were being publicly persecuted from historic allegations from Northern Ireland to the more frequent conflicts in Iraq and Afghanistan. It was due to this lack of representation that I decided to get involved in local politics. My intention was to become a local councillor so that I could represent this community and, if elected, my aim was to simply help one veteran – to save one life and to make that small difference.

Once elected, I immediately raised my concerns about the ongoing pandemic of veteran's suicide and the lack of mental health support that was available. This new position as a local politician allowed me to make immediate and substantial change by raising awareness to support local veterans who were struggling with their mental health.[i] Within my first year as a local councillor, I had achieved my initial aim, but this was not job done! One local veteran, who was suffering with severe Post Traumatic Stress Disorder (PTSD), informed me that I had prevented him from taking his own life by just being there for him and simply listening to his concerns.

It was this new appointment that allowed me to influence Wigan Borough's Health and Social Care Scrutiny Committee to annually review our Armed Forces community. From an annual report in Feb 2021,[ii] from the strategic manager for Wigan's Armed Forces, one particular point stuck with me. From this local study, in 60% of all veterans diagnosed with PTSD, their battlefield trauma was associated with childhood events. This got me thinking about my own continuous battles with my mental health and the therapy that I had received. My therapist was constantly probing into my childhood, which, at the time, I didn't understand. I was aware that growing up, I had a troublesome and neglected childhood, but I never really delved into it because, in my perspective, it was normal and I just accepted it. I suppose if you know the boy, you will gain a better understanding about the man, so, subsequently, that is where we must begin.

I am told that on the day I was born, it was a cold, grey and depressing Tuesday evening in late 1978, a typical winter's night in northern England. My mother would often joke about how red I was when she gave birth as she was convinced that it was due to her heavy appetite for rum throughout the pregnancy! I was the third of six siblings from a devotedly Irish background which categorically specified that I would be raised as a staunch Roman Catholic. Quite ironic, really, considering that four of us were conceived out of wedlock to different fathers. As a baby, I contracted meningitis and was admitted to intensive care. I was read my last rights by a priest as I was not expected to make it through the night. Everyone had given up on me, doctors, religion and even my family; they were preparing for the inevitable - my immediate death. Spoiler alert, I survived! I suppose even as a baby I was defiant and didn't respond well to authority and being told what to do. This characteristic trait would remain with me throughout my childhood and military career and would heavily influence some of my life-changing events.

Even as a child, I had never fully committed to the concept of religion as it seemed forced upon me by my parents as it had inevitably been forced upon them beforehand. Despite attending church every week and even becoming an altar boy for a short time, my home life contradicted every teaching within the Bible. Then, in the summer of 1999, I turned my back on religion for good as a direct consequence of personally witnessing the ethnic cleansing that had occurred in what would eventually be known as the country of Kosovo. Even to this day, I have trouble comprehending what had occurred in Kosovo, how one group of people could conduct such atrocities on each other because of different ethnicities and religion. Furthermore, the main instigators had been the Serbian Christians which made me question what little faith I had left. Whilst serving, I observed that religion was a convenient commodity for many soldiers, with many seeking out the 'Lord' in times of reassurance, which, more often than not, coincided with dangerous operational tours. This was their prerogative, of course, but I personally found this to be quite the paradox.

My early childhood had consisted of both mental and physical abuse that were the direct consequence of my parents' drug and alcohol misuse. My upbringing was quite a simple one of neglect and abandonment which, if I am being completely honest, would rationalise my dependency as an adult towards not just being part of the British Army, but my drive to being successful within it, regardless of the cost. As a small boy, it was not uncommon to be left alone for long periods without food or attention. Then, there were the physical beatings that were a regular occurrence from both my mother and father, and they got quite creative, ranging from belts to slippers or whatever was closest at hand. As a result of these beatings, I have many scars and burns but I have no memory of how they came into existence. Frequently, this was blanket punishment; if one of us did something wrong then we all shared the punishment. It was no surprise that I eventually concluded that if I was going to get punished irrespectively, then I may as well have committed the wrongdoing. Bearing this in mind, it would come as no surprise that I became quite troublesome, and, more often than not, used violence to expel my frustrations as a teenager.

Whilst growing up in 1980's Britain, there was a persistent prejudice towards the Irish community due to the ongoing bombing campaign by the Provisional Irish Republican Army (IRA). The IRA were constantly attacking the military with the Chelsea Barracks and

Hyde Park bombings being the most significant of my early childhood memories. Serving personnel were an easy target and then there was the potential assassination of the Prime Minister and her cabinet at the Conservative Party conference at the Grand Brighton hotel on 12 October 1984 to contemplate. These bombings by the IRA would establish a deep hatred and prejudice towards the Irish community in Britain. I would often be bullied and ridiculed due to my Irish heritage and was encouraged by my father that regardless of how many they were or how old, I had to fight for family and Irish honour.

Over the years and due to this inexcusable advice, I would like to think that I won more than I lost because if my father ever got wind that I lost a fight, then a more severe beating waited for me at home. At times, I frequently sought out conflict as a means to get my father's attention and, in a peculiar way, to try and make him proud. Ironically, I spent a summer throughout this period on a family farm in Sligo in Ireland and found myself fighting almost on a daily basis because I was, quite frankly, English. It was evident that I wasn't accepted by either community due to my Irish blood and English heart! In today's politically correct society, this would not have been tolerated but in the 1980s it was just accepted. Now, as a proud father myself reflecting back on this period of my childhood, I have trouble understanding why my father remained in the UK as he had such love and passion for Ireland. Why didn't he simply move back to Dublin as he never appeared to have any love or passion for Britain, let alone his family? My father died over a decade ago; needless to say, no tears were shed, and I didn't even attend the funeral, let alone grieve. There was no love lost there once I was old enough to understand what a shocking father and appalling role model he actually was.

My only outlet as a child was school. This was escapism where I could be a completely different person from the scoundrel that I had become at home. My Irish heritage was rarely the topic of conversation as my Primary Schools were always Roman Catholic which meant many Irish families attended. The reason that I say schools as a plural is down to the fact that my father would frequently beat my mother so badly that she would leave him in the middle of the night and we would move into a shelter before eventually being relocated in a new area. Then, routinely, once we were settled, like clockwork, my parents would make up and the cycle would inevitably repeat itself. I attended so many schools as a child that I honestly couldn't recite them if I tried. This destructive cycle would culminate in both my parents being imprisoned at the same time. I suppose that this was the trigger for social services to become involved and would eventually result in myself being admitted into a children's home.

My father was already serving a long-term jail sentence for assault at this point and this had left a void in my mother's life. One of her many flaws was that she always needed a man in her life, a man that she would always prioritise over her children. On one significant day, I recall that she had been out early, drinking with her current boyfriend, a man almost half her age. After the usual drunken argument and despite being heavily intoxicated, she had driven home but had hit a young girl with her car directly opposite our house. My mother was heavily under the influence of alcohol at the time and was a frequent drink driver. She had been banned from driving previously and had not learned her lesson. She then abandoned the scene, leaving this poor girl injured in the road, but not before parking up, entering the house and ordering me not to answer the door under any circumstances.

Hiding in plain sight was her ingenious plan! Within minutes, the police were banging on the door, and, like the loyal son I was, I didn't hesitate; I opened the door and pointed the police in the direction of my heavily intoxicated mother who was on the toilet at the time. One could say that she was literally caught with her pants down! I was appalled and ashamed by my mother's actions. I remember watching neighbours and passers-by help this girl lying helpless in the road and wanted my mother to acknowledge the consequences of her actions. As I watched the police arrest my mother, I was more concerned about the girl in the departing ambulance. I often wonder what injuries she sustained and how this incident affected her life. For my mother, she never showed any signs of guilt, or remorse for that matter, and I doubt that she ever will.

My mother would eventually be released early from her brief prison sentence due to the fact that she had children to 'take care of'. It wasn't long after that she got herself a new man and her inevitable cycle of self-destruction would start over. However, things had changed. I wasn't a small child anymore. I was an angry teenage boy who could challenge and be intimidating to my mother's partners. This would culminate in an ultimatum that I proposed to her, a decision that would indivertibly mould my future. In no uncertain terms, I had told her to choose between her partner or myself. I had blindly gone 'all in' in a life-changing poker game without even looking at my cards. I was certain that I had an unbeatable hand and that the winning pot would be the realisation that my mother should prioritise her children over whatever boyfriend she had at that particular time. Later that afternoon, I found myself bemused in the custody of social services and I never played poker again!

It was no surprise that I ended up in a children's home; my only astonishment was that it had taken social services this long! I did not do drugs and I wasn't a thief, but I was violent and had, by this point, already been expelled from two secondary schools for constant fighting. I had missed almost 2 years of schooling and my education appeared to be limited, but despite these setbacks, I always remained in most of the top sets when I was able to attend school. I had excelled at and enjoyed mathematics whilst at primary school and there was even the mention of grammar school at some point. However, within my family, no emphasis was ever put onto the value of education and I was often ridiculed for wanting to do well.

It's not that I didn't enjoy school, it was simply that all the moving around as a child had taken its toll; changing schools, making friends, getting settled, having routine, moving, losing friends then doing it all over again. Then, there is the fascination that surrounds the new kid at school. I was at that age where I knew that I was poor and was ashamed of my family, and it was my own insecurities that made me an easy target for bullies. The only difference was that I wouldn't take any crap and, by this point, enjoyed the thrill of the fight. So began the pattern of suspension after suspension before eventually being expelled.

After several evaluations, I was in due course sent to Ingledene Children's Home in Salford. My initial impression was that the place was a dump. The furniture was damaged, wall-mounted pictures smashed, and the floor and walls were ripped and full of stains. It was a mixed-sex home that dealt exclusively with secondary school kids. Entering a children's home is no different from entering a new school. There is a hierarchy in place amongst the established kids, a social structure, a balance of power that everyone understands and respects. I would eventually disregard this but not before I hit rock bottom.

My social worker had managed to pull some strings and get me accepted into one of the local schools on the sole provision that I wouldn't get into more trouble whilst attending. She was very precise that this was my last chance at an education, explaining unequivocally that under no circumstances was I to engage in any forms of fighting whilst at school. One week later, I was expelled! However, to this day, I would still argue that the fight didn't happen on school grounds, so technically, should I have been expelled? However, as I was wearing the school uniform at the time, I was still accountable. My social worker, as one can reasonably imagine, was pissed off at me and I can understand why. For the rest of the school year, I completed the occasional piece of work from home and had the usual end of year exams to sit. Surprisingly enough, I did reasonably well with little effort despite very little interest.

The only upside to being expelled (again), was that I was a hero within the children's home as I had gained a temporary cult status there. Even the older kids were impressed, some of them significantly older at 17 years old, and to gain their respect at that time of my life seemed important. The months quickly passed, and some kids moved on, the younger ones fostered or reunited with their families and the older ones progressing to a sixteen plus unit. Drugs were always being used by the majority of the other kids; they often attempted to peer-pressure me into taking them but unsuccessfully. I despised drugs as I had witnessed the damaging effects that they had on my family. In many ways, it was easy to be accepted by this group and, for a short time, I thought of them as my new family. At first glance, we had so much in common. We were all from similar backgrounds, had all been neglected or abused, some physically, some sexually and others both. They all gave the steadfast impression that they were all the toughest person in the room and, as such, were not to be trifled with. Challenge accepted!

Thieving was a common occurrence amongst the residents of Ingledene and this group would steal anything from anyone – there was no honour amongst these thieves. All of them smoked and took drugs, and for them, thieving was a means to an end. This was not fundamentally who I was, but I was desperate to fit in. I still refused the cigarettes and the drugs, but my short-lived cult status had expired and one of the older lads had recently discovered an unlocked and unguarded computer room at the neighbouring hospital. The plan was set, and I had agreed to take part, but only as the lookout. I wanted the slightest involvement possible, and it was in the early hours that we conducted our caper. I was oblivious and naive to what we were stealing, who we were selling it to and for how much. With less than fifteen minutes into my first criminal act, I had an epiphany. Despite my unconventional upbringing, I was aware that this was deeply and categorically wrong and that the path that I was on was a one-way street to prison. Something had to give.

Once I had abandoned my post and returned to Ingledene, I was aware that I would now be an outcast amongst the other kids. Although we shared so many similarities and experiences, at my core, I was different. I had a conscience and was unreservedly ashamed of what I had just participated in. I had anticipated that the other kids would be missing for a few days, revelling in the spoils of their criminality, but once they returned, I would have to face the consequences of my actions. My punishment came in many forms such as social exile, the theft of my clothes and personal items and the constant trashing of my room, but only the threats of being beaten up. This surprised me; why only threats? These were older kids, bigger than me - what were they waiting for?

It soon became apparent that these kids were only confident and aggressive when they were collectively together and if I wanted this torment to stop then the best solution would be to confront them individually, and that is exactly what I did. Lee was the oldest, by now sixteen years old and two years my senior. When passing the staff office, I carelessly informed the two members of staff who were sat casually drinking coffee, that I was going upstairs to move some furniture and that if they heard some bangs not to be alarmed. They secretly knew what was about to happen but didn't much care.

I recall kicking open the door to Lee's room and immediately saw a different side to him. He was afraid; terrified even. I had trained in martial arts from an early age and knew how to throw an effective punch but was surprised how effortlessly Lee was knocked to the ground. Lee was over 6ft tall but of a slender build, and during the previous months of hanging out and getting up to mischief, Lee had convinced me that he was a brutal fighter and had told many tales of his exploits. Now, the reality was that he was cowering and crying at my feet. I was confused; I hadn't expected this, so what do I do now? I kicked him in the stomach and informed him that things were going to change at Ingledene and for the better!

It didn't take long for the others to step into line as, at their heart, they were all cowards whether they wanted to believe it or not. The only ramification from my actions occurred a few weeks later in the hallway outside the staff offices in Ingledene. Lee was accompanied by another larger, stockier young man of around seventeen or eighteen years old. They were arguing, and it was getting heated until this bloke saw me. We made eye contact; everyone knew what this meant and what was about to happen. I charged rapidly at him, lunging low then high in a spear-type rugby tackle, knocking the wind out of him, then slamming him to the floor before repeatedly punching him with wild blows to the face. Lee abandoned his friend and ran off whilst the remaining two staff struggled to restrain me before Lee's so-called muscle also departed. Needless to say, I was never bothered at Ingledene again and I was about to make some productive changes.

Lee immediately requested to be moved to a sixteen plus, and once he had moved out, gradual changes were implemented. The staff explained to us all that being in a children's home could have many benefits. For a start, you get a gym pass, a clothing allowance as well as a cash allocation for weekly recreational activities, but only if you are well behaved, of course. I was always active as a kid and embraced the gym, played sports, and now studied karate at the local leisure centre. I persuaded the other kids not to damage Ingledene any more as this was our home and we had to live there. We gradually received new furniture, a pool table and the building was even redecorated. The residents gradually began to stop attacking the staff; however, some needed that little bit more persuasion than others. I look back fondly at these years, as, for the first time in my life, I was experiencing the much-needed stability and routine that I needed.

Ingledene provided me with a routine, no question. Mealtimes were rigid, we were routinely woken up for breakfast, had a curfew and fixed lights-out times. We had strict rules to follow and were rewarded for good behaviour although I did still occasionally break them. I was thriving inside this new environment and was even allowed back into Wentworth High School despite my previous violent acts. My social worker was a miracle worker and I was determined not to squander away this last chance at an education.

I returned to school mid-way through the fourth year of secondary school. I was no longer an angry frustrated young man as I finally had routine at home, albeit a children's home. I wasn't conscious of who I wanted to be but more so who I didn't want to be; in short, my parents. They would now become the motivation that I needed to succeed in life, but I was unsure of where I was going or what I wanted to achieve as adulthood loomed. Bizarrely, I was made a prefect at school, probably a first at Ingledene, and I achieved modest GCSE results with B grades in both maths and English. However, school was over, and I would soon be seventeen and wouldn't be able to stay at Ingledene for much longer.

Once I had finished my limited schooling, the next transition in the care system was to move to a sheltered sixteen plus unit and I knew that, from the outset, this wasn't the place for me. These were generally unsupervised bedsits where vulnerable young adults were exploited, and I knew that this was not the environment that I wanted to live in. The manager of Ingledene was a mountain of a man, a former prop forward for Widnes and he would heavily influence my career choices. We would often play chess together and he would fondly speak about his own son who was flourishing in the British Army. Maybe this was his way of planting a subliminal seed and I'm sure that he was happy when I decided that I was going to apply to sign up and follow in his own son's footsteps.

Whilst writing this chapter and reflecting back on some of my childhood experiences, I believe that I was very fortunate to be self-aware of my own actions whilst in my teenage years. It was this ability to analyse one's own actions that prevented me from slipping into a life of criminality. This ability would also be instrumental when self-analysing my actions throughout my military journey, then later on, by helping me acknowledge the symptoms of battlefield trauma within myself. Maybe this was a contributing factor that also led to, and subsequently fed on, my own deteriorating mental health, as from its very inception, I would often beat myself up about my failed actions or sometimes inaction. I would repetitively ask myself the questions, could I have done more? Should I have done more? More often than not, it felt like I was carrying the weight of the nation on my shoulders and at times, I genuinely believed that I was solely accountable for all military actions, but was this linked to childhood trauma?

Research has found that soldiers, particularly those who are minors and those from disadvantaged backgrounds, are more susceptible to the risk of some mental health problems than their adult counterparts. Those from adverse backgrounds were up to four times more likely to suffer with their mental health later on in life and from a 2016 study, it is argued that this is due to the development of parts other than cognitive in the brain throughout adolescence. [iii] I do acknowledge that there is some truth that links military PTSD to childhood trauma but in my circumstances, I do not feel that that is the case.

Whilst undergoing several different therapies to treat my own psychological trauma, I found that Acceptance and Commitment Therapy (ACT) was the most effective. I believe that this was because even as a child, I had accepted the trauma I had experienced instead of suppressing those memories. It was normal to be beaten on a regular basis by your parents, especially if you were troublesome like myself. However, despite this, one could quite easily conclude that it is the impact from your childhood experiences that moulds and determines your adult character and behavioural patterns. Therefore, childhood trauma would inevitably influence and sometimes determine your decisions later on in life. Nevertheless, I fundamentally disagree with the concept of what is categorised as a 'normal' childhood because, as a child, you have no control over the experiences and life lessons that effectively mould your character into adulthood. Thus, from a child's perspective, especially mine, all childhoods are normal.

Years later, whilst attending university, I would be introduced to the theory of social structures that essentially determines most of our adult characteristics, and, in most cases, sets the limits on our life opportunities. However, I would argue that the agency of individual actions is more definitive than the shackles of the social standings that we are born into. Thankfully, this book isn't about the social economic divide! (You're welcome). Having said that, it was my structure, a robust teenager from a council estate, streetwise, a scraper from a broken home who seemed to thrive in the British Army. It would be foolish not to highlight this relationship as it is no coincidence that there is a certain stereotype who are drawn into military service, more specifically the Infantry! In my circumstance, it was the romanticism that is associated with warfare that had attracted me to join the ranks of the British Army.

Chapter 2.
'Be Like Frank'

The romantic relationship between young men and warfare is as old as time itself, regardless of what the older generation may say to discourage them due to their own lived experiences. Young men will always seek out the soldier's adventure, some for glory, others for identity; for me, I simply had nowhere else to go! Let us not forget that warfare is continually celebrated throughout all cultures through mythology, history, religion, and even modern pop culture such as cinema. These countless tales are mostly focused on uncertain young men volunteering to go to war then becoming reluctant heroes in the process. They generally undergo trials and hardships, before almost always returning home as brave warriors and are paraded with medals. On return, they receive new-found fame, respect and most important of all, their new identity - the hero! This appealed to me and I wanted all of this.

I've never bought into the premise that we are all heroes in our own stories as this subjective outlook suggests that one is unable to commit any wrongdoings. I have always been a realist and was only too aware that even heroes have bad days and can make mistakes! Regardless of this, I was desperately seeking the heroes' journey and wanted the respect and more so, the identity that accompanied it, and the British Army, or more specifically, 'The Queens Guards' offered me this. Today, if you asked me the question, 'Do I perceive myself as a hero?' My response would be unequivocally no! I am now part of the lived generation that would discourage young men from joining the Armed Forces and this is regrettably as a result of my own detrimental experiences. I am no hero but did have the pleasure of working alongside many throughout my twenty-year military journey.

It is easy to associate and compare the institutional nature of a children's home to the institution of the British Army as they share many similarities, and this would be accurate. My seed was already planted for a career in the Army, but I was still unsure about the transition. The British Army recruiting adverts of the mid-1990s were focused around comradeship, extreme sports, global travel, and adventure under the marketing slogan 'Be like Frank.' I had thrived under the rigid conditions of being in an institution and wanted to continue to do well in the future, so the Army was an obvious choice; after all, I wanted to be like Frank.

It was no surprise that I was not the only soldier to successfully transition from a children's home into the Army and it was no coincidence that this was a frequent occurrence. I had unknowingly followed the recent footsteps of John Corcoran and Jim, both from Manchester, both from children's homes and both of whom had previously joined the Irish Guards. All three of us excelled in the military and we all revelled in the privileges and identity that was associated within the life of the Sergeants' Mess. I would serve closely on operations in Baghdad in Iraq with Jim, and in Kosovo, South Armagh, and Afghanistan with John. John would become one of my closest friends, the big brother I never had and would help guide me when I faced the many times of uncertainty and doubt. Unfortunately, John was haunted by the events of an insurgent ambush in Helmand Province, Afghanistan and would regrettably die from cancer a few years later. John's death left me devastated, knowing what he had survived on operations, then to be cruelly taken by cancer. I miss him daily; he was only 39 years old.

On entering the Army Careers Office, your job choices are very much made for you by the Recruiting Sergeant at the front desk. In my case, he was a Grenadier Guardsman. I recall how tall and methodical he was, and this, bizarrely, appealed to me as I craved structure. On completing the simplest of tests called the British Army Recruit Battery, or more commonly referred to as the BARB test, I was informed that I could apply for any career path, apart from officer training, of course, due to my humble background. Before going into the career's office, every adult I knew had advised me not to join the Infantry (cannon fodder), but to rather seek out an apprenticeship, a trade, a career that would be useful in later life. I had the option to train as an avionics technician, a carpenter, electrician or even a mechanic but I decided on the Infantry as I just wanted to fight, to be a hero; besides, I was a scrapper! At the time, I didn't see the reasoning in joining a fighting force to be a supporting logistical role, and let's not forget that I was heavily influenced by the Infantry recruiter, of course. Nowadays, I understand and appreciate the importance of all roles within the Armed Forces as one cannot function without the other. (But the Infantry is still the best!)

However, this bastard of a Sergeant pulled me to one side and told me that I was special and not in the 'I want to take you for a meal' kind of way. He quietly explained to me that he only recruits the best for the Grenadier Guards - proud Infantrymen with a dual role who also protect the Queen; I would become the Queen's personal bodyguard! My eyes sparkled with excitement and appreciation as he put on a video of Trooping the Colour. He had me hook, line, and sinker. I had never even been to London before and wow, that red tunic and bearskin! It was so iconic and seemed out of this world to me, immediately giving me a proud sense of identity. It was the Queen's Guards for me but only if they had an Irish Regiment, hence, I was recruited into the Irish Guards as I still wanted to make my family proud. Ironically, some years later, I would hold the same position of this Recruiting Sergeant and I would use the same technique to recruit gullible souls into the 'Guards,' having a private chuckle to myself every time this one-liner worked.

On hearing this news, my family had immediately raised their concerns about my application due to the very real threat of the IRA and their relentless attacks on British soldiers. I was conscious of this and was very concerned about being sent to Northern Ireland but thought to myself, 'what are the odds of that happening?' I remember being slightly conflicted, due to my strong Irish Roman Catholic upbringing, as some of my family despised the British Army. I was torn between my Irish heritage and English upbringing so joining the Irish Guards in the British Army ticked all the boxes for me. Years later, I would discover that an abandoned building on the family farm that I had spent my summers at in Ireland as a child, was once used as an IRA safe house shortly after the Easter Rising. The following year, I would be on foot patrol in South Armagh enforcing the border between Northern Ireland and the Republic of Ireland. Awkward Much!

I recall that I wasn't particularly phased by the army selection process. It was an overnight stay at a camp in Lichfield in the Midlands. This consisted of a medical, a military lesson and finally a fitness test before an interview the following morning. I came first out of my group on the 1.5 mile run with ease. I didn't put much effort in, if I am being honest, as I had always been a strong runner, but then again, I had to be. Growing up in 'Red' Salford, Manchester City fans were few and far between and I found myself running a lot!

At the final stage of the selection process was an interview. I can recall that the officer was attempting to poach me for his own regiment as he was impressed with my high levels of fitness. I still remember that he raised his concerns about my choice of selecting the Irish Guards over other Infantry Regiments as I was not particularly well dressed or smart. I was wearing a borrowed shirt and tie along with my school trousers and shoes which I had outgrown. In fact, the shoes were not even polished and were filthy, a point that was highlighted by this selection officer. He then mentioned my long hair and questioned my suitability for 'The Guards'. This was the mid-90s and Oasis mania was storming the nation. I was from Manchester, so I naturally had a Liam Gallagher bonnet and the unwavering attitude to suit. Reluctantly, the selection officer passed me despite being the scruffiest recruit there, and I was all set to join the Irish Guards.

The day was set, June 15, 1996 and I was apprehensive and having doubts about my decision to join the Army. Earlier that year, the IRA had bombed the London Docklands, killing two people in the process and this had raised some serious qualms. The weeks prior, I had already taken the 'Queen's shilling,' or £15, at my attestation where I had sworn allegiance to my Queen and Country. This money was meant to be used to buy toiletries for basic training, however my Recruiting Sergeant insisted that we celebrated my attestation at the pub opposite, The Shakespeare. Hence, my 'Queen's shilling' was spent indulging my recruiting Sergeant with ale, whilst I, sipping coke, listened, intrigued, to his 'war stories'.

The day had finally arrived, and I had mistakenly entrusted my travel warrant to my girlfriend at the time for safekeeping. She didn't want me to join the Army either and had conveniently lost my travel warrant to Brookwood Station in a desperate attempt to prevent me from leaving. I didn't have enough money for a replacement and began to panic. Desperately, I packed my bags and decided to travel to Piccadilly train station in the centre of Manchester; my plan was to explain my situation to the clerk at the ticket office, show them my enlistment papers and hopefully they could produce me a replacement ticket. If that failed, I would simply jump the train and my mind was made up; the Army was my ticket to a better life. However, getting to the station was the least of my problems! All of the roads were being shut off in and around the city centre. The police wouldn't tell us what was going on, apart from insisting that it was imperative for our own safety that we followed the diversions and under no circumstances should we enter the city centre; a coded bomb warning had been issued by the IRA!

I didn't listen to the police and eventually made my way through the roadblocks to about half a mile from the train station where I encountered a mob of police officers frantically running towards us! What were they running from, I wondered? Maybe, there was a bomb after all? The only road available to us to escape the city centre was conveniently pointed in the direction of my grandparents' house. They had always been good to me, but at times, distant and I was hopeful that they would pay for my train ticket. They were my last option; I was out of ideas! I was just over a mile past the outskirts of the city centre when the unthinkable happened in the form of the most deafening bang I had heard to date! The IRA had detonated a 3,300lb bomb, the second biggest in mainland Britain, which had just decimated Manchester City Centre. [iv]

Moments later, I eventually stopped at my grandparents' house, which is in Longsight, just over 1.5 miles from the city centre. Everybody was in their gardens looking up to the sky. Cars had stopped in the street and everyone was fixated on the large mushroom cloud that was now dominating the skyline. None of us could believe what had just happened, how close we were, or how lucky we had been. It wasn't fear I felt but rage! Manchester was my city, my home and this attack felt personal. I was now determined more than ever to join the ranks of the British Army to do my part in eradicating terrorism, but beforehand, I still needed some money for that train ticket!

I don't know if it was the shock of the bombing or that he just wanted rid of me, but my grandfather actually gave me some money for a replacement ticket. I found this strange as both my grandparents were Irish through and through and had no love for the British Army. My family, my girlfriend and, it would seem, even the IRA had reservations about me joining the British Army, but this had made me more determined than ever. I eventually was able to catch a later train from Stockport to London Euston Station, navigate through the London Underground, then eventually find my way to Brookwood Station and then finally to Pirbright Camp. I had made it to basic training!

To get to basic training, to say the least, had been a struggle. However, I had arrived late due to the IRA bombing and may or may not have had a few cans of beer on the train on the way. I clearly remember that the remainder of the other recruits were already in a lesson in the accommodation block when I eventually arrived. They were all dressed in green boiler suits and all looked very depressed, probably regretting their poor life choices that had led them here. It was in basic training that I became friends with Niall, a Southern Irish man from Cork. Niall was 25 years old when he had joined up, but despite the age gap, we instantly became friends. He would give me the short-lived nickname of 'Top Manc,' as at the time, everything in Mancunian terminology was 'top!' Top one, it's on top, that's a top jacket, etc.

Niall often jokes about my dramatic entrance, claiming that I bounced through the doors with northern swagger and attitude which I find hard to believe. Everyone else had arrived on time and wearing a suit; I didn't own a suit, nor could I afford one for that matter but instead, opted for shorts, my Manchester City football shirt, rucksack casually hanging from my shoulders, with accompanying football boots dangling from the straps, of course. It was summer after all and I wanted to be 'like Frank!' Let us not forget that my Recruiting Sergeant had sold the Army on the promise of sport and adventure, however, in training, this couldn't be further away from the truth!

For some strange reason, my stylish entrance had enraged the Sergeants who insisted on using my abs as a punch bag for a few rounds. I must point out that this was a bit of banter and after this rather formal introduction, I quickly got dressed in my green boiler suit and joined the rest of the platoon with a depressed look, contemplating and regretting my own choice as to why I had joined the British Army. Pirbright was where the Guards Division broke in and indoctrinated their new recruits; this process had been perfected over the generations and we would be no different. Behavioural training methods and military conditioning had been perfected from the lessons learned from the Second World War and were further reinforced from the recent lessons of the violent close-quarter fighting that occurred in the 1982 Falklands War.

Recruit training is designed to strip civilians of their previous identity and turn them into soldiers. This begins immediately by removing all of their civilian clothing and items with the aim to segregate the individual from their previous identity. For up to six months, every day is mapped out for them and recruits are told when to eat, sleep and shit and this forms the foundations of a co-dependency through routine. You are constantly shouted at and you instantly form a shared dislike towards your training Sergeants and Corporals. Unknowingly, this helps to build the foundation of military teamwork through this common ground. This process subconsciously establishes a strong bond between recruits through their shared hardships and often-difficult experiences. Years later, if two veterans meet up who were in training together, there is an unwritten mutual respect and bond between them that is unbreakable.

Next comes the standard recruit haircut. I had already prepared myself for recruit training by shaving my 'top' Mancunian bonnet after receiving the negative comments from my selection officer. I vividly remember watching the attitude, fight, confidence, and resolve drain out of my fellow recruits as the military barber shaved off their distinctive and individual hairstyles. Oddly enough, I still had to sit in the barber's chair and go through the process despite already having a short number 2 and unfairly, still had to pay for the privilege. Within 24 hours of this shock of capture, we were all shadows of our civilian selves as our previous identities were stripped from us.

In 1996, basic training consisted of six main military lessons that you were required to master within a cramped ten-week period in order to successfully 'pass out'. Phase 2 training for the Infantry was at the Infantry Training Centre (ITC) at Catterick, in North Yorkshire. This consisted of a further 17 weeks of tactical and platoon weapon training before we would finally progress onto our relevant Regiments as proud trained Guardsmen. Military training was a sausage factory with a high failure and dropout rate, with new platoons of recruits starting every 2-4 weeks.

I must point out that every subject had tests that recruits were required to pass in order to progress. If anyone failed one or was injured, those recruits would frequently be 'back-squadded'. This process was where recruits required remedial training and were placed in a junior platoon. More often than not, this was just two weeks, and although there was no shame in needing more time in mastering a new skill set, being 'back-squadded' was perceived as failure and weakness. Many of those who were 'back-squadded' left the Army due to this unproductive mindset. 'Back-Squadding' was also often used as a tool to motivate under-par recruits. I experienced this as I was often reminded that my attitude was always under par. I was even threatened with the prospect of being 'back-squadded' after asking a question regarding our flamethrower training. How was I to know that flamethrowers were now banned under the Geneva Convention?

Initially, there was foot and rifle drill to master. The main aim of drill, if memory recalls, is, 'to produce a soldier that is smart, alert and obedient.' I must point out the phrasing of the words 'alert' and 'obedient' as this is not necessarily terminology associated with human behaviour but more so on how one would train a dog. Drill is the embodiment of military discipline and recruits are rigorously marched around the camps and drill squares until they are universally working together as a formed body of men, a unit, a team. This is the basis of teamwork and several tests would have to be completed as a platoon before we progressed. It is also where the indoctrination process of the military begins. You are taught to react to words of command without question, without hesitation; muscle memory and reflexes take over as you are subconsciously reprogrammed. It is interesting observing the masses of veterans on parade at Remembrance, watching how, despite the fact that they are no longer soldiers, they still know and react to the words of command without question, without hesitation.... obedient!

Next is skill-at-arms training. This is where you learn the basics about weapons and how to operate them. Everything is now a 'drill', words of commands are yelled, and we automatically respond, again without hesitation, without question. Hours are spent stripping and assembling weapons until it becomes second nature, until the weapon feels like an extension of your body. Range work is gradually introduced, and recruits are taught to shoot at targets that resemble a soldier running towards you. I can recall the endless hours of imagining who this enemy target was, what was his back story, why was he so angry, as I repeatedly, then over time, instinctively, shot him through my sights. Eventually, shooting this lifelike human target became a reflex as we were all conditioned to dehumanise our targets. Yet again, standards of marksmanship are required before you can progress. Good results are rewarded, and poor results punished through reward-based incentive. Other subjects included:

Physical training, fieldcraft, map reading, first aid and how to survive in a nuclear, biological, and chemical (NBC) environment. Besides the detrimental military training methods that I believe restricted individual thought and had a long-term psychological impact on our mental health, we must also discuss the British Army's values and standards that were instilled into us.

I have always remembered these through the acronym of SOLID-C. Selfless commitment; respect for Others; Loyalty: Integrity; Discipline and finally Courage. I, like many troubled young men, needed guidance, structure and stability and these core values were the final part of the puzzle for the life that I desired. The two that always stand out for me are selfless commitment and integrity. The others, with the exception of respect for others, simply promote military lifestyle values; discipline, loyalty, and courage. Respect for others always seemed important to me and, throughout my career, I never experienced any racism due to skin colour or ethnicity as in the Infantry you were simply judged on your character and work ethic, which was, in many ways, refreshing. Sectarian racism, however, was evident throughout my career and will be covered much later.

There is no other job in the world where, on application, you essentially write a blank cheque for your life other than in the military. It would be these core values that I would later use to justify my sacrifices under the narrative that I was making the world a better place, freeing the oppressed, ending tyranny. Yes, this was the case in Kosovo in 1999 and to this day, I am still immensely proud of my small contributing part there, but what about Iraq? What about the now very publicly labelled 'illegal war', the illegal occupation and then, by association, the prolonged guerrilla war against the Taliban in Afghanistan?

Imagine that one justifies the sacrifices and horrors of warfare through these core values, and imagine that this helps one rationalise their actions. Now, strip away the integrity from the conflict and make the War illegal! How can a soldier comprehend and accept the trauma of war, one's selfless sacrifices, if the war is not just? What if the war is, in fact, illegal and his integrity as a soldier was in question? That soldier was me. This piggybacks onto the notion that we always perceive ourselves as the hero, after all, this is our story, but what if, along the way, the narrative had changed and somehow you had become the villain? How would you cope; what would you do?

Looking back, I actually enjoyed my recruit training at Pirbright. Although I didn't think it at the time, the training team from Egypt Platoon were firm, yet fair and they would heavily influence many decisions throughout my career. They were under pressure to produce results from a very demanding schedule and successfully achieved this. A few years later, basic training would be extended to 12 then 14 weeks to help alleviate this pressure on both the recruits and staff. This proved to be successful and increased the retainment rate, which, in turn, saved the taxpayer money. I would encounter all of the members of this training team in the years to come but would be saddened when one of them would take his own life, another victim of a dangerous mindset that was destroying good men from the inside...the increased rates of military suicide.

After a weekend break, or, to be honest, just the Saturday, I arrived at Vimy Barracks at the Infantry Training Centre Catterick to begin my phase two infantry training. I was immediately in awe of the barracks as there was a 432 armoured fighting vehicle at the front gate with accompanying pillar boxes at either flank. This would be a whole new adventure and I was excited at the prospect of learning how to use the vast array of infantry weapons systems. Maybe I would get to use that flamethrower after all! Sadly not, but we were trained in hand grenades, machine guns, mortars, anti-tank weapons and platoon tactics and let us not forget the very Infantry-relevant practice of bayonet fighting.

We had incurred substantial recruit losses at Pirbright through a combination of injuries, 'back-squadding' and those who had just decided that the Army wasn't for them. As a result of these low numbers, we had merged with the platoon that was ahead of us at Pirbright. We were a little jealous though, as these guys were just returning from two weeks' leave, whereas we had had our passing out parade on the Friday and were now starting at Catterick on the Sunday. By now, I had also bought a cheap suit; I had learned my previous lesson and I wanted to make a good first impression with my new training team!

Together, we would form 19 Platoon, part of Guards Training Company and would be competing side by side with a sister platoon from the Parachute Regiment in fitness, marksmanship, and drill for Regimental bragging rights. From day one, our new training team had a superiority complexion in comparison to those from Egypt Platoon at Pirbright. From their perspective, everything that we had previously been taught was either not up to standard or just completely incorrect. They would complain about how 'shite' our previous instructors were and how it was up to them to reteach everything on top of their already busy workload. I didn't buy into this due to the fact that they were basically saying that we were not good enough to pass out of phase one training and didn't deserve to be at the ITC.

Needless to say, I didn't particularly enjoy my phase two Infantry training and at times, the training team of 19 Platoon were simply cruel and exploitative. This new training team were also very physical and were not afraid to throw their weight around with many of us being punched and kicked along the way. On top of this, they would charge us to use cleaning materials, and even the electric hoovers had a weekly surcharge. We were even pressured to buy these crooks a present at the end of our training as a token of our unwavering gratitude. Years later, when I was in their position as a training Sergeant, I was adamant that my recruits never bought me anything for simply doing my job. Although, I did let some of them buy me a pint after they had passed out!

I never thought that I had been indoctrinated or reprogrammed in phase 1 basic training as I never felt that it was necessarily that challenging. Then there is the word association with the word 'basic' to consider. If something is basic, then one would automatically assume that it cannot be that harmful or have any long-term damaging effects. In this case, the basic foundations of the military mindset had been laid. The physical and mental challenges of Infantry training would build then feed on this and would culminate with bayonet fighting training at Catterick.

Close-quarter combat is brutal and unforgiving and is best avoided. However, we must remember that our Infantry training was primarily focused on the brutality that had occurred in the Falklands War. Besides, the British Army's ethos was to 'train hard to fight easy,' and we thrived at training hard! Infantry soldiers can only carry so much ammunition, therefore, it is imperative that they can still be combat effective with just the use of their bare hands and bayonets! Soldiers are taught to dehumanise the enemy as this makes killing that much easier. Engaging an enemy through a rifle scope at a distance isn't personal but at close quarters, this is personal, face to face, this is brutal, this is a different kind of warfare, this is bayonet fighting! Even now, writing this, my hands are trembling, and my mouth has gone dry; not due to the thought of training for warfare but rather being reminded of my own very real experiences from real operational tours.

At this point in our training, we had been taught that pain is weakness, emotions are weakness and we had been pushed to and beyond what we perceived as our mental and physical limits. I suppose, we were finally like machines that would react emotionlessly without thought or hesitation. Bayonet fighting training taps into all of this but allows you to finally vent all of the suppressed emotions and anger. Our instructors would psych us up in preparation by yelling 'what's a bayonet for?' and we would aggressively and barbarically reply, 'TO KILL'. Then, on the simple word of command, 'high port', you are expected to revert back to your calm self, machine-like. On receipt of the command 'ONGUARD', then 'ADVANCE,' soldiers are required to advance on stuffed dummies, then brutally and aggressively impale them, simulating killing another human being up close in the process. Through repetition and behavioural training, this becomes your new normal and some soldiers actually grow to enjoy it!

These dummies, depending on the creativity of the training team, would be filled with wallpaper paste mixed with red food dye, straw or even meat scraps from a local butcher for added simulation and effect. You would then proceed to lanes where you would run, crawl, and climb over obstacles, through streams and almost always uphill to kill these dummies with your bare hands – simulating close quarter fighting. This type of training made us emotionally numb and zombielike. I recall a short trainee Scots Guardsman unknowingly impaling his own bayonet through his thigh whilst crawling through this lane, completely oblivious to the pain. The training teams had successfully pushed him to both his physical and psychological limits and now he was fully indoctrinated into the Infantry mindset. Fearless, emotionless, questionless!

This, from my experience, was the final phase of my military conditioning and this had been successfully achieved through gradually changing my psychological mindset through repetitive behavioural learning. The term 'controlled aggression' was often used to describe such training methods; to be able to go from calm to killer, then revert back to calm again at a simple command. How does one go from civilian to a mindless killer on command in less than a six-month period? What structures need to be in place for an individual to be able to accept, then cope with this? What would be the lasting effects on the mental health in creating my generation of Infantry soldiers? I believe that it was the suppression of our emotions that allowed us to achieve this, but ask the question; what are the negative long-term implications associated with this type of training?

From a 2013 Ministry of Defence study, it was found that Infantry units have traditionally promoted aggression as a desirable trait and such units frequently recruit individuals who are socially disadvantaged and are likely to have low educational attainment.[v] This would suggest that the British Army purposely and deliberately recruited Infanteer's from adverse backgrounds who were poorly educated as these were easily conditioned. Alternatively, due to their low educational attainment, perhaps the Infantry was their only option? Regardless, this raises a pertinent question about what happens to these soldiers on discharge and is there a de-escalation of this process to revert them back into a civilian mindset?

It is no secret that soldiers, a product of their training and operational experiences, are emotionally numb and lack empathy. Bearing this in mind, it comes as no surprise that many of them (like myself) marry nurses who are their emotional opposite. We were taught not to show emotions but rather to suppress them and this has had a detrimental effect on our relationships and families. Eventually, by hiding, avoiding, and denying these emotions, something has to give. Imagine that soldiers' emotions are a pressure cooker, but constantly operating at a subconscious 80-90% pressure level. This allows them, through the use of 'controlled aggression', to conduct training exercises such as bayonet fighting where they can easily reach, then vent, 100% of their raw suppressed emotions through 'controlled aggression.' I fundamentally believe that 'controlled aggression' has been detrimental to all aspects of both our soldiers' and veterans' emotional outlook, as through military conditioning, they were deemed weak if they were to seek help. If it had taken six months to train us to act and think in this specific way, I ask the question yet again, why was there no mirroring training offered on return to the civilian sector? This would help to go a long way to explain why soldiers and veterans are victims of such high suicide rates and why trivial things cause them to emotionally explode![vi]

Before the bayonet fighting training had commenced, we were tormented throughout the night by being kept awake to perform mediocre tasks, then pushed to our physical limits through arduous exercise until we were physically and mentally exhausted. Then, and only then would the bayonet fighting be allowed to begin. I am all too aware that warfare is a dirty place and there is no black or white. Additionally, you cannot have an effective fighting force that reflects society, as what soldiers are required to do is not accepted within the laws of our society. Yet, once our service ends, there has been and continues to be a lack of emotional and psychological training to help us understand our mindset and it is our families who are left to pick up the pieces.

When you speak about the concept of indoctrination, one automatically associates this concept with a cult. However, on the 1 December 1996, on the Drill Square at Vimy Barracks, Niall and myself would have our first encounter with death. Private Brian Isherwood, a trainee with the Black Watch and only 19 years old at the time, would purposely patrol across the parade square, hallowed ground in military terms and not to be crossed unless participating in drill! Isherwood gazed directly at us, put his rifle in his mouth and blew his brains out to our immediate front[vii]. As the rifle ranges were close by, the sound of gunshots was a familiar occurrence, but this happened right in our line of sight, less than twenty metres away from us and we didn't move a muscle. This was not out of fear or shock for that matter, but because we were diligent trainee Guardsmen and whilst standing to attention on parade, it was indoctrinated into us that we didn't move a muscle.

I recall that our Platoon Sergeant, a fierce Grenadier Guardsman, was giving us final instruction before our pass out parade later that week. He had put the fear of God into us throughout the past 17 weeks of our Infantry Training and we were terrified of the consequences of interrupting him whilst he spoke. Time appeared to stand still whilst we were watching this horrendous situation unfold. Both our Platoon and Drill Sergeants had their back to the now-deceased Private Isherwood and were unaware of what had taken place until eventually I found the courage to mumble the word, "S..SS.SSS, Sergeant" to get his attention.

The immediate response for interrupting our Platoon Sergeant was that he was going to bite my face off, but before he could, Trainee Guardsman McLoughlin also spoke up. The rest is a bit of a blur as both our Sergeants attempted futile first aid. I do recall that Isherwood had died instantly as the impact from the bullet at such close range had left a gaping hole in the side of his head. Yet, oddly enough, I can still clearly see that one of his eyeballs, including the optic nerve, appeared unscathed almost like an escape pod that had landed several metres away from his body. It's only now, reflecting back on this event, that it has the appropriate, human, and empathic affect that was absent at the time.

Niall remembers our Platoon Sergeant unsuccessfully attempting to secure Private Isherwood's skull with his bare hands whilst concurrently screaming, "Ya dirty bastard!" as brain matter, blood and bone poured all over him. I don't believe that this was an insult aimed towards Isherwood but more of a coping mechanism to help him deal with what was occurring in his bare hands. I don't know what drove Private Isherwood to such desperate measures, but I do recall how little this phased me at just 17 years old. What concerns me now with the luxury of retrospect is why a platoon of almost thirty trained soldiers chose collectively to refused to flinch when another human being had committed suicide right before them.

As a Platoon, we had wholeheartedly bought into the concept of the 'Queen's Guards!' We were so disciplined on parade that not even this dreadful event would deter us, or maybe we had, effortlessly, been subconsciously indoctrinated into the mindset of the British Army. Now, looking back, I cannot help but wonder if it was the way in which we were trained, the way we were taught to suppress our emotions; had this type of behavioural reprogramming had a hand in his death? Documents obtained by the Northern Echo stated that between 1994 and 2003, there had been 23 reported deaths at Catterick, 5 of them being suicides.[viii] Many of these were training accidents, yet I find myself asking the question, 'Could these suicides have been prevented and what was the catalyst?' Was the way that we were trained, conditioned, and programmed in any way attributable to these deaths?

Whilst serving, soldiers committing suicide was a common occurrence. Corporal of Horse Wall (one of my instructors from basic training) hanged himself in 2004. An article would claim the added pressures of parking fines were a contributing factor to his death. Lieutenant Colonel Robert Shaw, (Irish Guards) shot himself in 2013 due to the ongoing pressures of work. Then there are those who had left the Armed Forces who unfortunately decided to take their own lives. This list is too big to mention, but these lost heroes were soldiers, friends, husbands, fathers, my brethren, many hiding their pain from the world until their untimely deaths.

It is the vast number of suicides that has and continues to occur that has motivated me to write this book. To ask the difficult questions about how military training, life, and operational experiences affected our psychological makeup. Why are so many veterans killing themselves? When I was diagnosed with PTSD in

2017, I felt ashamed – weak! However, I was very vocal about my struggle as I believed that speaking openly about my internal battles would encourage others to seek help. Several of my military friends informed me that they had always perceived me as being mentally robust; that I was the last person they thought would ever have any issues with their mental health. This is exactly the point! I had struggled almost daily for 20 years but had managed to hide my pain from the world and if I was successfully doing this, then other veterans and serving personnel were certainly doing the same!

When recently discussing Isherwood's suicide with Niall, who let's not forget was 25 years old at the time, we are both horrified at our lack of reaction. More so Niall, as with vast life experience under his belt, he is baffled at how he was unknowingly and unwillingly indoctrinated by military training. When asking the difficult questions of why didn't we react, why didn't we move, and most importantly, why didn't this bother us? I refer back to the term 'cult'. We had been successfully reprogrammed over the period of six months to act, feel, and respond differently than civilians and had successfully transitioned into soldiers, so maybe this was our final test? No counselling was offered as these were different times and I would hope that, in today's modern Army, this is not the case. Regardless, our training was now complete, we were now fully fledged Guardsmen and a new adventure of Battalion life awaited and that's all that mattered to us.

This well-oiled and drilled training cycle is a repeating cycle that is derived by the concept of reward-based incentive and would continue to be exploitative throughout all aspects of my military life. We were more focused and driven on attaining the rank and identity of a Guardsman than reacting to a fellow trainee's, a fellow soldier's suicide! This pattern of attainment is consistent throughout military life; let me elaborate. Once you complete phase one training, you are rewarded with a pass out parade. Your family and friends attend the parade and show their appreciation of your hard work and you receive a new identity in a new rank. You are now no longer a recruit but a Trainee-Guardsman! This gives you purpose and sets out a new set of goals to achieve. Once your training is complete, this pattern continues: you work hard and may get selected for promotion in rank, you go on operations and are rewarded with a medal. Once indoctrinated into this reward-driven mentality, you justify personal sacrifice as a means to an end; you buy into the concept that the Army's needs are far more important than your own. Let us not forget that we are selfless in our very nature as this is one of our core values. This would explain the high divorce rate amongst soldiers as they always prioritise work over their families and social lives.

Then there are the two types of career soldiers that tend to do exceptionally well within Infantry Battalions, both enlisted and commissioned to consider. How does this often-toxic environment affect them? There are enlisted soldiers like me, often from complex broken homes, to analyse. These types of soldiers need that approval from a figure of authority which is generally derived from childhood abandonment issues. The Army also provides much-needed stability and purpose for such soldiers but more significantly, a new identity. An identity that commands immediate respect in both civilian and military environments as, regardless of rank, there is always someone beneath you in the pecking order. Then, if you work hard and do well, you receive good annual reports as a reward. You earn the approval from a respected figure of authority that you crave and may also gain a new improved identity through promotions. You climb the ranks and get introduced initially to the Corporals' Mess, then, if lucky enough, the holy grail of the Sergeants' Mess. You experience frequent formal black-tie balls and are waited on daily at mealtimes. This is a million miles away from that poverty-ridden council estate in Manchester and the notion of 'work hard, sacrifice, earn your reward' is paying off. I justified my personal sacrifice through my status - the importance of self-importance.

Maybe I should coin the term "military Darwinism", as when you progress through the rank structure, it is very much survival of the fittest. I was very much testament to this as once I was injured, my progression ceased, and I was overlooked for promotion by more physically capable soldiers. However, this approach establishes an unbalanced and misguided co-dependency with the individual totally committed to the needs of the military. In my case for example, I was fit, loyal and determined to get whatever job completed regardless of the cost to my personal life. I genuinely believed that the Army was my life and, as such, I would unknowingly prioritise its needs above all else. Even whilst fighting a life-changing injury, I was determined to please, to make my superiors proud, to progress and earn my reward - the rank of Warrant Officer, but by then, my injury had taken its toll and I was unsurprisingly cast aside.

Now there are the commissioned soldiers to analyse. These are generally well-educated and from the mid-to-upper class within British society, or when we mention "The Guards", the aristocracy. Although, not from rough council estates, in fact, quite the polar opposite, these commissioned soldiers quite often share the same subconscious needs for approval due to their own abandonment issues. However, these are not from abusive households or broken

49

homes, but rather from the more stable upper-class affluent sections of society. The only negative side to this is that they often send their children to boarding schools due to family traditions or rites of passage. This absence of parents for long periods could potentially establish a co-dependency towards army life, similar to that of the less fortunate enlisted soldiers, the same need for approval of a consistent authority figure and the need for the same cycle of working hard, sacrifice and reward. The only difference is that they have an established social identity before and after their service which makes the transition to civilian life that much easier. Yet, regardless of this pre-military identity, once part of the same military indoctrination machine, they are very much, like the enlisted soldier, consumed by it.

When you consider that enlisted Infantry soldiers undergo over six months training to transition into the military mindset, commissioned soldiers at the Royal Military Academy Sandhurst (RMAS) participate in 12 months training before they are commissioned as officers and before they undertake their infantry training, this raises one important question. Why is there no training available for veterans to be psychologically prepared for a return to civilian life? When I served, the fundamental purpose of Infantry training was to prepare civilians mentally for warfare, to give them the skills that would enable them to ultimately close with and engage the enemy at close quarters, in order to bring about the enemy's defeat. The aim was to transform them from 'weak civilians' into what was commonly referred to as lean, green killing machines, the key word here being KILL!

Again, I ask the question, 'Where was the de-escalation training to prepare us for civilian life?' Niall, who successfully reached the rank of Warrant officer Class II, put this into perspective when he said that on leaving the British Army after 24 years, he felt like he was being stripped naked to his very core. One day, you are suppressing your emotions, many from your battlefield exploits. Your outlook is through the prism of your military status, then the following day this identity is taken away. Where are all of these caged emotions supposed to go and what are you to do with them? Many, including myself, simply carried on as normal (pretending that we were ok) and denied their very existence. From my personal experience, by doing such, my deteriorating mental health manifested and fed on this. From the outside, I looked and pretended that I was fine but internally, I was very conscious that something was seriously wrong. I was in pain but was too embarrassed and proud to seek help!

Reflecting back on our training experiences, by no means am I attempting to point the blame at any of the training staff for doing the jobs that they were trained to do; rather, I am attempting to analyse and understand the long-term psychological impact that recruit training has on the individual. It comes as no surprise that recruit training has to be both physically and mentally demanding. In many ways, it is also a cultural transformation. The process introduces you to a completely new environment, a unique and violent world within itself. Let us not forget the importance of the concept of identity as this process is designed to change your mentality and thought process and this can be extremely traumatic and detrimental to the individual's long-term mental health. Soldier 'G', another veteran from my generation, described this process as being 'beaten into submission.' After all, the purpose of basic training is to break the individual down and rebuild them into what the British Army requires of them.

Having been through this process and then some years later being on the other side of the looking glass as a recruit trainer myself, I can confidently refer to this process as indoctrination! Now, many years later, I find myself asking the questions: where does the soldier stop, and the civilian begin? Was this process of behavioural learning in anyway responsible for creating the psychological instability that allows PTSD to thrive? I am by no means a psychiatrist, nor do I have any qualifications regarding the study of mental health; I am merely asking these questions from my own experiences. Still, why is there not an equivalent process available when you leave the forces? Why is there no effort made to reverse this harmful destructive process and mentality? Where is the aftercare? Where is the support? Maybe, I expect too much from a society that sent me to war, a society that trained me to conduct and witness inhuman acts, the worst that mankind has to offer! I will never be able to entirely revert back to a civilian mentality after witnessing the horrors of war, but perhaps a little help to understand how to transition back from a soldier to this society would have been appreciated.

Training Photo 1996. I am stood left of centre. Niall is bottom right.

Canada 1998. Frank and myself days before he would jail me!

Chapter 3.
Boy Meets World

The previous six months had been hard. We had been pushed to our limits, yet it was worth it as we were now Guardsmen and had arrived at our Regiment - the 1st Battalion of the Irish Guards. The rank of Guardsman is the equivalent to that of a private soldier, however, as Guardsmen, it was 'drilled' into us that we were superior. The Battalion would receive 5 new excited Guardsmen, two from the Republic of Ireland, a Scouser, a Mancunian, and a South African, four of whom (including myself) were Catholics.

The initial few days when joining a Battalion are a real culture shock. Again, we had received no leave and were to report directly to our Battalion, our first stop being at the Guard Room. The Guard Commander and the Regimental Police Corporal would initially have a little fun by having us perform stupid tasks for their amusement. I would later learn that these two, despite being non-commissioned officers (NCOs) lacked any respect within the Battalion and this was one of the few times that they had any authority by harassing the new guys! After this short-lived bit of drill, we were then put into temporary accommodation for the evening. I remember feeling very insecure as we were now very small fish in a very large pond.

The following morning, we were introduced to the Commanding Officer and the Regimental Sergeant Major. We were then informed that we would be joining Number 4 Company and that we would be deploying to Northern Ireland in the following March. By now, I wasn't concerned or fearful about deploying on an operational tour as this was the job that I had trained so hard for and my excitement outweighed my apprehension. I was still only 17 years old at this point, a boy, and I was about to be introduced to a man's world!

The accommodation at Elizabeth Barracks was very dated by today's standards and for Guardsmen, this consisted of sharing 8-man rooms. For the next few days, the 5 of us hid away in this room, curtains drawn, and door locked. Eventually, the duty Sergeant for 4 Company, or in military terms the 'Sergeant in Waiting', found us and we were introduced to our new Company Sergeant Major (CSM). Growing up in Manchester, when being introduced to a new group, the first question was always, 'what football team do you support?' In training, this had changed to, 'Where are you from?' Now, this had evolved again with the Company Sergeant Major asking us what religion we were. I thought to myself, 'What has this got to do with anything?'

Once the Company Sergeant Major had established that we were mostly Catholics, his demeanour changed. He then happily informed us that we were joining a predominately protestant Company and that we were going to inevitably get 'filled in' (military slang for beaten up). If we were a bit of a fighter and fought back, then the NCOs would fill us in and if we somehow managed to fight them off, then he would fill us in. Either way, we were getting filled in. Being 17 and naïve and not one to ever back down from a fight, I thought to myself yet again, 'challenge accepted.'

I remember feeling disappointed at the lack of respect that we were receiving and, if I'm being completely honest, at this point, I didn't understand what sectarian racism was or the history of Ireland, for that matter. Regardless, if forced to, I wasn't afraid to fight and I wasn't afraid to stand up for myself. The following day, my whole perception changed when we were introduced to our equals, our fellow Guardsmen. I would have trouble understanding and accepting the seniority structure within the sub rank of my peers. Some of them were almost 30 years old and had been in the Battalion for twelve years, whereas we had just arrived. I had mistakenly assumed that we were all equal as we had earned the same rank and this lack of understanding would make my initial year in the Irish Guards and my new home in 10 Platoon a living hell.

I cringe now when I recall some of the belittling events that would frequently occur, particularly 'Chair'. A senior Guardsman would yell 'chair', and I was required to get on all fours so that he could sit on me. The intimidation of the mob and the peer pressure of the masses had immediately knocked the fight out of me, or maybe this was a result of the six months' behavioural conditioning that I had endured. I had become submissive and can only conclude that this was the result of my training. We were nominated for every shit job and I couldn't comprehend why this was happening as we were all the same rank, all Guardsman, all equals - weren't we? I would speak up about this only to find more jobs and 'chairs' coming my way.

Niall was smart; he just cracked on and was eventually left alone. Looking back, I can't help but think, 'Why couldn't I have been more like Niall?' It's not that these were bad guys, this was just a rite of passage that all Guardsmen went through. Regrettably, years later, when I was a more senior Guardsman, I would also be part of the pack and bully the new guys. I am ashamed by this, especially having been through a horrendous experience myself as a new Guardsman, but unfortunately, we were all institutionalised and this was our normal.

I will never forget the night of my 18th birthday; we were all fast asleep in our eight-man room when our door was kicked in. A large group of Guardsmen stormed the room screaming wildly the name of one of my friends; it was obvious they were all drunk. They then proceeded to beat the crap out of one of the guys who I had passed out with, but why? The previous day, we'd had snacks at a nearby café at the neighbouring barracks where recruits were trained. We had confidently jumped the queue which was not an uncommon act for trained soldiers to do, however, at the till, the lady cashier didn't believe that we were trained soldiers - Guardsmen - and thought that we were recruits just trying our luck. We collectively explained that we were and thought nothing more of the uneventful incident. Unbeknown to us, this was one of the wives of a senior Guardsman within 4 Company and despite what we had perceived as a monotonous encounter, the senior Guardsmen and his wife felt differently.

My buddy reluctantly sat up in his bed and was quickly surrounded by this drunken mob and they proceeded to interrogate him about the incident at the café whilst the rest of us were told to go back to sleep as this didn't concern us. This kangaroo court would determine that it was because we acted like Guardsmen - trained soldiers and had jumped the queue at the café, but evidently, it was speaking to the senior Guardsman's wife that was somehow the real crime. She did ask my buddy's name and by confidently providing this, we had condemned him to a midnight beating in his bed. Yet again, I look back and I regret my inaction at just lying there and I am sure that the other four feel the same. Within two weeks, the constant belittling and sectarian abuse had knocked all of our confidence, so we just lay there listening to the thuds and yelps as one of our friends was beaten to a pulp in his bed beside us.

The next morning on parade, it was obvious what had occurred as my friend had a head like a smashed cabbage. No questions were asked, and I couldn't help thinking to myself, 'Was this beating due to his religion? Was that even a thing?' The use of excessive violence was the norm in most Infantry Battalions in the 1990s; the men were trained to fight, to kill and often vented on each other but this felt different and I couldn't understand exactly how. That afternoon, I remember attending the junior ranks' Christmas Party in the cookhouse. We were intentionally positioned together in the corner of the hall so that the rest of the Guardsmen could throw food, cans of beer or whatever they could find at us. This had nothing to do with our religion but more so the fact that we were the new guys, and this institutionalised behaviour and bullying was just accepted at the time.

The Ministry of Defence and senior officers would never like to acknowledge the fact that Sectarian racism was rife within the Irish Guards; a famous Regiment that was the Queen's fourth regiment of footguards and was always in the limelight. As a child, I had witnessed national racism and, of course, racism was rife in the 1980s, but this was derived from ethnicity and skin colour. Initially, I couldn't understand sectarian racism as wasn't this Irish versus Irish? Were we not all in the British Army? Had we not all sworn an oath to the Queen? As a company of men, we were training for our deployment to Northern Ireland, more specifically South Armagh, the notorious 'bandit country,' so surely, we should be working as a team.... together?

It was no surprise that we were nominated for guard duty over that Christmas leave period in 1996, and this was quite a calm and refreshing period for us. Two weeks with only a skeleton crew within the barracks. We would be required to conduct guard duty for a 24hr period then have a whole day to ourselves but most of all, we would be left alone. I enjoyed this luxury as my feet were yet to touch the ground ever since that first day of training when I had turned up late with just my Mancunian swagger. I would use this downtime to improve my fitness on the vigorous training area of the Pirbright hills. I would run for hours in the freezing cold and found this very therapeutic. I would contemplate my decision to join the Army, the assurances that I was given by my Recruiting Sergeant about sports and adventure and conclude that I had made a grave mistake. However, it was too late, and I was committed to three years' service.

When the Battalion returned from leave, we were thrown straight into Northern Ireland Training but not before a fitness test. I had excelled at fitness in training and had narrowly missed out on receiving the 'Best PT' trophy due to misdemeanours. In basic training, Niall was set to receive the award for 'best recruit' but we had sneaked out of barracks whilst on adventure training to get some beers and were inevitably foiled in the process. As such, they downgraded Niall to my award, and by reading my recruit reports some years later, I now realise that I was just fortunate to pass out. Even to this day, Niall enjoys reminding everyone how he was the fittest in training, as it was, he and he alone who was presented with this prestigious accolade. Even at Catterick, I would always have difficulty keeping out of trouble and now in Battalion, things would appear to be no different.

The British Army's basic fitness test has been called many different names throughout the years but was essentially a 1.5-mile race after an energetic warm-up. This was conducted after 2 minutes of a maximum effort of sit-ups and press-ups. I was determined to prove to the Company that I was one of them and desperately wanted to be accepted and concluded that I would be accepted through my fitness. How wrong I was. I shot off like a bat out of hell then quickly realised that I didn't know the route so slowed down a little. I was confident of my running ability as I had always come first or second during my training and could complete the 1.5-mile run in just under eight minutes. My aim was to finish in the middle third of the Company but to my surprise, no one was catching me. Eventually, two of the other Guardsmen would catch up; we broke away from the main group and a race was on.

I was ecstatic with myself having finished second, however, the Guardsman who had won the race wasn't even out of breath. He was an army boxer and his fitness levels were simply insane. Much to his disappointment, my future best friend, Frank, would finish third and this would mark a fitness rivalry that would bond us during our careers. My pal who had been beaten up in his bed a few weeks prior was as fit as me if not fitter, but to my surprise, he made little or no effort on this test. I suspect that this was due to his unjust beating as he was just trying to go unnoticed under the radar. On return to our Company Offices, all of the Guardsmen received a collective 'bollocking' (telling off) regarding how poor their personal fitness was as several of them had failed the test. I was then highlighted as a beaming example of what the older, more experienced soldiers should aspire to! Oh no, I thought to myself; this is only going to make things worse.

Normally, after being on guard over the Christmas period, you take your leave in the January, but for us, our Company was halfway through their pre-deployment training for Northern Ireland and we needed to play catch up, hence, leave was cancelled. This catch up never came; we were not given any remedial training and were just expected to know all of the operational training methods. Then, if we did something wrong, we would be ridiculed and punished for not knowing the answers to a subject matter that we were never taught! Eventually, I had decided enough was enough and that I would tackle these bullies one at a time, just like I had done previously whilst in a children's home.

We were at Lydd Ranges in Kent at the time; it was February and we were in a patrol base simulating a scenario from our imminent tour of Northern Ireland. I found myself in a sanger with one of the head protestant bully boys, so I decided to antagonise him. After little effort, he threw a punch at me, which I anticipated, blocked, then pinned him up against the wall. I told him that this victimisation had to stop or the next time I would hurt him and that was that, job done, or so I thought. Our pre-deployment training was coming to an end and we were going on leave in a few days and I didn't want to be deploying on operations with any animosity amongst us.

I vividly remember that after being on the ranges most of the night, I was in my sleeping bag in temporary accommodation awaiting the Platoon Commanders briefing for the following day. The next thing that I knew, I was held down and the zip of my sleeping bag was pulled to the top above the hood and I was trapped, cocooned inside. I was then beaten to a pulp, unable to fight back or even defend myself. It was the Northern Irish Mafia. After what appeared to be a lifetime, I could hear that our Platoon Commander and Sergeant had entered the room. The beating finally stopped but not before they lifted the base of the bed ninety degrees up towards the ceiling, trapping me between the wall and the bedsprings. I was then, and still am now disgusted that neither my Platoon Commander nor my Platoon Sergeant did nothing to stop this. Instead, they chose to ignore what they had just witnessed and carried on with their briefing like this was a normal daily occurrence. As one can easily imagine, I was seriously regretting my decision to join the Army at this point. I couldn't help but think that I had been victimised and beaten because of a religion that was forced upon me and that I wasn't too fussed about to begin with. Furthermore, I also acknowledge that I was a cocky and very opinionated young man, and this may have been a contributing factor that led to this brutal hiding. Maybe, if I would have kept my head down then this beating may not have occurred or would have been significantly less vicious, but that was just not in my nature and further beatings would follow.

Around the time of my sleeping bag beating, Lance Bombardier Restorick had been shot and killed by the IRA at Bessbrook Mill in South Armagh in the early February of that year.[ix] We were training as a Company to deploy to this very base and this was an unwanted reminder of the dangers that awaited us. Maybe this had something to do with my sleeping bag beating? Maybe, Restorick's murder at the hands of the Roman Catholic IRA felt personal to the Guardsmen from Ulster, so maybe by beating me they would be able to vent some of their own suppressed emotions and anger and if this was in fact the case, I have something to say to this mob; you're welcome!

Historically, as a formed body of men, the 1st Battalion Irish Guards were not allowed by the Ministry of Defence to deploy as a unit to Northern Ireland. They had completed just the one tour as a Battalion in East Tyrone in 1995. This was due to the simple fact of security, as British Soldiers were often the priority targets for the IRA. Therefore, soldiers from Ulster were an easy target and those from the Republic of Ireland would often have to keep their service a secret. At the height of the troubles, it was not uncommon for soldiers to be killed whilst off duty or at their homes with their families and this was the reason why so few Irish Guardsmen had previously deployed to Northern Ireland.

Therefore, as the Irish Guards had a large contingent of soldiers from Ulster, the risk was considered far too great to deploy them as a Battalion. Furthermore, many of these Guardsmen may have had ties, through family or friends, to paramilitary organisations on both sides of the conflict, whether being the IRA, or the UDF, UDA, or UVF. The other reason that was never mentioned was the increased tensions of the underlying sectarian racism that existed, and this was evident also through our unpleasant experiences in 4 Company. Roman Catholics and soldiers from the Republic of Ireland would often be referred to as 'dirty Finnian bastards' and this was widely accepted as just good healthy banter.

One must also analyse the familiarities and history between Ireland as a country and the Irish Guards as a Regiment. Both of them had strong links to the Roman Catholic Church, with the Irish Guards being the only Regiment in the British Army to be specifically allocated Catholic priests as military padres. Then, there is the more important internal fighting for sectarian dominance to consider; the split between the Republicans and the Loyalists from the historic troubles within Northern Ireland. This hereditary hatred for each other was instilled from birth and, despite now being on the same team as part of the British Army, always subconsciously remained.

After ten months of high intensity and traumatic training, I was finally granted 10 days pre-deployment leave. I hadn't enjoyed my Northern Ireland training for obvious reasons, and I was seriously considering going AWOL (absent without leave). I was crashing in my little brothers' room in my mother's house and I didn't particularly like this situation, but it was better than staying in barracks, so, I reluctantly headed home to Manchester. Then, on 14 March after a heavy night out, I would find myself in the accident and emergency department.

The previous night I had lost my keys and had attempted to climb through my brother's first-floor bedroom window but had slipped at the last moment. I had landed awkwardly on my back, unfortunately on the lip of the concrete steps below. I initially thought that I was just winded and was able to pick myself up off the ground before making my way to the back door that was ironically left open for me. 'Just typical,' I thought to myself. The following morning, I felt slightly stiff and was planning to go for a morning run when it finally dawned on me that I may have seriously injured myself. I was unable to put on my shoes and socks; panic started to set in! The pain was not my concern, let us not forget that I was now a tough, robust Infantry soldier and pain was weakness. It was the lack of independence and not being able to dress myself that worried me. Reluctantly, I persuaded my mother to take me to the accident and emergency department for an x-ray.

Accident and emergency departments are a fun place to people-watch. It was Friday morning after all, and during the long wait, I had amused myself by imagining how all of the other 'idiots' had ended up there. Due to the fact that I had walked into the department and that I had normal sensation in my legs, the doctors and nurses were not particularly concerned about my little accident. This was until the results of my x-ray were reviewed. I have always been cheeky and recall that I was having banter and trying to chat up the nurses as I had convinced myself that I had only pulled a muscle and wasn't predominantly concerned. However, these nurses were now ignoring me and looked anxious before eventually returning to my cubicle with two doctors, one of them being a spinal consultant. Now I was extremely worried!

The first words out of the consultant's mouth were 'What are you doing walking?' I jokingly replied, 'It's like running but at a much slower pace.' Nobody laughed. He then explained that I had fractured my L1 vertebrae and that there was a risk that this could sever my spinal cord, paralysing me from the waist down. The jokes ceased – the realisation that I had broken my back began to set in! The consultant would later explain that this was a 'miracle break' and I was tremendously lucky that my spinal cord wasn't damaged in the process and that any sudden movement could potentially damage my spinal cord. I didn't feel lucky; I felt disappointment. My only concern was that I was abandoning my comrades as I would be unable to join them on their imminent tour of South Armagh.

Looking back on this period, regarding my negative experiences in the early years of my career in the British Army, I can genuinely empathise with the Northern Irish protestants of 4 Company. They had lived through the troubles, and, before they had even joined the British Army, had been fighting for Ulster to remain part of Great Britain. They had been taught from an early age to despise Catholics and it was this generational hate that drove and motivated their future actions. However, this does not excuse them from their inexplicable behaviour. Nine years later, when I was a member of the Sergeants' Mess, I would accidentally bump into Lance Corporal 'F', now a civilian, detached from the military mindset and now a completely different person. Lance Corporal 'F' couldn't apologise enough, was tearful, genuine, and full of regret for the way in which he had treated me. I acknowledged his apology and quickly moved on as I had accepted this for what it was at the time, a combination of Sectarian racism and institutional bullying.

I do not accept that the trauma of my early experiences of sectarian bullying in the Irish Guards attributed to my often-poor mental health, as this was a reflection of society at that time, thus accepted. I believe that for me, acceptance was a key factor in my ability to manage this; besides, I had been taking beatings my whole life and this was no different. However, years later, when I was a section commander, I would discover that some Ulster Men from the Drums and Pipes Platoon had previously and violently initiated some of my lads, including 'Mad Dave', into the Ulster Volunteer Force. This inexplicable act was conducted with the use of balaclavas and pistols and would have been very traumatic for the young men who had no familiarisation or understanding of the affairs in Ulster.

When the news of this encounter surfaced, we had just returned from the War in Iraq and we had all been drinking heavily. By now, 'Mad Dave' had fully grown into his ironic nickname as before the War he was the polar opposite, timid and quiet. Nevertheless, we all wanted revenge! Reflecting back on the brawl that would inevitably occur, this was my way of subconsciously seeking payback for the way that I had previously been treated by the cruel protestants of 4 Company, and I will cover this event in more depth in a later chapter.

The lasting effect of this sectarian bullying is the slight and unwanted subconscious prejudice that I once had towards Northern Ireland Protestants as a result. This is despite having many good friends from this demographic and one cannot help but wonder if the old saying, 'violence incites further violence' is actually true?

The following Monday after breaking my back, I was due to report for duty to deploy to Northern Ireland and telephoned the Company Offices and spoke to one of the Sergeants in an attempt to explain my unfortunate predicament. This particular Sergeant was only too aware of the bullying that I had received and concluded that I was making excuses to avoid deploying to Northern Ireland. He persisted to scream and shout down the phone to the extent that a nurse grabbed the phone from me and gave him a telling off in the manner that only nurses can! He then, more reservedly, wished me a quick recovery. Nurse 1, terrifying Sergeant 0! The following day a doctor would inform me that it would be a long two weeks before I was allowed to stand unassisted and it was unclear to whether or not I would make a full recovery. I had been admitted to Hope Hospital in Salford, the very hospital where, a few years beforehand, I had been part of a limited caper to steal some computers. Looking back on this from my hospital bed, I was so ashamed of my younger self. The doctors had told me that I wouldn't be able to walk unassisted for three months, run for six months and that it would be very unlikely that I would ever be able to carry weight on my back ever again. I was devastated as this had put an end to my military career before it had even started. 'What's the good news?' I nervously joked.

I was later fitted with a full-torso cast and was told to wear it for a minimum of 8 weeks and returned to barracks. The medical treatment I received from the Army was second to none with the

Battalion bringing in physiotherapists to treat me once daily to begin with, then twice daily as my recovery progressed. Once the cast was removed, I went under intense rehabilitation and was gradually allowed to return to the gym. My aim was to re-join my Company in Northern Ireland as I still felt an overwhelming sense of abandonment towards them! This would motivate me to prove everyone wrong, get back to full fitness and finally deploy with my Company to South Armagh.

It was during the summer of 1997 that I first encountered Soldier 'G'. Soldier 'G's' career would almost mirror my own through operational deployments and postings. Not that it is relevant to you or me, but in the Irish Guards, he was a Southern Irish Roman Catholic and depending on where you were sent, this could be a bad thing in this period. Soldier 'G' came from a family with a rich military background from within the Irish Defence Force and was motivated to join the British Army under the premise of soldiering on operations. Like myself, he was very much captivated by the romantic relationship between young men and warfare, but in Soldier 'G's' case, this desire for soldiering never left him and this would always be his priority throughout his distinguished career. Like myself, Soldier 'G' had joined 4 Company straight from training and, after a few weeks, would be deployed to South Armagh before me. I was envious, but this motivated me even more.

Finally, my determination and hard work had paid off. I had been purposefully and relentlessly running past Battalion Headquarters twice daily, often in full military equipment, to catch the Commanding Officer's and Adjutant's attention. The order had come through - at last I was deploying for the final 10 weeks of the tour. Four months prior in a hospital bed, I had questioned the prospect of alternative careers as mine as a soldier appeared to be over. I recall being overjoyed with the physical recovery that I had made and, specifically, being in the company stores receiving my operational body armour. Then, we all heard a single pop of nearby gunfire.

Another soldier had just committed suicide. This time, a member of the Sergeants' Mess from the Irish Guards. Sergeant Nash had asked to inspect a loaded rifle from one of the sentries guarding the back gate, then, without hesitation or warning, shot himself. I never knew this member of the Irish Guards and as callous as it sounds, in that specific moment, I wasn't really bothered about it. I was exclusively focused on fulfilling the Army's needs of deploying on my first operational tour which had now become my own needs. I am shocked with myself for not having had an emotional response to this incident at the time - perhaps I did, but I was using the tools instilled through my behavioural training to suppress these certain emotions.

Soldiers have an unhealthy relationship with death. This is a combination of our training, where we are programmed to deny our basic survival instincts; we are taught to run towards danger rather than away from it. Then, there is both the military mindset to consider as well as those who ignorantly choose to deny the dangers of soldiering. This would become more relevant on the more attrition tours of Iraq and Afghanistan when far too many soldiers thought that they were impervious to enemy action. It was not uncommon for soldiers to frequently survive dangerous firefights, improvised explosive devices, and mortar fire. These persistent brushes with death every now and then would generate an invincibility mindset within some soldiers, yet sadly, this was not the case and often proved to be fatal.

Like many soldiers, the first time that I was to travel on an aeroplane was not to go on the traditional family holiday, but rather to deploy overseas. In my case, I was doubly excited as it was my first time on an aeroplane, and I was also deploying on my first operational tour to Northern Ireland. I would then be taken to Palace Barracks for an in-theatre briefing before being flown by helicopter to Bessbrook Mill in South Armagh. I felt overwhelmed with jubilation and was looking forward to linking up with 10 Platoon. Since breaking my back, I had felt guilty for not being able to deploy and guilt for abandoning my comrades. I had worked hard on my rehabilitation to get here and I was determined to make up for lost time. I had convinced myself that the lads would be happy to see me and would appreciate the struggle that I had undergone to get here. Yet again, I would be mistaken.

On arrival, I was quickly thrown into guard duty at the helipad at Bessbrook Mill. The more senior Guardsmen also made me do their guard duties and I quickly became the fall guy for every shitty job and task. If someone needed their washing doing, I was tasked, if someone needed something from the NAAFI (the shop), I would get it, if extra guard duty was required, I was nominated, if extra security of the helipad was required, you guessed it, it was me. I was having no downtime and very little sleep, but Niall had advised me to stop answering back to the more senior Guardsmen and not to speak up for myself. I concluded to myself that if I tried to fit in then I would eventually be accepted. I had noticed that Niall was a shell of his former self, quiet and lacking confidence but this is what I longed for, so I just knuckled down and hoped for the best. Years later, Niall would turn his back on soldiering and retrain as the military tailor for the Battalion and I cannot help but wonder if our early experiences of sectarian bullying motivated him to do so.

South Armagh was a notoriously dangerous province to operate in as it was mainly rural and bordered the Republic. Cross-border shoots were frequent and road vehicles were banned due to the amount of improvised explosive devices; and then there was the IRA .50 calibre sniper team to contemplate. In short, it was a dangerous place! The terrain is arduous and can be unforgiving and then there is the high Catholic anti-British population to consider. When on foot patrols, we would be frequently abused verbally, and the kids would often throw rocks at us. I initially found this difficult to comprehend as this was part of Britain, yet somehow kept undisclosed from the general public on the mainland and is why I fundamentally believe that the events of Northern Ireland will always be perceived as a stain on British history.

About a month into my tour or almost five months for everyone else, I recall that we were coming to the end of a 24-hr patrol and everyone was tired. As usual, I had carried all of the Electric Counter Measure (ECM) including spare batteries and even my patrol commander's flask. We were operating in a four-man team but part of a multiple of two other such teams. I recall that we had gone firm and were waiting to be collected by our helicopter and naturally, I was on guard whilst the others rested. It was a hot summer's afternoon and the patrol had been uneventful when it began to rain. 'This was odd,' I thought to myself as there wasn't a single cloud in the sky. Then it dawned on me! Two of the Guardsmen from another team were pissing on me to the rest of the multiple's amusement. I would have the last laugh, though, as these Guardsmen would have to sit next to me on the chopper ride back to Bessbrook Mill whilst

I was stinking of piss. What is disappointing to this day is that none of the junior commanders intervened or even disciplined the culprits.

A week later, I recall that we had been on a night patrol and my team commander, who was notoriously bad at map-reading, had taken us to the wrong pick-up point for the helicopter. He would often ask the locals for directions or let one of the other Guardsmen map-read for him. Due to his navigational error, he decided that we would patrol on the roads through a small town called Silverbridge to make up for lost time. At the time, this didn't trigger any red flags because I was inexperienced, but Silverbridge was an out-of-bounds town area and was even marked with red on our maps. Silverbridge was a small border town with a strong IRA presence and, as such, for our own safety, under no circumstances were we allowed to patrol through it. My team leader, however, decided that he knew better.

Despite it being in the early hours of the morning, he had gambled with our lives that this route was safe. I was the fourth man on the patrol, the rear man, the most inexperienced and was carrying all the heavy kit and equipment. I vividly remember that the town was dead; the sun was coming up to our front which was blinding our vision and by the time that I had entered the town, the metal dustbins were already beating like jungle drums. Not long afterwards, a crowd started to gather, and rocks were being thrown at us. I started to panic at the prospect of being snatched as I was the last man. We were all aware of the infamous death of Captain Robert Nairac and I decided that this was not going to be my fate and started to run towards the rest of my team. As the hostilities increased, they too had begun to increase the pace. By now, I was the second man out of the team and before long, I was the frontman leading our extraction despite the fact that I alone was carrying all the heavy equipment.

Even to this day, I sincerely believe that if I had not initiated the hard extraction from this patrol, one of us would have been snatched or, at the very least, seriously hurt. Once out of the town and at a safe distance, we looked back to see the large angry mob of Republicans that had gathered. We were lucky and laughed about our potentially dangerous encounter and my patrol commander asked us to keep it a team secret, so I did just that hoping that on return to Bessbrook Mill, I would be treated slightly better.

I continued to be quiet and just accept all of the crap that continued to come my way for the rest of the tour in an attempt to fit in. However, I finally snapped one evening towards the end of the tour when we were granted a night's rest and recuperation. We had all been drinking and I may or may not have started a small scuffle which ended up with two NCOs beating me with an unplugged iron. Once the fighting had finally finished, my multiple commander gave the order for me to stand to attention, and like the obedient drone I was, I did as I was ordered and didn't move. Then, my team commander repeatedly hit me in the face with the iron. The following year, this same team commander would later be thrown out of the British Army for bullying. He was a dinosaur of the previous generation where physical bullying was rife and institutionally accepted. These particular NCO's were not fit to lead; they believed that respect was best earned through fear and violence which had a harmful knock-on effect on the Guardsmen.

I have taken many managerial and leadership lessons from this experience and would use these horrendous examples to mould my own leadership style later on in my career. I had always believed that no matter how bad a life experience was, that I must take something positive away from it. In this case, it was how not to lead and manage soldiers. I firmly believe that it was the NCO's lack of ability to cope with the demands of the operational pressures that created a toxic atmosphere within my multiple. These few bad eggs were by no means a reflection on the Irish Guards as a whole, as they were just that, a bad batch. As I progressed through the ranks, as a commander, I would use humour as a positive tool to ease the operational stresses on the Guardsmen and be as informal as possible when appropriate. I would make mistakes along the way but tried to be the polar opposite of the bully boys of that early period of my career.

I do not feel that my early experiences within the Irish Guards had an impact on my mental health as, by now, I was institutionalised, and this treatment was just accepted at that time. My childhood had made me tough and my experience of bullying was probably not too dissimilar to many other soldiers of that period. What is relevant, though, is how the majority of the non-commissioned officers, or commissioned officers, for that matter, didn't give a crap about the welfare of the Guardsmen. Don't get me wrong - there were some who were brilliant, such as 'Swifty', but sadly, in my early experiences, only a few. Mental health awareness was not a popular topic for discussion; after all, poor mental health was rammed into us as weakness and we were not weak! Therefore, it is important to understand the mentality of the British Army in the late 1990s, as some of these poor junior commanders would eventually become the senior commanders of the future, more pertinently, throughout the prolonged 'War on Terror' in Iraq and Afghanistan that would leave its hidden mark on so many of my brethren.

Chapter 4.
Living the Dream

It is amazing how quickly the turnaround of the morale in a military unit can occur. For the men of Number 4 Company, this came directly as a result of the leadership from our new Company Commander, Major Charlie Knaggs, and his Company Sergeant Major, Ray Collister. Both of these men were natural leaders and they both had a relaxed temperament about them which made them approachable. Unlike most of their peers at this time, they were competent and gained the respect of their men through leadership and ability rather than fear, violence, and bullying. These were the first two inspirational soldiers that I had the pleasure of working under and they genuinely cared about the men under their command. Under their leadership of Number 4 Company, the bad eggs were weeded out and we gradually became a family and an effective fighting unit.

My first encounter with Major Knaggs was on the rugby field; well, a few of us were actually just casually playing rugby with a water bottle after an exercise session and he had decided to join in. I remember hitting him hard in a tackle and was in shock at his response as he threw several punches at me, then wanted to throw down; the man was a lunatic! Knaggsy wasn't afraid to get down and dirty with the men and this earned him instant respect. He also took the time to learn about all of his soldier's families and he understood the importance of morale. Like Napoleon, Knaggsy recognised the importance of high morale to the fighting troops. Napoleon was convinced that the high morale made the men under his command fight three times as hard and in Knaggs's case, even more so.[x] In fact, we would have run through walls for Knaggsy and would have confidently followed him through the gates of hell as he was the finest commander that I ever served under. When he took command of Number 4 Company, the Company was fractured and we were pending a Battalion move to Germany, but things were about to change and for the better. I would use Knaggsy's compassion and leadership lessons later on in my career when I was a commander myself, but regrettably, I witnessed very few officers at his level who shared his attributes and compassion throughout my career.

Once the Irish Guards moved to Germany, we would all have to be retrained to facilitate our new job roles as Armoured Infantry. For the next five years, we would be stationed at Oxford Barracks in Munster, and these were some of the best times in my military career. Initially, all of the soldiers would have to complete Warrior Armoured Fighting Vehicle familiarisation or crew conversion training. For me, this meant that I would be trained as a Warrior driver/commander and be responsible for the maintenance and tactical manoeuvring of a 26-tonne vehicle with a Roll-Royce Perkins 17.4 litre air-cooled turbocharged engine. As we were Number 4 Company, all of our vehicles began with the letter 'D'; therefore, my Warrior was named Donegal, radio callsign '1,1.' I can even remember the number plate, 35 KG 46, as this tracked armoured monstrosity was essentially my first car! But this was a car with caterpillar tracks instead of wheels, with an accompanying 30mm cannon and 7.62mm chain gun as added extras.

10 Platoon would be allocated four Warriors and we were split into two daily working groups. The vehicle crews, which consisted of the drivers, gunners, and commanders, were responsible for the maintenance and daily upkeep of the vehicles. The Infantry dismounts were known as 'blades' or 'fox hounds' and each Warrior would have an Infantry section of seven 'blades' allocated to them. Their daily training would consist mainly of Infantry v's tank training as our training methods were still focused on a Soviet invasion of the West. Most days, we would finish work at 1330hrs, and we would be able to have plenty of downtime to relax. I would work hard on my fitness and often completed three exercise sessions a day before joining in with the Platoon antics. I would share a room with Frank and we soon became best friends. Frank had always had career ambitions and was quite serious, whereas I was more the Platoon clown. On paper, our friendship shouldn't have worked, but at least at work I was professional, and we had always had mutual respect for each other on the fitness front. Even to this day, we argue who was the fittest and despite the fact that I am now classed as physically disabled, in my mind, I still believe I could beat him!

I would routinely come up with bad ideas that would usually end us up in trouble, whereas Frank tried at least to be by the book. We were both overly keen soldiers and Frank would be rewarded for his hard work by being promoted to the rank of Lance Corporal after successfully completing his junior non-commissioned officers' cadre along with Niall. I was pleased for them both, but I was happy being one of the lads and having no responsibility - apart from the maintenance of my 26-tonne armoured car, that is. Frank often spoke about his plans to climb the ranks and even fancied himself as a future Regimental Sergeant Major. My ambition, back then at least, went as far as the weekend and the future planning of the next Platoon block party. These ranged from toga to Vietnam-themed and were usually out of control!

The weekends were wild, to say the least, with these very block parties and the supplementary shenanigans that one would expect from a frat house. Then again, this is exactly what we were as our Company lines where we lived became extremely territorial and isolated from other members of the Battalion. This did have a positive outcome as it made us closer as brothers which, in turn, made us a more effective fighting unit. We were young men based in the centre of Europe and it was not uncommon to play map roulette at the weekends and just head off to explore a random city. The Pound was strong against the Deutschmark and we seemed to have endless amounts of disposable income which made our time in Germany even more enjoyable. This was the adventure that I had been sold by my Recruiting Sergeant and I was finally enjoying life in the Army despite my bumpy start. Furthermore, the strong leadership from the senior level of Number 4 Company had positively stemmed its way throughout the command element, to the benefit of all of the Guardsmen as we felt valued and trusted our leaders.

Most of our Wednesday afternoons were spent at the large Aasee Park in the centre of Munster, playing sports. Additionally, we would frequently form up in our combat fatigues with large packs on our backs and head out on a high-intensity combat march only to make our way to the Aasee. However, our backpacks more than often contained beer, footballs, boom boxes and civilian sportswear. European culture, especially the acceptance of nudity, fascinated us. We were all red-blooded young men, after all. Women would frequently sunbathe topless in the Aasee Park, so naturally, our footballs would always be 'accidentally' kicked in their direction. Then, there were the naked saunas! This was my first life lesson about the realisation of fantasy v's reality. On our first and only trip to a German sauna, we had all imagined that it would be crammed with young sexy naked German girls, whereas the reality was that it was just us and old fat German men! Regardless, I was nineteen years old and living my life to the full, but I never returned to that sauna again.

Later that year, we were deployed to Canada for a culmination exercise at the British Army Training Unit Suffield (BATUS) in Alberta. BATUS was a vast training area where we could war game and put all of our training to the test. This would determine if the Irish Guards as a Battalion were fit to deploy on combat operations as Armoured Infantry and was a test that we needed to pass. The vehicles' crews had become very close in the past year and my Gunner, Soldier 'B', shared a special bond that made us a formidable crew. We could anticipate each other's combat decisions as a result of repetitive training and our friendship. On top of this, he was an exceptional gunner and we had trust in each other's ability. Midway through the exercise, a turret malfunction crushed the legs of o popular and experienced vehicle commander O.D., and he w have to be replaced by a very inexperienced 2nd Lieuten Ormerod was fresh out of the factory and had not even any Warrior conversion courses yet, but because mys 'B' had a reputation for being, if I'm being modes were given a baby-sitting role that we would in

Maybe we were slightly arrogant, b commands from Soldier 'B', to the dissa

Mr Ormerod. We were just two teenage Guardsmen, the lowest rank in the British Army but as a Warrior crew, despite our limited experience, we thought that we outranked a junior officer, as he had none. On this particular exercise, I vividly recollect that we were liaising with Battalion Headquarters, which was several kilometres away and on our return journey, we had new orders for Number 4 Company. Soldier 'B' was encouraging me to go faster and I needed very little encouragement to put my boot to the floor. Mr Ormerod pleaded with me to slow down but Soldier 'B' was insistent that we could increase the speed. Warriors have a top speed, cross-country, of around 30mph, but this one was like a race car as the engine limiter must have come loose, so I increased the pace as we approached a huge artillery crater. It was too late to slow down, and time began to come to a standstill as this 26-tonne mini-tank became airborne! In the seconds that we were in flight, I panicked and attempted to ineffectively fasten my seat harness as I knew that this emergency landing was going to be painful!

Our Warrior came to an immediate violent stop and the force of

of dust around us. Soldier 'B' and Mr

ust what is commonly

d had been wedged in

h. There is a reason for

around us, there was a

ther side of the crater

our irresponsible feat. As

k the damage and, to my

s were still intact. As the

I recognised it was our

nd I could tell just by his

body language he was not pleased. Knaggsy calmly asked who my commander was, then just as calmly asked Mr Ormrod to have a private word with him at the back of the vehicle. Let's just say that words were said and ironically, Knaggsy then called Soldier 'B' and I to the front of the vehicle and ordered us not to take commands from Mr Ormerod anymore and that Soldier 'B' was in charge of our Warrior. Both of us kept quiet and let Mr Ormerod take the fall! Integrity was one of our core values, but neither of us wanted to disappoint Knaggsy, so we kept quiet.

The six-week exercise would be brought to a halt with the untimely and upsetting death of Guardsman Connor Lilly, who would be killed when a Land Rover lost control on the dangerous gravel of Rattlesnake Road that accessed the prairie. I always remember that the Army flew Guardsman Lilly's family out to Canada, and this gave me great confidence in the British Army's welfare policy. With the risk assessment of such exercises, it is accepted that deaths can and will occur and, in some cases, it would take up to six deaths for certain training exercises to be halted altogether. It was at this time that Major Knaggs spoke to me about the prospect of attending my own junior non-commissioned officer cadre. To his bemusement, I declined as I was happy with being just a Guardsman, but Knaggsy wasn't the type of commander you said no to and none of the men under his command, including myself, wanted to disappoint him. That was it then; I was now reluctantly on the next course for promotion.

Once we had completed the exercise in BATUS, we were required to hand over our armoured vehicles in the same condition as we had received them. For our crew, we had an uphill battle as we had damaged several road wheels on the caterpillar tracks as a result of our airborne antics. It would be 48 hours before replacement parts would become available and we were all desperate to experience the Canadian nightlife. However, we were not permitted to leave camp until our vehicles were sufficiently repaired. Consequently, due to our impatience, it was suggested by one of our Sergeants that I 'acquired' these road wheels from one of the permanent staff's vehicles that were in the adjacent hangar close by. I remember that I was just unscrewing a second road wheel when I was foiled and sent to jail for disciplinary action. In true 'Guards' fashion, before I was charged with theft, I would be rigorously marched to jail in the camp's Guardroom. My best pal, Frank, had recently been promoted to the rank of Lance Corporal and was ironically tasked with 'locking me up'. Unfortunately for me, the Guardroom where the cells were located was over a mile away from the vehicle park and Frank would have to put our friendship aside and perform his military duties by rigorously marching me to the jailhouse!

Initially, this was comical as we were having some good banter between us, but after a few falls on the ice in the sub-zero Canadian temperatures, my outlook began to differ. Then, to my disappointment, when we arrived at the Guardroom, we were informed that they had no cells for me to be put in, so then, like a Benny Hill sketch, I was marched at the same rigorous pace back to the vehicle park for further instructions. At this point, I had had enough, and I could have easily just mentioned that I was 'following orders' from my Sergeant, but instead, I asked what the charges were. Once I was informed that I would be charged with theft, I merely pointed out that I was taking one item of military property and relocating it to another location. This enraged the senior commander who had wanted me formally charged, then fortunately, my

Company Sergeant Major appeared and suggested that as no formal charges could be pursued as this wasn't technically theft, he would discipline me 'in house.'

My punishment would be kept from my permanent military record and I would be required to complete company fatigues for the following week whilst the rest of my friends partied in the vibrant town of Medicine Hat. There were several such incidents throughout my career where I narrowly avoided being formally charged, whereas Frank was never so fortunate. My luck would ensure that after 15 years' service, I would be presented with my Long Service and Good Conduct Medal to everyone's, including Frank's, disbelief. The crime, as they say, was 'getting caught', or in my case, getting formally charged. Although I often joke with Frank about him missing out on this medal, he would argue that 'jailing a thief,' his best friend, was a worthy substitute.

It was in Canada that I would be introduced to the skiing world. All of the soldiers had the choice to either spend seven days Rest and Recuperation (R'n'R), at the tourist city of Edmonton or participate in a week's adventure training. This was a no-brainer for me and Frank as both of us had joined the Army for adventure and we were currently living that dream. I received a quick starter course at the Olympic Ski Park in Calgary, before heading to the Sunshine Village Ski Resort in Banff. The staff had even opened the resort four days early to accommodate us, so we had the mountain to ourselves. Soldiers are fearless and a good example of this is when I unintentionally skied off a small cliff; bizarrely and like lemmings, I was followed by Frank and Soldier 'B'. We were all novice skiers but would attempt the advanced black runs and our fearlessness would more often than not end up with us painfully hugging trees! Then, once we were joined by the public, we were intentionally using them to stop. In hindsight, this is probably why they opened the resort early for us as once we were joined by the public, it was mayhem! I would continue to ski throughout my career, and this was just one of the many perks of being a soldier in the British Army.

On our return to Germany, rumours began to circulate about ethnic cleansing and acts of genocide that were happening in Europe. We were all aware of the breakup of the former Yugoslavia due to the United Nations (U.N.) intervention in Bosnia, but none of us was aware of the region known as Kosovo. We were informed about the 250,000 Albanians that were being forced from their homes by Serbian Soldiers and this was well documented and hyped up by the press. Just before Christmas leave, the tempo and excitement began to grow as our deployment readiness was increased. Frank, Soldier 'B', and I were super--excited at the prospect of 'going to war', as we were young men who were blinded by the romantic prospect of combat. We were young and naïve but had joined the Army for adventure and excitement, and throughout 1998, we were not disappointed as the Army had delivered. We were overly eager to test our skills, our tradecraft, and especially to put our newly acquired armoured warfare training to the test. My promotion course was put on hold, but I didn't mind as the prospect and glory of warfare superseded any career ambitions.

On return to Oxford Barracks in the early January of 1999, the operational readiness was significantly increased again, but unfortunately, all of the readiness was prioritised towards Number 1 Company. To my frustration, they would deploy to Macedonia in the February and come under the command of the King's Royal Hussars Battlegroup. Number 4 Company would lead the Irish Guards commanded Battlegroup and to my frustration, we would have to wait slightly longer for our operational deployment orders. Whilst we eagerly waited to deploy, we would continue to train hard but would equally party as hard.

One would automatically conclude that our off-duty shenanigans would be put on hold due to our imminent deployment, but this was far from the case. The weekends were still frenzied, and when looking back, the added enthusiasm of a war in Kosovo may have made us much worse. The Regimental Police and the Barrack Guard were regularly called to our lines to put an end to our block parties and were often met with violent resistance. I don't recall any fear or apprehension about the prospect of going to war but maybe subconsciously this was just our way of coping with this pressure as we were all clearly acting out. Come Monday mornings, we were all professional and performed our duties admirably, but on the weekends, we were feral! I remember in the following years that Frank and I witnessed a fridge seemingly fall from the sky from the downstairs window of the 4 Company lines. Then moments later, two of the most unexpected and unlikely of soldiers, Pez and Greeny, chased it down the stairs to retrieve their beers that were still inside. This was not out of the ordinary as it was classed as 'normal' behaviour' and was accepted as long as everything was back to normal come Monday.

At the time, Kosovo was a prominent Albanian region of Serbia, which had a deep and complex history regarding its autonomy and identity. By the mid-1990s a guerrilla campaign was established by the Kosovo Liberation Army (KLA) and was well underway. This was a direct result of Albanian leaders declaring independence, a rise in ethnic tensions and civil unrest.[xi] Tensions further increased in the

March of 1998 when Serb forces rolled into the Kosovan village of Prekaz, using tanks and armoured personnel carriers. Their target was the family of Adem Jeshari, the founder of the KLA, and the house was levelled, killing all inside, 57 members of the Jeshari family in total. The Prekaz massacre was reported by the world's media and changed international opinion, especially regarding the KLA as a terrorist organisation. The KLA made good use of new multimedia advances such as the internet to successfully report their persecution, and this gained them more international support over the Serbs.

The murder of the Jeshari family had also inspired thousands of young Albanians who had rallied to join the ranks of the KLA and this unfortunately incited further Serbian acts of genocide. In January 1999, more massacres were reported outside the village of Racak, when 45 Albanians were found dead after another Serb attack.[xii] The UN feared a repeat of Bosnia and the atrocities that could have been prevented there with more decisive military intervention such as the Srebrenica massacre. There was still one main obstacle to overcome and that was that Serbia had the support from Moscow and this only raised international tensions further with the terrifying prospect of an all-out war with Russia!

After the peace talks had stalled between Serbian President Slobodan Milosevic and the U.N. to halt the ethnic cleansing of the Albanians, diplomacy had fundamentally failed so, as a result, military action was authorised. After all, war is essentially an extension of diplomatic failure. In the March, an air campaign began to target military and strategic targets in Belgrade to put additional pressure on Milosevic. Then, in the May, and after months of frustration, we would finally get the call to deploy but not before uparmouring our Warrior Armoured Fighting Vehicles with additional Chobham armour. This is when I realised that I was driving a bullet magnet and questioned the need for further armour. We finished by spraying 'KFOR' on our vehicles, which was short for Kosovo Peace Implementation Force before they were shipped out to be ferried by sea to the Greek port of Thessalonica. We would come under the North Atlantic Treaty Organisation (NATO) which was basically the sword to the U.N.'s shield, which implied that we were going to war. My excitement outweighed any fear, or doubts, for that matter, as I was young, full of beans and was fully engrossed with the romanticism that is associated with warfare. Like many of my military brothers, I was more than willing to make the ultimate sacrifice as I believed in what we were doing and would happily welcome an honourable death on the battlefield.

After a short stay in Greece, we travelled to Petrovec in Macedonia and began the final phase of our training. I was genuinely concerned (not afraid) about my Warrior being immobilised and not being able to influence the fight. Therefore, I had anticipated that if such an event actually occurred, I would dismount and continue to fight on foot as an Infantry soldier. As a result of this potentially happening, at every given opportunity, I would make use of what we had on the vehicle to use as a makeshift gym. I would run to and from the vehicle park, which was now a dustbowl, as a high level of fitness is a prerequisite of a capable Infanteer. I would train hard with a fellow Guardsman, Dale McCallum. Dale would later transfer to the Scots Guards and was sadly killed by small arms fire in the Lashkar Gah district of Helmand province in 2010. When I knew Dale, he was so full of life and one of those guys that everyone took an instant liking to. The sad thing is that within the military machine, people are moved on so frequently that you often lose touch with them and this would be the case with Dale. I value the limited time we spent together and always remember him for his warm smile. Regrettably, he wouldn't be the only one of my military brothers to fall in battle, but being a realist, this is just an accepted consequence of life as a soldier.

10 Platoon was appointed a new Platoon Sergeant in Wade, who had just been posted in and as such, Wade had little experience in Armoured Warfare. He was appointed our vehicle commander and it was up to Soldier 'B' and I to get him up to speed. Wade was a really good guy, despite being a Manchester United fan. He had a soft Northern Irish accent and was straight down the line and by the book. I would learn a lot from Wade, and he became a role model for many of the Guardsmen in 10 Platoon who went on to have extraordinary military careers. Our Platoon Commander, on the other hand, well, that's a different story altogether. He lacked experience and even forgot his own burgan (large backpack) after taking it off to rest on a night patrol when training in Petrovec. Come on, these backpacks are massive; it's not like losing a set of keys!

The only downtime that we ever experienced in the forest camp of Petrovec was in a small tent which housed an even smaller TV. Fortunately for us, one of the channels played British football and it was rigged with the sound from BBC sport from a separate radio, and this enabled us to watch the big games. I only attended this tent once as it was often inundated with senior ranks and we Guardsmen never felt comfortable in there. The highlight for myself was being able to watch the Division 2 playoff final between my beloved Manchester City and Gillingham on 23rd May. 'Manc' Evans, John Corcoran and I were all good buddies as we had a lot in common.

We were all Manchester City fans, all from Manchester and were all in the Irish Guards. 'Manc' Evans and I were in 10 Platoon whereas John was in the Reconnaissance Platoon, but we never held that against him. After 90 minutes, the tent had emptied as City were 2-0 down and I was the only one left when Kevin Horlock scored. John quickly returned to the tent and, to our disbelief, City scored again in the 95th minute to equalise and we went on to win on penalties. That night, we got drunk with a bottle of ouzo that I had smuggled in from Greece but instantly regretted it the following day as I was on the ranges in the scorching Macedonian sun! Rumours did circulate about three men streaking that night, but nothing was ever proved, and the culprits still remain at large!

Occasionally, we would be tasked to patrol the mountains to the North, bordering the region of Kosovo and we had a front-row seat to watch the ongoing bombing campaign against the Serbian military and strategic targets. These mountains were a sight of natural beauty and I remember watching the most stunning sunset from this elevated location before the main event, which would be observing the allied bombings of Serb military targets in the distance. A U.S. F-117 stealth fighter had previously been shot down by a Russian Sa-3 Goa surface-to-air missile and this only made these border patrols more intense as these planes were supposed to be hidden from radar. These patrols never frightened me and throughout my time in Macedonia, I don't recollect any of our Platoon being afraid, for that matter. We were well trained, and we were actually looking forward to finally being able to put our training to the test!

By early June, our training was stepped up and we began the more aggressive drills such as bayonet fighting. Every man went through this, even the vehicle crews and this prepared us psychologically to kill the enemy and, let us not forget, to dehumanise them. We were preparing for war and this is what our training always consisted of. It was physically brutal as the ethos at that time was to 'train hard to fight easy'. I remember that no training was conducted to provide any form of humanitarian relief and little language training was provided as we were allocated interpreters. Everything was now conducted at a high tempo pace with the focus always being on aggression, fighting through and different ways of killing the enemy. I recall that we were all pumped, wound up and ready to be unleashed. We were dogs of war, we were ready, well trained, drilled and mentally focused for the battle to come.

Our mission and training were primarily focused on defeating the Serbian Forces in the region of Kosovo. We had been training aggressively for this and when the mission began to change to a more peace-keeping task, all of us felt a sense of underwhelming disappointment. We were all young men who had undergone years of behavioural training, conditioned to go to war, to defeat the 'evil' enemy. We wholeheartedly believed that we were the 'good guys' and were willing to participate in aggressive military action as we all undoubtedly believed in our mission to save the Kosovar people. We had been given daily briefs on the ethnic cleansing and one must remember that we were still living in a bipolar world, where the remnants and scars of the Cold War were still at large. There was still a great deal of international tension and a distinct lack of trust between East and West and the Kosovo crisis could quite easily have been the powder keg to start another war.

We received our orders to deploy into Kosovo on the morning of 12th June and after months of preparations, we moved from the cover of the Petrovec woods and leaguered up into neat military columns. I recall being in awe of the military might that was now on show and that the air was swarming with helicopters. This was a multinational operation and we were the main effort to secure the roundabout at the Southern access point to Pristina but were starting at the rear. The plan was to 'peel in' so that we would be fresh from any fighting once we arrived at the outskirts of the Kosovar capital. Once we were in position, we received a motivational speech from our Commanding Officer before having a Battalion blessing from the Padre. I found this 'prayer before battle' quite hypocritical as many soldiers who rarely took religion seriously were now praying because their lives were in imminent danger. Some soldiers were only religious in times of need which was a concept that I couldn't really buy into.

Our route was to drive along the E65 Macedonia Highway into Pristina, and we were greeted with Albanian refugees as we passed through Skopje, waving us on and supporting us from the side of the road and on bridges. This gave us enormous pride and added purpose. We had a wealth of operational experience within the Platoon that ranged from the 1991 Gulf War and Bosnia to Northern Ireland but none of us had ever experienced anything like this. As we left Macedonia and entered the Serbian Kacanik Gorge, a mountainous valley, our armoured columns suddenly felt extremely vulnerable. Fortunately, we had elite soldiers from the Parachute Regiment and the Royal Gurkha Rifles flown in by helicopters to provide flank protection for our armoured vehicles. We were constantly delayed by Serbian mines and obstacles that had to be cleared by the Royal Engineers and this was a very tense time as we were static and open to attack.

It was 1530hrs by the time we finally passed through the potentially lethal Kacanik Gorge and I was relieved. The tunnels were crumbling from the inside and had no light, whereas the bridges barely forded the weight of the armoured vehicles. It was a feat in itself just to get the armour along this decaying and dangerous mountainous route. In fact, the Royal Engineers had to build several bridges for us to use as the current ones were not sufficient or safe enough for our heavy vehicles. If we had been forced to fight our way through this valley then we would have taken an immense number of casualties, and if defended properly, then possibly we would not have made it at all. I wrote in my diary that I had hoped to have entered Kosovo aggressively with Serbian resistance, but after seeing the landscape, the reality of this made me cold and shiver. I wrote that I was relieved that we were entering as a peacekeeping force due to the nature of this landscape[xiii]. As we entered the former Yugoslavia, there was an eerie ambience as there were no signs of life in the neighbouring villages and towns. Cars were burnt out and buildings demolished; what had happened here?

As the ground levelled out, we were fast approaching our goal, Pristina, which was now only 50km away when the heavens opened up. This was not just any rain but a tropical thunderstorm which reduced our visibility and resulted in the convoy slowing down. About 30km out, the convoy came to a halt as the third section in 10 Platoon, Warrior callsign one three, had crashed into a truck. However, this wasn't just any truck, but a Serb military truck full of landmines! The truck swayed off the road and crashed with the impact from the armoured Warrior, then all of the occupants, Serbian soldiers, fled in fear for their lives. All of our Infantry dismounted but not before they were reminded not to stray off the hard standing of the road because of the danger of landmines. The irony - it would seem that nowhere was safe from the Serbian mines!

Just after 2200hrs, we received new orders to go firm for the evening. It seemed as if our mission parameters were changing hourly. The plan was now to take Pristina the following morning at first light. We were only 20km away and we could visibly observe the lights of the capital in the distance. Throughout the night, Serbian forces would pass us heading North with the occasional T54/55 main battle tank aiming its cannon at us. If one single soldier lost their nerve and engaged these forces, then it would have started an all-out war. Thankfully and despite the tension, we all kept our cool. In my diary, I noted that these military convoys were also accompanied by civilian vehicles from some of the Serbian population. These civilians were fearful of repercussions from the returning Albanians as well as from us NATO soldiers and sought refuge within mainland Serbia. Our interpreter explained that the Serbian-affiliated population of Pristina had evacuated the city the previous day and at the time, I didn't really understand why, but in the following months, it would become all too clear.

After breakfast on the 13th of June, we mounted up and drove at speed to Pristina only to be halted by some Italians who were blocking our advance. The radio was filled with slightly racist phrases such as 'get these fucking spaghetti-eaters out of the road' as our goal was to be the first into Pristina and the race was on! When we arrived at our roundabout, the three platoons of number 4 Company tactically manoeuvred into our pre-planned and rehearsed positions in all-round defence and secured the large roundabout at the southern entrance to Pristina. We were surrounded by the world's press; they had been there waiting for us since the previous day, but the heavy rain had delayed our advance. This didn't really seem like an aggressive land advance if the press were already waiting for us, but we still had a job to do and there was still danger lurking everywhere.

Then, the plan changed yet again. Our Company Commander screamed on the radio for us to withdraw as the city had not been cleared for entry and that we shouldn't have secured the roundabout. Most units who were involved in the liberation of Kosovo will take credit and boast that they were the first NATO forces into Pristina. I am not bold enough to make such a claim, but the men of number 4 Company were certainly in contention for such a military accolade. We withdrew to the outskirts of the city and the Company Commander gave us all a brief in person, informing us that the situation was continuously evolving! Our new orders were to secure the main supply route through Pristina. However, by now, some of the withdrawing Serbian forces were becoming aggressive and were attempting to antagonise us by firing small arms wildly at us in our general direction. We were now informed that our mission was to force the Serb forces out of Pristina and to secure Kosovo for its future people.

Chapter 5.
Kosovo Now

T he time had come; I mounted up, climbed into my driver's cab, and flicked the power switches on my driver's instrument panel before flicking the starting motor and powering up the engine. The 17.4-litre engine roared and seemed almost as excited as I was. This was our big moment; we were about to liberate a nation from oppression and the whole world was watching. The radio was full of chatter as we made our way along the main road to Pristina. This was a beautiful city, full of history and culture and could have been any number of cities in Eastern Europe, but something was amiss. Where were the people? This city was a ghost town and the only signs of life was the odd stray dog. Bullet holes decorated the fronts of all of the buildings and burnt-out cars littered the streets; this was something one might expect from the apocalypse and it certainly felt like it was just that; there was an eerie feel about our presence there. As we cautiously patrolled through the abandoned streets, Soldier 'B' and Wade observed from the top of the turret for any hostilities, but there was nobody around - Pristina was deserted; it was a ghost town!

It was only 0900hrs when we eventually came to a halt at the north of the city at the junction of the historic Ottoman Xhamia e Llapit mosque. 10 Platoon had led the way through the city, and at this point, I remember thinking to myself, 'where the hell is everyone?' Then the order came across the radio for all of us to go firm and to replace our helmets with our berets. This made no sense to me at the time as Serb forces were still extracting and taking the occasional pot-shot at us. Looking back, the strategic thinking behind this was to make us appear less aggressive and to de-escalate the tense situation that all of us were in. The air campaign had destroyed all of the Serbian communications and it would be weeks before all of them would be successfully withdrawn; some Serb troops didn't even know that we were coming. Furthermore, NATO forces had bypassed thousands of Serb troops on our advance to Pristina and without prior knowledge of our arrival, it's a miracle that all soldiers on both sides kept their cool. Personally, I was in full-on war-fighting mode and I didn't trust anyone who wasn't wearing a British Flag on their arm.

Then there was movement from a sewer to our rear. I grabbed my assault rifle and made my way to the top of our Warrior; I hated being static in the built-up area as I was ineffective in my driver's cab. Concurrently, our Infantry section dismounted to provide us with some protection for the impending threat. To our surprise, an Albanian family emerged in tears to greet us; God knows how long they had been living down there, hiding in fear for their lives. Then more and more Albanians began to emerge from their refuge and began to emotionally break down in tears before us. These people had been oppressed, beaten, and murdered because of their ethnicity and we were in the process of liberating them. An excited young male then attempted to climb onto my Warrior and was met with my size 10 boot. I didn't like this situation as we were all distracted from the real threat and that was the withdrawing Serb Forces. We didn't know who to trust and none of us knew what to do as we had trained hard for the past six months for war and now, we were in the centre of a humanitarian mission! It was difficult not to be overwhelmed with the joyous and euphoric ambience, but we were disciplined soldiers and still had a job to do. We were being greeted like rock stars, heroes, but the mission parameters were still fluctuating, and this put enormous pressure on all of us. Soldiers like to plan for all eventualities, yet we had not anticipated this current scenario.

We had trained relentlessly for war and now we were greeted with peaceful indebted crowds of Albanians; we were liberators, and this was hard to process for our pre-programmed Infantry mindset. I have no idea where all of those pink flowers came from but within minutes, my Warrior Armoured Fighting Vehicle was completely covered in them and it resembled a parade float that wouldn't be out of place at Pride! The Albanians were overcome with happiness and joy and began to cheer, then sing. Some offered gifts such as their watches and jewellery, which we obviously refused. These people had nothing but were so thankful for the small part that 10 Platoon had played in their freedom that they were offering us all they had in unconditional gestures. The crowd then began to grow and intensified even more as some KLA freedom fighters wearing UCK insignias emerged. I didn't completely trust the KLA, but we were there to help them, and one must not forget that they had played a key role in Kosovo's liberation. It was no coincidence that as the KLA emerged, we could hear gunshots and small battles that were now ongoing from within the city. It was time to move, investigate and secure Pristina.

The KLA made our mission more difficult as they persisted in ambushing the withdrawing Serbian Forces at every opportunity which was against the peace agreement that had been brokered days earlier. This put all of us on edge as we couldn't trust the KLA and I don't really think that they trusted us in return. Then, as we began our investigation, I recall that we were patrolling through a residential area of the city when we were forced to come to a halt due to a roadblock of cars that had created a killing zone to our immediate front. To our right-hand side, where once stood 2 small houses, was a Serbian T54/55 main battle tank that was pointing its main 100mm armament directly at us. Wade immediately commanded Soldier 'B' to aim our 30mm cannon toward this main battle tank in a show of equal force, but Soldier 'B' responded with the words, 'Paul, get us out of here...drive!' I put my boot to the metal and easily drove over 2 small cars then over a tractor before clipping the side of a small shop. Soldier 'B' and I didn't fancy getting hit with a 100mm tank shell at close range and I think that Wade was also relieved by Soldier 'B's' quick thinking.

We eventually met up with some fellow Irish Guardsmen from another company who were providing first aid to some Serb soldiers who had been shot up by the KLA whilst looting. One of these was clearly dead and a quarter of his skull was missing on the right-hand side. The bullet had left a hole that I imagined could have easily been caused by a large axe and this was completely different from the previous head wound that I had witnessed some years earlier in training. Regardless, he was dead, and we had to take the body to the morgue at the hospital. We wrapped this soldier in a poncho and Soldier 'B' and I launched him into the crew compartment in the back of the Warrior, however, we threw him with such force that he cracked his head on the corner of our boiling vessel. This made a dull thump, the kind of sound where everyone around goes 'oooh,' then rubs their own head acknowledging the pain. Soldier 'B' then persisted to ask if the corpse was ok, as skull, blood and brain matter dripped from the poncho!

As I drove to the morgue, I began to joke about the dead Serbian in the back of our vehicle. I was still the class clown and insisted that he was moving and that I could hear him screaming for help. I continued with the prank and told the lads in the turret that he was clawing at their feet and, to my amazement, they were buying it. By the time that we had arrived at the morgue, both Solder 'B' and Wade were practically sat on top of the turret out of fear of a zombie bite! Then, to our amazement, shock, and horror, when we opened the back door of the Warrior, this perceived zombie corpse was sat up slightly! Soldier 'B' apologised again for cracking his head off the corner of the boiling vessel as I fixed my bayonet to make sure that he was actually dead. Now, even I believed in zombies! Talk about a joke backfiring! I don't know whether it was the vibrations from the Warrior that made this zombie sit up or if we had gone over a bump, or maybe it was just gas within the corpse, but this was the last time I joked about the dead!

The access to the morgue was at the gable end of the building through what appeared to be a fire door. There were plenty of black stretchers at this entrance, so we were at the right place. I promptly grabbed one and Soldier 'B' assisted as we loaded up our zombie friend. Then Soldier 'B' asked why these stretchers were not white, and the realisation hit us both at the same time as we reluctantly advanced towards the corridor to the morgue. These stretchers were white but had been stained with so much dead blood that they were now black! Our high morale from our proud good-spirited morning was about to change to desolation and all of our lives would be forever changed as we entered this tomb of death.

Pristina had been without power for some time so the first thing that hit us as we approached was the ungodly smell. You could actually taste the death, chew on it, in fact, from a good distance away. The rotten smell of decomposing human flesh consumed us. Even now, writing these words, I can taste, smell, and feel the morgue, a smell so bad that it makes your skin itch; even crawl! The temperatures were well over 30 degrees Celsius that summer and both sides of the corridors were lined from the floor to the ceiling with mainly women and young children. This left a narrow walkway only a few feet wide so I kept my head down and tried my hardest not to look to my left and right, but I just couldn't help myself. These people had not died from natural causes - they had been beaten, mutilated, raped, tortured, and murdered! Some were missing limbs whereas others were burnt or just too badly decomposed to observe their wounds to determine how they had actually died. I was gagging on the smell and my eyes were watering and I just wanted to run out of there and scream, but we still needed a place to dump this corpse.

Eventually, we found a widening where some doors were, and we set down our zombie Serb. Then, almost like a moth to a flame, in my direct eyesight there was a 10-year-old boy decomposing right in front of me. His chest cavity was non-existent, black and was full of maggots eating away at him. I could only imagine what had inflicted such a wound; a shotgun up close, a burst from a heavy machine gun or just maybe, he had been there that long that the maggots had just eaten away at him. I had a younger brother back home around the same age and all that I could think about was that if he had been unfortunate enough to be born in Pristina, then this could have well been his fate. Soldier 'B' recalls becoming overwhelmed by witnessing so much death and began to lean on a 'shelf' for support, only to find that this was not a shelf but in fact a set of mutilated feet. I don't recall leaving the morgue that day or how we returned to the rest of the Platoon, and I never wrote about this in my war journal...I didn't need to as it has stayed with me and haunted me every day since.

That afternoon, we returned to the jubilant scenes at the corner of the Ottoman mosque and despite the party atmosphere, I didn't feel like a liberator or a hero anymore; I felt only despair and anguish. Part of me died that day in that morgue and I became numb and emotionless, an empty vessel. Liberating the people of Kosovo came with a lifetime's debt of psychological suffering and pain. I was an optimistic boy that morning when we entered Pristina and in the space of several hours, I had lost faith in humanity along with the hopes and the romantic innocence associated with my childish pursuit of warfare. This was an unwanted, unwritten truth about the darker sides of warfare that is never taught, that you can never prepare yourself for. None of us ever spoke about our experiences of that morgue to the rest of 10 Platoon as this was our cross to bear and we didn't want to dampen the morale of the rest of the lads as they were still being festooned with flowers, hugs and kisses from the citizens of Pristina.

The very same day that we had entered the capital, the Russians had also uninvitedly landed at Pristina Airport. This could have potentially triggered an all-out war with Moscow, but they had not landed there to fight us. They were there to protect the Serbian nationals who wanted to remain in Kosovo and they too were greeted like heroes by the Serbian villagers who were as much afraid of NATO as the KLA. That night the city was alive with skirmishes, looters, and the still ongoing ethnic cleansing between the factions, so as a result, none of us slept! The following day, things seemed to calm down slightly as there were fewer Serbian troops in the capital, and we were all relieved that the Russians were very happy to work alongside us.

During the following days, we would escort the remaining Serb forces out of Pristina as they feared that the KLA would ambush them and they were right to think this way. The KLA were becoming more and more difficult to work with and would continue to attack Serb communities, hence we were caught in the middle as our mission had evolved to a more peacekeeping one. From my war journal, I noted that we escorted approximately 15 Serbian trucks full of loot ranging from electrical goods like TVs and stereos, to foodstuffs like tuna and mayonnaise. There was a clear scorched earth policy put in place by the Serbs and what they couldn't physically take with them, they burnt or destroyed, leaving nothing for the returning Albanian refugees.

In the days that followed, we made a local MUP (Serbian Police) station our temporary home on the outskirts of Pristina and were informed that the KLA were in a period of decommissioning, but this was all talk as they never really voluntarily handed in any of their weapons. They were always patrolling their own Albanian areas and even set up their own vehicle checkpoints. We would frequently come across highly fortified buildings with AK-47's pointing out of the windows and KLA banners proudly flying high. Having a permanent base allowed me to participate in foot patrols which I relished and on one such patrol, I recall that we were trying to haggle for some fresh milk from a local farmer but somehow, we found ourselves in the centre of a minefield. The farmer must have confused milk with mine. We carefully and instinctively relied on our training and exited the minefield by slowly retracing our steps and we all felt very lucky indeed. Needless to say, we never approached the locals for milk again! What was quite the spectacle though, was that a gigantic U.S. cruise missile had landed in this farmer's house and he was still living there like everything was normal with this huge unexploded rocket sticking out of the side of his building. We reported this like it was a normal daily occurrence then continued on our patrol.

Mines were an ongoing danger in Kosovo. We had been trained prior to our deployment on all of the different variants and we would frequently hear them exploding in the distance. This made patrolling on foot that bit more dangerous as we could easily wander into an unmarked minefield and this happened far too often. We had no idea where the Serbian soldiers had left their mines as they never marked them and neither did the returning Albanian refugees. Cattle would also be blown up by mainly anti-personnel mines and at one stage or another, we all had to deal with civilian casualties as a result of this malicious parting gift from the Serbian soldiers. These were mostly shrapnel wounds and breaks to the lower limbs with the bones more often than not protruding. Even back then, it was always the injuries to the children that bothered us; it was always the kids who seemed to suffer as a result of warfare.

We would eventually move to a small town to the west of Pristina called Obilić, and this would be our home for the rest of the tour. Our first priority was to gain intelligence from the surrounding local villages to determine their population, ethnicity, and wellbeing including food, power, and sanitation needs. I recall from my journal that the first village that we patrolled through had been decimated, burnt out, destroyed. There were no bodies but there were signs of death everywhere. Stale blood patches stained the ground, bullet holes marked the walls, and not one building was left intact. It was obvious to us all that something bad had happened here, something inhumane! Then the dark squaddie humour kicked in acting as an emotional deterrent, with Wade suggesting that a decent plasterer could make a mint here. This was by no means disrespectful but rather a coping mechanism that allowed us to function in a demanding and emotionally overcharged situation. We all joined in with the inappropriate comments and this helped us escape the very sombre atmosphere.

I remember that the last building was a farm complex, and, like the other buildings, it was in complete ruin. Thick smoke was coming from it as it was still on fire. A tiny elderly woman then emerged. I wrote in my journal that she was filthy and hadn't washed in weeks, her clothes were not her own and her shoes were several sizes too big. This distraught elderly lady immediately broke down in tears and collapsed in front of us and we knew very little of what she was saying but we didn't need to. It was clear that she was explaining what the Serbs had done to her village. Then, from the surrounding hills, a small number of villagers emerged and tearfully greeted us. From my journal, I noted that they were so welcoming and modest. These people had lost everything but somehow were still able to offer us hot drinks and bread. We gave the children boiled sweets and chocolate and provided the villagers with our spare rations; it was the least that we could do. I even gave my Manchester City top to a young kid who needed clothing. The villagers insisted that we ate and drank with them and even had alcohol in the form of Slivovitz, the deadliest drink known to man. I am still to this day humbled by the hospitality that we received from the Kosovar people in a time when they had lost everything and had nothing.

We would frequently patrol through countless villages and this pattern of destruction and death became our daily norm, especially around the town of Obilić. Obilić was a multi-ethnicity industrial town and is best described by Major Bridge, the commander of D Squadron, the King's Royal Hussars, who explains the cultural make-up in the following statement:

"One could not be bored. Almost unique in Kosovo, the Irish Guards' Battle Group still had large populations of Serbs and Gypsies as well as Albanians. D Squadron Group's Area of Operations was perhaps the most multi-ethnic of all. There was sufficient of each ethnic group to make them prepared to continue the struggles. The clashes between Serbs, Albanians and Gypsies - not forgetting Turks and Moslem Slavs - would keep us busy for the remainder of the tour; incidents involved murders, grenade attacks, drive-by shootings and the occasional riot."[xiv]

Obilić was indeed diverse and this made our job even more unpleasant. From my diary entry on 26th June, I documented that we had returned to one of our villages in our area of responsibility and were devastated at what we found. There had been reports of gunshots targeting this Gypsy-occupied village the previous day. The Gypsies' Village consisted of poorly constructed buildings and the sanitation ran directly through the main street. They had power and we would always clip these makeshift cables with our Warrior vehicle antennas when passing through. The children would always greet us, and we would give them boiled sweets and rations as they had nothing. On our previous visit, Wade had lost it when we had caught some Gypsies looting other Gypsies' homes and he really gave them a mouthful. This was the only time that I saw Wade ever lose his cool. We didn't need an interpreter to get our point across and although this was just a bollocking, these Gypsies had genuine fear in their eyes and expected to be shot! Maybe because we were uniformed soldiers, they had expected to be punished the Serbian way, but we were British, so a good telling off was as far as it went!

We had patrolled the area frequently, but we had nine villages and areas to patrol. We simply didn't have enough manpower to be everywhere at once to provide security and once we had patrolled through a village, atrocities from different factions often followed. Due to the imminent threat to this Gypsy village, we were accompanied by members of the Royal Military Police and a special forces soldier from the Special Air Service (SAS). We had patrolled this village in the early hours of that morning, but on our return at first light, we could see thick smoke from a distance and realised that the village was on fire. As we drove closer, we were all aware of what had happened in the several hours that we had been elsewhere. As we approached, the smoke became thicker and we were greeted with the stench of burning flesh; the smell of death.

As we patrolled through, the dismounted Infantry checked the remains of the buildings that were still burning and reported Gypsy corpse after Gypsy corpse on the radio. The buildings that were left standing were now full of bullet holes and all of the windows had been smashed. Blood was everywhere; the Gypsies had been massacred! We didn't know who exactly had committed this atrocity but intelligence from our accompanying military policeman informed us that it was conducted by Albanians. We never found out whether this was returning refugees, or if it was, in fact, the KLA who were responsible for this massacre, and nobody was ever held to account.

From my journal, I logged how we had to return back to the morgue with these burnt Gypsy bodies, but I have no recollection of this, and my journal entry is brief. However, I wrote how I couldn't comprehend how people could do such atrocities to each other. I logged that the returning Albanian refugees were initially saddened at seeing their homes, livelihoods and possessions obliterated and their friends and family members murdered at the hands of the Serbs. Their sorrow justifiably turned to rage towards the remaining Serbian villages and now, as peacekeepers, our role was to protect the Serbians from the wrath of the KLA and the returning Albanian refugees.

Once we became settled in Obilić, we would rotate our patrols in and around the key infrastructures of the factory, power plant, quarry, and coal mine. It was at the power plant that we had our most dangerous brush with death to date, but this would come from within! 10 Platoon was being used as a battlegroup asset and wherever there was trouble or tensions, we were deployed to assist. For the first two weeks in Kosovo, none of us had very much sleep and this fatigue would eventually take its toll. Drivers were throwing tracks from their Warriors and soldiers were falling asleep on guard and this was blatantly due to fatigue and operational burnout. Then, after yet another night of continuous patrols and limited sleep, on leaving the power plant for yet another village protection patrol, I heard a loud bang and screams from the back of my Warrior. I instinctively opened the back door using the button next to my driver's instrument panel anticipating the worst, grabbed a field dressing from my med kit and scrambled over the top of the Warrior to the rear. I had expected blood everywhere, as by now it was obvious that one of the Infantry dismounts had accidentally discharged his rifle in the confined space of the crew compartment where seven soldiers were crammed in like sardines.

We were passing another section and crew from 10 Platoon when this event happened and it soon became evident that Guardsman Chambers had a negligent discharge (ND) and had accidentally fired his weapon, narrowly missing another soldier's face in the process. When I arrived at the back of my vehicle, the dismounts were all dazed and confused and Butch, a driver from the one 10 crew, had Chambers pinned to the floor and was screaming at him. We were all physically and emotionally shattered and we could have quite easily taken our frustration out on Chambers, and Soldier 'B' remembers that is precisely what I did. On inspecting the interior of my vehicle, it soon became apparent the bullet had penetrated several of the 94mm Light Anti-Tank Weapons! These warheads were designed to penetrate the armour of main battle tanks and it was a miracle that they had not detonated as everyone close by including our sister section would have been annihilated.

As a consequence, we were now grounded until these powerful explosive rockets were deemed safe. Within hours, two soldiers from the Explosive Ordnance Disposal (EOD) arrived and would later explain how fortunate we had been, as the bullet had narrowly missed two of the lethal warheads. As a result of this near-fatal incident, we were given some stability and routine with a three-day patrol cycle followed by a day of administration and vehicle maintenance. We had all been working 24/7 and were at breaking point and there is only so much the human body can take. I have always been a firm believer that out of every experience, good or bad, you have to take something positive away. For 10 Platoon, this near-death experience brought us stability and routine, which meant sleep, and this was a positive outcome.

There are many events that happened in Kosovo that I have chosen to forget. One such event is when I went for a swim in a small lake. We didn't have any showers so this was one of the few ways in which we could keep clean and we had randomly come across this lake whilst on a routine foot patrol. Frank was the patrol commander and we had all agreed that on such a hot summer's day, a swim was in order. However, this would be conducted in a 50/50 split and whilst half of us went for this refreshing swim, Frank and the remainder of the patrol would provide cover from the high ground close by. As much as I would still like to deny the events that occurred on this day, they have been verified by several other members from 10 Platoon. Once Frank was in position on the high ground, he could clearly see that we were not the only ones using this lake and that, in fact, it had been used as a dumping ground for bodies. From his elevated position in overwatch, Frank could clearly see that we were swimming above corpses and that this lake was a mass war grave. I still deny that this ever happened, or maybe this is just my subconscious protecting me from this memory and the associated trauma. Frank and I, to this day, still continue to agree to disagree on the matter!

We would routinely patrol through the main village in the centre of Gračanica, which was heavily populated by Serbs, on route to our most eastern vehicle checkpoint (VCP 4) and we were never made welcome. Why would we? The Serbs who remained in Kosovo perceived us as foreign invaders who were aiding and abetting the KLA, a terrorist group, and they still classed themselves and the region as Serbian! The residents of Gračanica manned barricades to both the Northern and Southern Checkpoints and the Russians would often accompany us on these patrols. VCP 4 was never dull and after a while, some of the Infantry dismounts had made friends with some of the local girls and were invited to a party. Wade wasn't aware of this and believed that the lads were just going on a routine foot patrol and I can recall that I was annoyed with him as Wade had insisted that I stayed with the vehicle.

With just over an hour gone, we heard a bang from the direction of the foot patrol from VCP 4. Wade messaged the patrol on the radio, but we never received a reply; panic began to set in! Eventually we were informed that a Serbian sympathiser had thrown a hand grenade at the foot patrol but had miscalculated their whereabouts and had targeted the wrong window in the flats where they were at. The music was so loud at the house party that the British Soldiers were unaware of the grenade attack against them. Fortunately for them, it was the wrong window and, as a result, two elderly civilians were injured. Once they became aware of this, they answered us on the radio and quickly extracted to our vehicle and Wade was none the wiser, well, that is, until about a week ago when I informed him of the truth about what the patrol was actually up to that day. Even 22 years later, and despite the fact that I am no longer a soldier, I still sensed his disappointment in knowing that I was aware of this reckless act!

On a different day at VCP 4, a car of Albanians sped towards us and slammed on the brakes. Two men then frantically rushed out of this vehicle with their injured sister who had a gunshot wound to the face. The two brothers had been playing with the pistol and it had accidentally gone off with deadly consequences, but she was still alive. The closest Helicopter Landing Site (HLS) was on the other side of this Serbian barricaded village and they would not willingly let Albanians through, which was a sensitive issue that we would have to ignore. We put the casualty in the back of our Warrior, and we shot off as fast as we could, aggressively smashing through the barricades in a vain attempt to save this young woman's life. Once we arrived at the HLS, we performed first aid, but she was having unremitting fits and spasms and fought us at every step. The helicopter ambulance swiftly arrived, and she was evacuated, but we now had to evacuate ourselves as an angry mob of Serbians was forming around us. The young lady would later die of her wounds which was really disheartening as we had fought so hard to save her, and this was not the only occasion we would encounter the Serbian mob!

Then there was the Gračanica riot that we unknowingly and accidentally drove into on return from VCP 4, where we had to fix bayonets! Members of the Recce Platoon had had weapons stolen by the residents of this Serb village in Gračanica and had taken it upon themselves to conduct an unauthorised house to house search to retrieve them. They had been successful in recovering their weapons and had also retrieved some military grade Soviet-era weapons but had stirred up a hornet's nest in the process. We had no idea that our Recce Platoon was even in Gračanica that day and it was only by pure chance that we were able to rescue them. John Corcoran would always argue against the term 'rescue' and insisted that we merely assisted them with their safe extraction. Regardless, they were exhausted and about to be overrun by a very angry mob!

As soon as we approached, Wade instantly radioed the other vehicles from 10 Platoon for backup, something that maybe the Recce Platoon should have done as soon as they were overrun. When we arrived, the Recce boys were in a ring of steel with bayonets fixed and were being hit with rocks, bottles, bats, and whatever else the Serbs could get their hands on. I revved my mammoth engine and slowly forced my way into the angry crowd. Within moments, the mob were like ants swarming a beetle and had climbed on top of my Warrior and were hitting Wade and Soldier 'B' with baseball bats. The Serbs were helping themselves to a game of whack-a-mole at Wade and Soldier 'B's' expense! Two more Warriors promptly turned up from 10 Platoon and they were able to split the crowd, which was now in the region of 200 strong! The dismounts were ordered to fix bayonets and assist the Recce Platoon who were now in serious trouble due to fatigue. I genuinely believed that we would have to shoot our way out of this as the Serbs were barbaric and it wasn't just the men; it was all of them, including the elderly!

Our 20 'blades' from 10 Platoon then aggressively dismounted and attempted to separate the mob from the Recce Platoon, and this allowed some respite, but now, they were bearing the brunt of the mob. This allowed the Recce Platoon to safely extract on foot with all of their weapons, but we were now fighting for our lives. This was a ferocious riot and the men of 10 Platoon didn't have any riot gear and, as such, were just brawling with the Serbs to avoid being snatched or overrun! This was not how soldiers are traditionally taught to respond in such scenarios, but the brutality of the Serbians' attacks could only be matched with equal violence. The last thing that we wanted was to open fire but thankfully, the men of 10 Platoon were tough, disciplined soldiers and it never came to that. We then lined the Warriors up to block the road and this allowed us to separate the lads from the mob and the vehicles took the burden of the riot. Once safely past the barricades, the mob dispersed, and we were able to extract to the factory for some rest and repairs. More riots would follow, especially in the aftermath of funerals and we would eventually be provided with riot gear which made managing these situations that little bit easier.

Soldier 'G' would experience similar riots in the Serbian-bordering town of Podujevo to the North of Pristina. The Serbian paramilitary group the 'Arkan Tigers' had a presence there and were always antagonising NATO forces and were wanted for war crimes. After a grenade attack in the marketplace, a riot had followed which left Soldier 'G' and his team of Irish Guardsmen overrun and if it hadn't been for the assistance from the Italian element of NATO, then Soldier 'G' was adamant that they would have been overrun and killed by this guerrilla force. These types of riots were terrifying to be part of and happened all too often, especially surrounding funerals. Both Niall and Frank, as junior commanders, would frequently bear the brunt of these ferociously violent events, whereas I was always safely surrounded by Sheffield steel within the driver's cab of my Warrior. I suppose this was a perk of my delayed promotion!

My last engagement in Kosovo came when we were living at the Obilić football stadium; I recall that it was the middle of the night and we were being engaged by sniper fire. We were a skeleton crew, less than section strength, but I was able to locate the firing position and encouraged another Guardsman to accompany me on a stalk. We crawled for over 50 metres using a nearby concrete wall as cover before reaching the firing point of the sniper, which was a two-storey building, 10 metres to our left. After a short quick dash through the open ground, we clinically entered the ground floor of the sniper's building, ensuring that we were covering our arcs and checking the corners before making our way to the stairs. My heart was beating fast, and I switched my rifle to fully automatic as we cautiously made our way up the stairs to the first floor. I wasn't out of breath or tired, but my heart was beating like never before with adrenaline as we cleared each of the upstairs rooms. The sniper had extracted but his empty cases remained. We had found the firing point but he or she was still at large. However, this sniper would be someone else's problem as our time in Kosovo had come to an end.

On our return to Germany, no consideration was given towards our poor mental wellbeing and no counselling was ever offered, for that matter. Post Operational Stress Management was foreign to the British Army at this time. Soldiers in the 1990s dealt with their emotions like 'men,' and drank themselves into oblivion and this was an accepted practice throughout military culture. I had opted not to fly back with my brothers from 10 Platoon and instead volunteered to sail back on a ship from the Royal Fleet Auxiliary with all of the armoured vehicles. This five-day cruise had given me time to reflect on our time in Kosovo, however, despite my best efforts, I was still reliving that day in the morgue. I was having difficulty processing all of the needless death, the very worst of what mankind has to offer with all of the ethnic cleansing that we had witnessed. Over time, most of these horrific memories began to blur and disappear into my subconscious and if it wasn't for my own personal journal, they would have been lost forever.

A U.S. State Department report from November 1999 acknowledges that the U.N. Security Council had received reports that more than 11,000 civilians had been killed and were scattered in 529 reported mass graves and killing sites in Kosovo. Furthermore, 1.5 million Kosovar Albanians were forcibly expelled from their homes and these were, more often than not, burned to the ground. In total, an estimated 500 Albanian villages were reported to have been destroyed in March 1999 alone. Mass rape of the Kosovar women was encouraged by Serbian military commanders with hotels being used to facilitate this, but these numbers were under-reported due to the stigma that is associated with rape within Albanian society. The aftermath of these atrocities, after NATO's intervention, saw some revenge attacks on Serbian villages with between 200-400 residents killed. Nevertheless, after what the Kosovar people had endured, one could easily empathise with them, particularly after the 500 sites of summary executions were found. [xv]

Today I still have tremendous difficulty in understanding what happened to the people in Kosovo. We witnessed first-hand ethnic cleansing and the inevitable retribution that followed. I still cannot comprehend the evil that some men, soldiers, men of honour are capable of doing – these inhumane acts of savagery. One thing always stands out throughout my horrific ordeal though, and that is the kindness and generosity of the Kosovar people. Even when they had nothing, they would offer us everything and always made us feel welcome and this gave me a glimpse of hope for the future of humanity. In the years that followed, I would become distant and machine-like and more withdrawn. I began to drink heavily to the point of blacking out and not remembering the previous evening's events. It was easy to hide my underlying pain as many other soldiers at that time were doing exactly the same thing. The military machine didn't care as long as come 0800hrs you were on parade and ready to put a shift in.

After the tour, I finally completed my junior non-commissioned officer cadre and came top out of all of the Irish Guardsmen. I had previously accepted a posting to the Army Training Regiment as a personal administration instructor and I was looking forward to the new challenge. I was offered the opportunity to join the Battalion on a centenary trip to South Africa and to complete my next promotional course within a year as a reward for my hard work. The only caveat was that I had to turn down my posting to the UK and remain in the Battalion. However, my mind was made up as I just wanted to get away from everyone and everything that reminded me of Kosovo, and as a young man at this point, I wasn't motivated by career opportunities and progression. My only drive was to remove myself from everything and everyone that reminded me of the true cost of war - the avoidable casualties, the preventable deaths.... those mutilated civilians in the Pristina morgue.

My baby, 'Donegal' in Petrovec Macedonia, May 1999.

June 13 Pristina - trust nobody!

Chapter 6.
The Road to Hell

I desperately needed a break from my Battalion and Germany, as everything there was a daily reminder of Kosovo. For the next two years, I would learn some invaluable lessons as a Barrack Room Instructor at the Army Training Regiment in Pirbright. Four years before, I had been a recruit here and now, with two operational tours under my belt, I would be returning as an administration instructor. My role would be to assist the Platoon Sergeant with the day-to-day running of the platoon as well as helping the recruits with their own personal administration. I would experience military life outside the self-absorbed bubble of the Irish Guards and thoroughly enjoyed working with different Regiments, including those instructors from logistical support units. Then, in my second year, the world would change forever in the aftermath of the events on 9th September 2001.

Everybody knows exactly where they were when the terror attacks were carried out by Osama Bin Laden and Al Qaeda. For me, I was in the platoon office of Talavera Platoon listening to Virgin radio when the news broke. I immediately made my way to the Corporal's Mess and watched in horror as the day's events unfolded. Part of me was secretly excited as I knew that someone or some country would be held accountable for this unforgivable act and I knew that a war was on the horizon. The following day, Frank and I asked to be returned to our Battalion as they were deployed in the Middle East on a tactical exercise in Oman as we were primarily

Infantry soldiers over recruit instructors, however, our requests would be immediately denied.

By this point, I had forcibly drunk away my memories from Kosovo and had successfully boxed them away in my subconscious. I had become driven and competent at work and that's all that mattered to me now. If I wasn't beforehand, I was now fully indoctrinated into the military, and, unlike Frank, I was returned to the Irish Guards shortly after the events of 9/11, with the prospect of another high-intensity deployment on the horizon. I was psychologically broken after Kosovo, a shell of my former self, but after two years away from my Battalion, I had thrown myself completely into work and this had helped me to cope with my internal demons, along with alcohol, of course. Frank would narrowly miss out on the initial war in Iraq and I believe that he consequently volunteered for so many future deployments to make up for this perceived loss. Looking back, I probably played a significant part to play in his frequent deployments by mocking him about missing the 2003 War, which was childish and immature, yet at the time was perceived as 'banter.'

In the winter of 2002, I had finally been selected to attend my next promotion course called the Section Commanders' Battle Course (SCBC). I had heard all about the legendary horror stories of the Brecon Beacons in Wales and this didn't deter or worry me in the least, as I never shirked away from a challenge. This course would qualify me for promotion, and in 'The Guards,' that meant a fast track into the Sergeants' Mess with the rank of Lance Sergeant but more important than that, I would get the opportunity to command men in the coming war!

I didn't find this course particularly difficult and actually thoroughly enjoyed it. The preliminary skill at arms phase was what essentially qualified you for promotion due to the instructional qualification and, as a result, two of my friends would drop out of the secondary arduous tactical phase (once qualified for promotion, of course). I recall being drunk for the majority of this initial phase but still passed with relevant ease. I was still drinking heavily to repress my memories from Kosovo and would bluff my way through this instructional phase by always putting my hand up to volunteer to take the lessons. A dark art known as Brecon bingo! You are taught to never volunteer for anything in the military, but I did quite the opposite in this classroom and it worked. I embraced my time at the Infantry Battle School in Brecon and was excelling, which was only achieved by suppressing and denying my battlefield trauma by unreservedly hurling myself into work.

The secondary phase focuses on section and platoon tactics and in the early tactical and planning classroom lessons, I was very vocal in debate and some of my course work was even put-on display as an example for other students to follow. This was rare, as it was normally reserved for students from the SAS or other special forces background. Naturally, fallout was expected, and the other students would put apples on our instructor's desk and even the odd romantic note from myself; this was some good banter. In the early tactical exercises, I was tasked to lead the 'difficult' anti-armour ambush and succeeded with flying colours. I was suppressing my trauma from Kosovo by unreservedly throwing myself into this demanding course. This was my coping mechanism and how I would continue to manage my poor mental health throughout my career in the Army - Work! Work! Work!

Next up was the dreaded but iconic 'fan dance.' This was a long-range tactical insertion over the most arduous and mountainous land in Wales, Pen y Fan. It was an inter-section race but with platoon weapons including the heavy General-Purpose Machine Gun (GPMG or Gympie). Naturally, I volunteered to carry the 'Gympie' for the first phase as I was the fittest in my section. Then, on the second phase and eventually for the whole race. I remember bumping into Frank at the top of the 'Fan', and, despite the blizzards and the heavy snow, I automatically recognised him running towards me. He was on a map-reading instructors' course and we had time for a quick chat whilst I waited for the rest of my section to catch up. We often still joke about this random encounter as I had left my section behind despite carrying all of the heavy equipment!

After this event, my instructor informed me that he had never seen a student carry the 'Gympie' for the whole duration of the insertion and was eager to know why I did it. I joked that due to the harsh winter weather conditions, the 'Gympie' was 'warm kit' and had kept me from freezing to death. He chuckled and informed me that if I kept things up, I would be on for a distinction grade! This didn't happen though as I have always tended to say the wrong thing to the wrong person at the wrong time and that is exactly what I did.

During the final exercise, I was approached by the Company Commander, a Major from the elite Pathfinder Platoon. He approached me to consider attending selection for his special forces' unit which I disrespectfully declined. My snub had angered him because of my blunt and direct refusal. I had pointed out that as the Pathfinders were an advanced reconnaissance unit, there was no appeal for real Infantry soldiers such as myself who craved combat. Besides, orders had come through that the Irish Guards were going to war and that was all that was important to me now. I would get the opportunity to lead men in battle, to test our metal and put our training to the test. Who cares about an average pass? At least I received an A grade for my fitness which is something Frankie failed to achieve when attending SCBC. This is something that I still frequently remind him about as we still argue about who was the fittest throughout our service!

It was on this course that I first got to know Bob. Bob was already a Lance Sergeant but was attending a similar course called the Platoon Sergeants' Battle Course (PSBC). This was a course I would also later complete to qualify for my next promotion. Bob would become a dear friend and we kept in contact even after our service had ended. He was a member of the Reconnaissance Platoon in Kosovo and was part of the Gračanica riot and is another one who claims that they had the situation under control! Bob would later be shot in the chest in Iraq and would almost die from his wounds. However, he would make an incredible recovery and reach the rank of Captain before leaving the British Army in early 2021. Bob became immensely angry after the war in Iraq and I believe that this was as a result of the lack of welfare support that he received when recovering from his near-fatal gunshot wound to the chest. Yet again, no psychological support was offered for his mental wellbeing.

Once the course was completed, I returned to the Irish Guards in the January of 2003 and went back to my old Platoon in Number 4 Company. I loved 10 Platoon; in fact, my loyalty is still to the men who served in this Platoon and is something that I will always cherish. I was given my own section and also assigned a Warrior crew. This was a dream come true for me and I was uncontrollably excited. We were aware that Iraq was ruled by the tyrant, Saddam

Hussein, and that the Iraqi people were oppressed; furthermore, that they had (suspected) weapons of mass destruction (WMDs). Then there were the additional 'intelligent' links to 9/11 to contemplate. As a child, I had enjoyed watching the live scenes from the 1991 Gulf War pan out. I had read the books and played video games based on this conflict and now I was going to lead men in battle in its sequel. Regardless of the reasons or the politics, I was in heaven - I was going to WAR!

My section second in command (2i/c) was a well-built Northern Irish chap called Stevie and, at the time, we never saw eye to eye. Iraq would be his first operational tour and he was nervous, but he showed this, especially in front of the men. There is nothing wrong with being afraid, we all were, but as a commander, you have to always put on a show of confidence for the Guardsmen. He had also decided to leave the Army and had already handed in his twelve months' notice which I misinterpreted as lacking commitment to the team. I didn't really acknowledge his point of view at the time, and this didn't help our relationship. All I wanted to do was to please my commanders by excelling on the battlefield, whereas I felt that Stevie just wanted to survive the impending war and return home. The Army was not for him and he wanted to return to civilian life which I can now understand and respect, but I was young, stubborn, egotistical, and completely indoctrinated.

As a regiment, the Irish Guards were disseminated to supplement and increase the manning of other battle groups. For the men of 10 Platoon, they would be sent to support the 1st Battalion of the Royal Regiment of Fusiliers (1RRF). Our desert warfare training began in Celle, a small garrison to the northeast of Hanover, during an unforgiving traditional German winter. Our platoon was strong, and we promptly outshone the soldiers of Y Company 1RRF that we were now attached to. This would result in 10 Platoon being disseminated and separated even further as we were split down into section strength. I was attached to Y Company's second platoon and given the call sign 23/C.

The men of Y Company were good soldiers, but we were an exceptional Platoon that was well-led and combat-hardened, and I can understand why they separated us. Y Company's Commander, Major Nanson was one of the best officers that I had the pleasure of working for and was an inspiring leader, second only to Major Knaggs. After the war, he pulled me to one side and said that I was one of his best section commanders which was a huge compliment as I was from another Regiment. This was unexpected due to my strong opinions which meant that I often clashed with senior commanders such as himself.

In early February 2003, I had volunteered to deploy early to Kuwait as part of the advance party. This made perfect sense to me as I had no family or girlfriend and was overly eager to get stuck in. This would allow the rest of the guys to have a few more days to relax and say their goodbyes to their families. My first night in Kuwait was one that I will never forget. Tommy and I would be dropped off by helicopter in what appeared to be a random part of the Kuwaiti desert and were told to start planning. Planning for what? I was a low-level commander and Tommy was Warrior Crew, a Warrior Commander to be precise, and his exploits during the war would earn him the nickname of 'Tommy the Gun,' as a result of his battlefield feats.

The desert can be freezing at night and there was an unforgiving wind that was cutting right through us. However, we were able to build a windbreak out of a large plastic panel that we found, and this offered us some relief. We then set out our sleeping bags and called it a day. That night, whilst we were attempting to sleep, I felt something large jump onto my legs. In a reflex motion, I kicked my legs upwards not knowing that this was a large camel spider which was now on a collision course with my face! I automatically thought of the face-huggers from the Alien film franchise as this furry monstrosity rapidly approached my face. Fortunately, the camel spider bounced off my head as I embarrassingly let out a very loud feminine scream! I then recall stabbing and slashing the surrounding sand for the next few minutes with my bayonet in a blind panic whilst Tommy laughed uncontrollably. I have never been afraid of nature, but this was the exception as camel spiders are not from this planet!

The following days saw more and more troops arrive at our location before eventually, all of the 1RRF Battlegroup had arrived. The fighting elements of the Battlegroup consisted of 42 Warrior armoured fighting vehicles and 14 Challenger 2 main battle tanks from the Queen's Royal Lancers (QRL). We would be part of the much larger 7Th Armoured Brigade, 'The Desert Rats' and our mission would be to capture the southern Iraqi city of Basra.

We trained vigorously for the next three weeks, participating in realistic battle scenarios, but surprisingly, no bayonet fighting. I don't believe that this was due to the climate but rather because it wasn't necessary as we were already pumped and ready to kill. There was also a real danger that chemical or biological warfare would be used against us and, as a result, extra training was conducted in this discipline. We had already been given our anthrax injections before being deployed and now we were ordered to take our nerve agent pre-treatment pills every eight hours. This was intended to help us fight longer during a chemical/biological attack and I gave all of my lads the personal option to take these pills with some, including myself, opting out. We were also issued with atropine pens that we were to self-inject to help prevent muscle spasms if we were subjected to a chemical/biological attack and we all genuinely believed that at some point, Saddam Hussein would use these weapons on us. Let us not forget that this was part of the reason that we were going to war to begin with - the search for the weapons of mass destruction.

I remember the first time that we came under a suspected chemical attack. I was over halfway to the portable toilets that were located about 800m away from my vehicle when that attack alarm went off. Everyone was shouting, 'GAS, GAS, GAS!' An Iraqi scud rocket was in flight to our location and I was stuck in no man's land. I had two options; return to my vehicle to safety and probably poo myself and be ridiculed by my men or should I continue to the portable toilets and risk death? Let's just say that I made the right decision and maintained my dignity. Luckily, the rocket overshot us, but this was a stark warning of what was to come. As a result of this attack, I chose to increase the intensity of the training of my section which now included further training in our limited downtime.

I would mark out Russian trench systems with tape on the desert floor and I would drill my section relentlessly until we had our movements perfected. We would practice in different roles with the most junior soldier leading so that every member of the team knew what the other members' responsibilities were. We would do the same for buildings and I was insistent that every soldier knew and could anticipate exactly what the others were doing. This battlefield awareness would be crucial in the coming months and would help to keep my men alive.

I would arrange familiarisation training of the more specialised battalion weapons, such as the 81mm mortars and the Milan anti-tank weapons, as I wanted my men to be trained and prepared for anything. I was conscious of the lack of bayonet fighting so, as an alternative, at the end of every day, we would sharpen our bayonets for an hour or so. I believed that this was best for my men as it would prepare them mentally for the hard battles that would follow. This would frustrate my Platoon Sergeant as British Army policy forbids the sharpening of bayonets except in times of war. Every evening, he would inform me that this was illegal, and he was correct, but when were we expected to sharpen them? Just before we needed them? I think not, so every evening, I defied his orders.

The road to hell is paved with good intentions and all I wanted to do was to prepare my men as best I could for the pending conflict. In the weeks that followed, I noticed that Dave had become slightly withdrawn and not once did I ask why or question his mental health which is something, in retrospect, that I sincerely regret. Dave had recently completed training, in fact, apart from Pez, all of my Guardsmen were fresh out of the factory and all of them were teenagers. Due to this period of self-solitude, Dave was given the nickname of 'Mad Dave', which is, regrettably and ironically, what he became.

In hindsight, I do think that in the build-up to the war, I was oblivious to the additional pressure that I put on my team. I was still suffering from the emotional trauma from my time in Kosovo, and I pushed my men to their physical and mental limits. My sole priority was to fulfil the Army's needs and no consideration was ever given to the welfare or mental wellbeing of my men. From their perspective, this was their first operational tour, they were preparing to have chemical/biological weapons used against them and we were already being engaged with medium-range rockets. Then there were the two divisions of Iraqi armour waiting for us across the border and the vast Iraqi Army that outnumbered us man for man on our mission to Basra. Not once did I ask my men how they were feeling or if they had any concerns. My job was to lead my men into battle, to close with and engage the enemy at close quarters; it was the section commanders who would win this war and, as such, there was no time for emotions, for doubt, for weakness!

The team of men in my section seemed confident and ready on the outside but, looking back, this was just a charade, a false front. Yes, they were well-drilled, and I was confident in their abilities, and even 'Mad Dave' had come out of his shell, but one could never tell how they really felt. We had all been institutionalised, reprogrammed to suppress our emotions and this had established a toxic alpha mentality that was detrimental to the mental health of all of my generation of soldiers. Dave had come out of his shell and was now overly confident which had a knock-on effect that helped to inspire the other Guardsmen. Looking back, I believe that this was the turning point when his mental health began to deteriorate.

Mac, Ski and Ricky were all from the same area of Birmingham and shared a dark sense of humour. They had given their rifles names such as 'the widow maker' and had even named our vehicle 'the Middle East Beast.' I had opted for the name 'Gulf club 7' after the 90s band but had been outvoted. Pez was a drinking buddy of mine and a good friend; he was the joker of the pack and would provide us with some much-needed boosts to our morale. Pez was the complete opposite of what you would expect from a warfighting Infanteer, but he was the much-needed heart and soul of our team. As our training intensified, I recall that we were all in good spirits when we heard a pop and a scream. One of the Irish Guards in another vehicle had accidentally shot himself in the neck. 'Diggler' was cleaning his rifle with his magazine on and, in doing so, had accidentally discharged a round. He was really lucky that this negligent discharge had only grazed his neck as it could have been fatal. This incident was an unwanted reminder of why we were here and what dangers awaited us across the border in Iraq.

It was now mid-March and news had come down the chain of command that President George W. Bush had threatened Saddam Hussein with nuclear retaliatory action if he used chemical or biological weapons on coalition forces. Saddam Hussein had previously used chemical weapons on several occasions, including on his own people. The international community had condemned the Halabja Massacre when Saddam had used chemical weapons on the Kurdish population in 1988, killing 5000 of his own citizens in the process.[xvi] We were all in genuine fear of being 'gassed' but now there was the added dangers and mental stress of a nuclear war to contemplate. I had reassured my men that this was not the case and that the only fighting would be conducted in the traditional attrition way. We had superior equipment, better weapons and were highly trained. The Iraqis had been given a 48hr deadline to surrender and by now, we were in the final stages of our planning process known as battle procedure. We were ready and the plan was to invade on the 20th March when the call came forward; 'all commanders report to Major Nanson immediately!'

This was the 19th of March and I was halfway through delivering my orders to my section for an attack the following day. I grabbed my rifle and respirator (gas mask) and sprinted towards the Company Commander's vehicle for the best news that I had ever received, some quick battle orders. Major Nanson was brief and direct and stated that 'two Iraqi armoured divisions were approaching from the North; we all know our jobs and have been well trained. Mount up; we're going to War!' I was overjoyed with the romanticism of the pending battles and was certain that my men felt the same; didn't they?

I quickly returned to my Warrior and briefed up my men with the same quick battle orders that I had just received and was taken aback at their lack of enthusiasm. As I counted my men into the vehicle, it suddenly dawned on me how young and afraid they actually were. Ricky was the last one in and had just turned 18; in fact, he had celebrated his birthday whilst in Kuwait. I'll never forget the realisation and the burden of command when he pulled me to one side and asked me to make sure that he came back alive! There is no training that can prepare you for the emotional weight that commanders have to carry, especially in the unpredictable environment of warfare, so I lied. I told Ricky that of course I was going to bring him home alive. I had to maintain the confidence of my men whatever the cost. The mission was all that mattered now.

As we advanced to the Kuwait-Iraqi border, we came under heavy mortar fire. These were not the anticipated high explosive bombs, but rather, C.S. gas bombs. We were already in our full chemical suits, boots and gloves and were now required to put our respirators on. The conditions in the back of a Warrior vehicle are extremely cramped and uncomfortable at the best of times and now our bodies were under additional strain due to the heat and these chemical suits. Every now and again, the back door would open, and we would get out, go firm and observe for the enemy but we were still in Kuwait and there was no sign of any Iraqi forces. I remember Pez having what could only be described as a tantrum as he could no longer take the heat and claustrophobic conditions in the back of our Warrior. He ripped off his respirator and asked someone to shoot him, to put him out of his hell!

I now had a difficult command decision to make as it was obvious that my men could not sustain themselves for long periods in their full chemical suits and respirators. They were losing the will to fight and, in Pez's case, the will to live! I reluctantly gave the command for them to remove their respirators until they were needed and that everyone needed to hydrate. The lads then began to sing songs as we approached the border and I believe that this calmed them. I was listening to the ongoing battle on my radio and was talking to the vehicle crew but as we crossed the Kuwait border into Iraq, they were singing 'We're all going on a summer holiday,' by Cliff Richard. The order would later be given to remove our chemical suits as we were not combat-effective whilst wearing these in the Iraqi desert, especially when you bear in mind that we had trained for this war in the snow in the sub-zero temperatures of Northern Germany. I suppose Pez had already anticipated this!

For the next few hours, we would hear the loud bangs of bullets and explosions from the confines and safety of our armoured vehicle as the battle unfolded around us. This was until it was Y Company's turn to lead the invasion. The 1RRF were designated the lead armoured battlegroup and the British Army's doctrine is one of a basic rule of three; assault the enemy, suppress the enemy and then be in reserve. It is every military commander's dream (or was mine at least) to lead men in battle and I would now get my first chance on an advance to contact in war.

We were now at the very tip of the spear and I began to brief my team on the environment that awaited them outside the safety of the Warrior. I explained that we had two additional Warriors to our rear and two friendly tanks to each flank. Then the vehicle commander, 'Dicky', began to count us down from 10 to 1, before we deployed on the unfamiliar ground in Iraq. I looked at my men and gave them a quick brief and reminded them to trust their training. I told them to look for cover and that they should advance no farther than the small ridge, just before the road to our immediate front. Ricky was sat opposite to me and I purposely smashed my helmet against his to gee him up and told him to stay close. I was adamant that I had to be the first man out; this was against protocols as our doctrine stated that a Guardsman should always be the first man to deploy, a sandbag! I disagreed with this and wanted to set the example to lead my men, but I was slightly unsure if the others would follow. We were about to deploy from the safety of an armoured vehicle into our first firefight and I could sense that they were afraid. Therefore, it was vital that my second man, Ricky, immediately followed my lead and, like the brave and courageous men I knew they could be, they all overcame their fears despite the incoming enemy fire.

I remember thinking that it was nice to get out and stretch our legs and the small ridge to our front would provide ideal cover from view and shield us from small arms fire as we tactically advanced, keeping low and moving fast. It's amazing how fast you can crawl when the enemy is trying to shoot you! Once at the ridge, I gave the order to 'watch and shoot', or, in layman's terms, if you see any enemy, engage them at your own discretion. The battle appeared to be going very well and I was very proud of my men and how they were handling themselves in their first engagement. Even my 2i/c Stevie, who I had former doubts about, was doing an exceptional job; all my previous concerns were now quelled, and the men of 23/C operated as a single organism. Then the RPGs and mortars began to rain in. This was accompanied by heavy small arms fire and suddenly, I felt outgunned.

Whilst we were under heavy fire, the Company Commander had asked for a situation report as the advance had halted. I informed him that we were taking both heavy direct and indirect fire from the village approximately 600 metres north of our location. Major Nanson acknowledged my report and halted our advance and mentioned that he was going to request battlegroup assets to assist us. I encourage my men to keep moving and to change firing positions frequently, to watch out for snipers and to conserve ammo; that they should only shoot what they could positively identify to avoid unnecessary civilian casualties. We then witnessed this disappointing battlegroup asset as a single U.S. Super-Cobra attack helicopter conducted a fly-by over the village.

'Is that it?' I thought to myself! Moments later, a squadron of these harbingers of death let loose all of their payload on this village at what can only be described as a truly epic and marvellous sight. I remember thinking that this was overkill, this show of superior firepower, but at the same time, this was some good old-fashioned American shock and awe! It was now obvious that the first helicopter must have been identifying all of the enemy positions for the rest of the squadron to target.

I can still recall the relief and sense of total euphoria as the village burnt before us. We were all jubilantly high-fiving each other as the enemy were no longer shooting at us; they had been effectively neutralised by our American aviator cousins. This euphoria would quickly turn to despair as a civilian in a pickup truck rapidly approached us waving a white flag. I shouted, 'Possible suicide truck!' and told my men to prepare to engage when I noticed that this truck was full of civilian casualties, mainly women and children. This was just the first of many and before we knew it, we were inundated with civilian casualties from the airstrike that, moments earlier, we had been celebrating. This was not what I had envisioned being a leader of men and modern warfare would be like. My misguided romanticised association with warfare left me that day and I immediately thought about the morgue in Pristina. I no longer perceived myself as the hero as I now felt more like the villain. This horrific incident would make me completely numb as I shut down emotionally and tried to forget this massacre, this acceptable collateral damage, the untold darker side of warfare.

We were trained to dehumanise the enemy, reprogrammed not to hesitate, and to kill through the use of controlled aggression and behavioural conditioning, but there will never be any sufficient training that could have prepared us for this slaughter. I had previously witnessed the worst that mankind had to offer during my time in Kosovo, and now, I had played my own role in the death and mutilations of these Iraqi women and children. Once we were no longer in danger, I gave the command for my delta fire team to provide battlefield first aid to these unfortunate civilians. I told my team to use all of the spare medical supplies, but this was nowhere near enough. I can still and quite vividly see the shocked look on my men's faces as they attempted complex first aid on the wide range of injuries that we were not adequately trained to deal with. It was evident that we needed help.

I recall that one of the casualties was a young girl, aged no more than 10 years old. She had some minor shrapnel injuries, but her right foot was facing the wrong way and the back of her thigh bone was protruding through the skin on the wrong side of her body. This was an open complicated fracture and Ski, our medic, just looked right at me in complete shock. I barked at him to use one of our first field dressings to make a doughnut bandage to prevent even more blood loss, and he did just that. Next, there was a heavily pregnant woman with shrapnel injuries to her back. She was in a full black burka and the trauma had induced her labour. Her husband was lost and looked to us for guidance. 'Put her on all fours!' I yelled and mimicked the position and she soon copied. There were countless men, but we paid little attention to them, we never did. We eventually ran out of medical supplies and were unable to assist the remaining children suffering from burns and blast wounds.

New orders were coming in through my radio as I was failing to manage this array of complex casualties and we were ordered to mount up and continue the advance. I thought back to my time in Kosovo and my regret about not being able to do more to help the civilians there and decided that I was going to make a stand, to break rank and defy my orders. My callsign, 23/C, was not going anywhere until I had armoured ambulances on my position, with qualified medics and doctors to help these dying civilians. Major Nanson was furious and sent my Platoon Commander forward to coerce me into mounting up and to follow his orders. I understood that he was controlling a whole battlegroup and that this was not a priority for him, but for us, this was our only priority as we were to blame. Hence, to his frustration, I continued to ignore his orders.

When my Platoon Commander finally arrived, he nervously crawled forward in a crab-like motion as we were now on the receiving end of some more small arms fire. I walked over to him in plain sight as bullets flew past me. I had no regard for my own safety as my only priority was the medical care of these civilians. I was no longer concerned with the mission and, for the first time, the Army's needs were not important to me. My Platoon Commander then popped up and saw the aftereffects of the air strike and wholeheartedly agreed with my decision to request medical support for these poor civilians - acceptable collateral damage.

Words cannot describe the carnage that had occurred, and he agreed that we owed it to these civilians to treat them and that is what eventually happened. Once the armoured battlefield ambulances arrived, we provided protection as the casualties were loaded up. Then, almost immediately, I was ordered to mount up and advance. This time I complied, and the next few days became a blur as I was traumatised and unable to process the events of what had just occurred. I thought that I was battle-hardened as this was my third operational deployment. I had never been more mistaken, and I can only imagine how this event affected my younger, less-experienced soldiers and the trauma that it continues to cause.

In the years that followed, Ski would write a letter from his prison cell to the Guardian stating that it was this event along with a string of others that had initiated his own deteriorating mental health. I believe that this traumatic event was, at part, the reason why he had been incarcerated. Yet, this is something that the Ministry of

Defence has always denied as after the war they diagnosed Ski with a personality disorder rather than PTSD. He wrote.

'On one of the first days after we breached the border, our section went firm while the American gunships' Cobra helicopters cleared a village. It was an awesome sight, but an hour or so after it was chaos as cars came racing out of the village. I remember one car came up to me. Immediately, I knew there was something wrong as the driver started to get out. His wife and kids had been shot to pieces and were bleeding badly. This man brought them to me to help them. All I could do was look at them in shock knowing that we couldn't use our kit on them to help because we only had enough for ourselves.'[xvii]

Pez has also been haunted by this incident and only really occasionally speaks about it when blind drunk. He explained that he pushed it down deep so that he doesn't have to remember it. Pez vividly recalls a white Land Rover-type vehicle approaching us when I gave the command to prepare to engage before I paused the order when an Iraqi man exited, distraught and in tears. His wife appeared to be dead in the front as he made his way to the back of the vehicle. He then advanced towards us, crying, desperately seeking help, cradling his daughter who appeared to have been shot multiple times in the back. Pez broke cover, removed his morphine pen and instinctively advanced towards this young girl to help, only to be aggressively commanded by myself to stay firm and 'watch and shoot.' This was not a tactical act but more so a human response and because Pez has always been all heart, he impulsively wanted to save these people.

From Pez's perspective, all he wanted to do was to help these civilians and he believed that I lacked any compassion in preventing him from doing so. Maybe I did, but whatever compassion I had left from my continued indoctrination was to my men, and our limited medical supplies were exclusively for ourselves. Pez recalls that after I refused to allow him to apply first aid, I directed the civilian casualties through the lines to a medical aid post to our rear and that's when he began to see his one-time drinking buddy in a different light and our friendship was no more. This would be only the first wave of civilian casualties and it would seem that yet again, it is the collateral damage and the true nature of warfare, the accepted civilian casualties that always have a lasting impact on our soldiers' mental health.

Pez would go AWOL in 2004 for six years before being dishonourably discharged in 2010. No questions were asked as to why he had gone absent to begin with, and I can only speculate that it was due to the emotional trauma suffered from this incident. What is interesting is the fact that closing and engaging with the enemy has not affected Pez as, like many of us, the Iraqi Army and its soldiers seemed fair game. When asked if he was aiming to 'shoot to kill,' he unequivocally replied with a yes, but he went on to state that it was honestly hard to acknowledge 'who actually shot who' because of the amount of firepower that we had at our disposal. As I have previously mentioned, Pez was an average combat soldier at best, yet, when called upon, he didn't hesitate, his training took over and every time he pulled the trigger, he was intent on killing another human being, for which, even today, he has no remorse. I cannot help but conclude that this was a direct result of our behavioural training and the way in which we were taught to dehumanise the enemy.

Ski would be the first of my team to succumb to his battlefield trauma. He would be followed by Mac, Dave, Stevie, Pez, and eventually, myself. Poor mental health can often manifest itself in many different ways. Personally, I chose to deny this traumatic incident and suppressed its very existence for almost fifteen years. The rest of my men were not so fortunate as the trauma of the darker side of warfare would have an almost immediate effect on all of their lives. Five members of my team would show signs of poor mental health, PTSD and battlefield trauma in the years that followed. After the war, we would be separated and go our different ways. Then, one by one, they would be consumed by the horrors of war that they had not only witnessed but had also a hand in. As for Ricky, I have no idea if this incident affected his mental health in any way, but what I do know is that we would have to face more challenges as we advanced onwards to complete our mission; to capture the southern Iraqi city of Basa.

Chapter 7.
The Battle for Basra

I don't know if it was the lack of sleep, operational stress, the battlefield trauma of witnessing the civilian casualties or maybe a combination of all, but the days seemed to disappear until we arrived at Basra International Airport on the 23rd of March. Allied airpower had once again flexed its superior muscles and had decimated most of the Iraqi forces. This was supported by the artillery and tanks from the 1RRF Battlegroup which had resulted in the less-equipped Iraqi Army being easily defeated. By the time we had dismounted to assault Basra International Airport, we were just clearing out any stragglers who were brave enough to remain and fight.

It was our job to clear the terminal buildings and we dismounted several hundred metres away to allow the tanks and Warrior crews to provide adequate fire support. As we advanced, our first priority was to clear the runway of any Iraqi infantry, however, as we thoroughly cleared the Iraqi defensive position and vehicles, there was no resistance whatsoever. By now, the runways were a graveyard of charred Iraqi soldiers and dismembered body parts. Once you have been up close and smelt the burnt remains of what once was a person, the smell, the taste stays with you for life. At the time, this didn't bother me and as we prodded these corpses with our bayonets for signs of life, this was our new normal. (This was a necessary evil as we had received intelligence that some soldiers were hiding amongst the enemy dead, attempting to ambush us).

Until you have experienced warfare first-hand, it is impossible to contemplate the soldier's mindset. Your fear and anxiety are gradually taken over by a numbness as you emotionally shut down to an almost dormant state of mind. Your training kicks in and all of the death, destruction and the darker side of warfare become just a normal daily occurrence as you enter a zombie-like state. This process is inevitable and varies in the time it takes, but personally, and for the men of 23/C, this had happened on the first day of the war. I would remain in the emotionless mindset for the many years that followed as this prevented me from acknowledging my own battlefield trauma - memories that I would suppress in a hopeless attempt to forget the collateral damage, the death of civilians, the darker side of warfare.

I recall that we entered the terminal building at international arrivals; ironically, a week previously, this was my perfect summer holiday and now it had turned into a summer hell. We swept through the airport, swiftly clearing room by room, corridors and lounges. My men were fluid and proficient and moved as one; I was proud of their professionalism. We could hear firefights close by and I was monitoring the battlefield radio for updates and new orders when I suddenly noticed a sign for the duty-free shop. I knew that several of my team were smokers and had run out of cigarettes, so it was time to raise the morale of my men. Let's take a detour to the duty-free.

I could still hear Iraqi resistance close by and then some loud screams of, 'room clear,' and 'corridor clear,' from other British soldiers. The race was now on for the spoils of war, for the duty-free. To my surprise, we were not the first soldiers to think about this and a fellow section from the Irish Guards had beaten us there and were already stocking up on 'essential supplies'. We grabbed a few packs of smokes for the lads as they didn't deserve any additional stress, a few chocolate bars, and a bottle of Jack Daniel's, then returned to mission.

Looting is illegal but the welfare of my men superseded this little misdemeanour. We had all been exposed to the harsh reality of warfare and needed a pick-me-up. After all, one of the key principles of war is 'maintenance of morale' and my men needed this boost to their morale to sustain and prepare them for the battles to come. That night, we slept in the airport and a battery of AS-90 self-propelled guns moved in close by. The persistent loud firing throughout the night comforted me and helped me catch up on some much-needed sleep in the same way a lullaby is to a baby.

In the following days we were resupplied and rested and the battle preparation and planning was now fully underway to assault the southern Iraqi city of Basra. I can only suspect that I was being punished for not following orders on the advance to contact as my team were always tasked for rear protection and vehicle checkpoint duties during our stay at the airport. We were now all together as a Company and the other Irish Guardsmen would mock us for being put on these duties as they were tasked with more offensive missions. However, they were unaware of what we had been through and none of us spoke of what we had witnessed. In fact, none of my men have ever spoken to me about their poor mental health or the incident at the village in the years that followed. This is the way things were back then and, of course, one must not forget that we were trained to ignore our emotions. We were all psychologically fragile, and, looking back, maybe we were given these boring duties not as a punishment but as respite?

For the next ten days, we would siege the city of Basra in what in military terms is called an investment phase. British Forces would strategically put a ring of armour around the Southern section of the city and gradually creep forward until we were in the best tactical situation to assault the city or 'break in'. I cannot recall the exact date, but I do remember conducting a relief in place at night with some American forces and it was something that you would expect straight out of a Hollywood movie.

We had dismounted and were moving forward through the lines of U.S. soldiers. I was at point and was asking the American soldiers for directions to their commander for orders. There was no stealth involved here as a loud tank battle was ongoing around us and everything was quite chaotic and very loud. As I approached the front of the battle, I stopped and paused for a minute to take in the whole picture. American Abrams main battle tanks were hitting the inferior Iraqi tanks relentlessly. Some were in flames, but others just emitted white sparks as if they were hit by fireworks. My panoramic view was then lit up by illumination rounds from the artillery AS-90 Battery stationed at the airport and I saw the commander I was looking for. I approached the commander and explained that we were here to relieve him. This American Cavalryman was well over six feet tall and was wearing a Stetson cowboy hat; he looked awesome! He excitedly began to break down the battlespace and gave me a brief on the ongoing battle.

I had now chosen to forget the incident in the village that had happened less than a week ago and was in total awe of this Texan. He had explained that the Iraqis were sneaky and had attempted to outflank his forces, but he had cut them off and had warned me about the threat to my armour due to the Rocket Propelled Grenade (RPG) teams. I could have observed and listened to this Texan all night but interrupted and asked where the pre-dug Infantry positions were located. He condescendingly replied, 'Are you a grunt?' before mockingly giving me the once over. 'The grunts are that way!' he then pointed to his left and we moved off to find our pre-dug positions. I never caught this Texan's name, but he was a charismatic and inspiring commander, even for a Yank!

Eventually, we found some of the U.S. infantry and conducted our relief in place and can recall that I was shocked that the Americans were just lying in the open without any cover. I questioned them as to why they had not dug any trenches to be told that the ground was too hard. I then called my section over and explained that we would be digging three trenches, and this would provide us cover and protection from RPGs, tanks, and artillery, as well as from small arms fire. I added some extra incentive by explaining that the Americans didn't dig in because the ground was too tough for them. It didn't take long for my lads to break the tough top surface of rocks with pickaxes and our trenches were taking form well before the American soldiers departed. In fact, as soon as they had left, my lads' enthusiasm and work ethic suddenly dwindled. It's amazing how a little international rivalry can motivate soldiers.

The following day, we came under intense artillery fire and we were thankful that we had worked throughout the night to dig these trenches. Initially, the artillery fire was nowhere near us. It was a few hundred metres to our front, and we joked amongst ourselves at how incompetent the Iraqi soldiers were. Then, the next was 150 metres to our rear, then 100 metres to our front, and so on. This was no longer funny as they were 'bracketing' us; a technique used to find the correct range of your target, and it wouldn't be long until they were right on our position.

My Platoon Commander then gave the order for all dismounts (us) to return to our vehicles for safety. This was by far the worst place we could be during an artillery bombardment. 10 soldiers crammed in a vehicle like sardines surrounded by thousands of bullets, shells, anti-tank weapons, grenades, and explosives. Furthermore, the top of these vehicles has some of the least amount of armour and, as such, this is their weakest area. All it would take was one bomb to land on or near our Warrior vehicle and all of us would have been killed. These vehicles were packed with explosives and, in this situation, a powder keg; this was the wrong call!

I was unaware whether the rest of the Platoon had dug trenches that night, but my section had worked tirelessly digging our own trenches. We had dug three trenches that were five feet deep and over thirty metres apart and this was difficult to achieve as we had to smash through the top layer of rock and had sacrificed our sleep to achieve this. Then, we had reinforced them with sandbags in anticipation of enemy action, especially artillery or mortar fire, and, as a result of this, my men were going to stay in our trenches.

The worst type of scenario you can find yourself in during combat is when you are under effective enemy artillery fire, as you have no idea where the enemy are firing at you from due to the ranges involved. Normally, with small arms fire (standard guns and rifles), it is relatively easy to identify the enemy's position. Through training and experience, this can be achieved, but from indirect fire from mortars and artillery, it is near impossible to identify due to the vast distance of these weapons systems. Therefore, all we could do was observe from the safety of our trenches until the shells were on top of us. At this point, no matter how brave we all pretended to be, you hug the person next to you and hope for the best. Pez chose to hug me and as I didn't want to be considered rude, I hugged him right back!

In his very open public letter, Ski describes this incident as the following:

'We got hit hard by enemy artillery which was landing 10 to 15 metres away. It was the most awful sound and it felt like the ground just opened up and tried to swallow us.'[xviii]

I unreservedly agree with Ski, as the sound of the artillery bombs was deafening and all we could do was hope that one of these Iraqi shells didn't hit us directly. Then, there was the added risk of being crushed to death if a shell landed close enough to compromise the integrity of our trenches. I recall this ordeal as being terrifying as I was no longer in control. There is a warranted sense of helplessness when you are on the receiving end of artillery fire, and, for me, I no longer had any influence over the fate of my men. I was unable to return fire, unable to influence that battle as Pez and I held tightly onto each other.

Yet again, it would be the American Super Cobra attack helicopters that would come to our aid and moments after they flew over our position, the artillery barrage ceased. However, this time there were no high fives, no jubilation. We were all thankful that the artillery had stopped firing, but at what cost? The Cobra attack gunships had engaged the artillery within the city of Basra, a densely populated civilian area. For a brief moment, I wondered about any potential civilian casualties before dismissing this unwanted afterthought and going to check on my men.

We were all shaken by the artillery barrage, but my men seemed ok on the outside; or maybe, like myself, they had now become emotionally numb. From a commander's perspective, this significant attack had now emphasised that the Iraqi Army was more competent than we had previously given them credit for. We were planning to cross the Basra canal and advance on the city, and I was concerned about battlefield fatigue and the physical sustainability of my men. It had never even crossed my mind that this artillery attack may have been traumatic for them as no training was ever provided to educate commanders to consider the mental wellbeing of their soldiers. Besides, I was suppressing my own emotions, as taught, and this was aiding me to manage my own battlefield trauma.

After this artillery barrage, we were happy to be advancing forward and we were all relieved. This was courtesy of the armoured element of the Royal Engineers. These brave soldiers had advanced forward to dig huge berms that would provide the Infantry with cover and the armoured elements with protection for their hulls. These berms were at a suitable height that the tanks could still fire whilst offering some protection from small arms and RPG fire and we mounted up and advanced a few hundred metres closer to the city. Then, once we dismounted, we began to immediately dig in again. This time though, trenches were not needed but the shallower shell scrapes. We were now part of a combined defensive front in a baseline of three Warrior crews, two tanks, two Milan units on their flanks, snipers, and an American forward air controller. One of our objectives was to prevent the destruction of a vital bridge on the 31 Highway. There were two other such bridges to the south and all three were critical to the battle plan.

These bridges covered the large man-made Basra Canal and were critical to our operational planning, so, as such, lethal force was authorised to ensure the survival of these structures. Leaflets were dropped daily over Basra to warn the civilian population not to attempt to cross these bridges. There were even giant speakers set up blasting this message across. Surely, the civilian population had received the message. Unfortunately, this was not the case and I can recall several vehicles being destroyed by British Challenger 2 main battle tanks that approached the bridge. I do not know if these were genuine civilians, but the tanks engaged all vehicles that attempted to cross these bridges.

Our tank crews had some difficult decisions to make as we had previously received an intelligence report that the Fedayeen were planning to send civilian vehicles laden with explosives towards these bridges in an attempt to collapse them and stall our impending advance. The repercussions of this would be inevitable coalition casualties and this was a heartless tactical decision that a senior commander had made. It is easy to give such an order but is immensely difficult for the men of those tank crews, who had to fire on potential civilian vehicles, to carry out. This is just another example of the darker side of war, the acceptable collateral damage and calculated loss of human life (civilians).

We had not been under artillery fire since the Cobras had neutralised the Iraq battery in the days prior, but the RPGs were coming in thick and fast. I recall one such day when Ricky was on stag (guard duty) on top of the berm when an RPG whizzed close by. The majority of the rest of the section, including myself, was in our shell scrape to the rear playing cards when Ricky yelled, 'They're firing RPGs at me!' We all broke into frantic laughter from the safety of our shell scrape and, of course, the berm. From the tone of Ricky's voice, it sounded as if the Iraqis had specifically and exclusively only targeted him. Pez began to heckle Ricky as the Gympie let out a thunderous burst. The snipers also engaged as more RPGs fizzed over us. Pez was our own personal jester and always lightened the mood, but he soon became very serious when I informed him that it was now his turn for stag, and he had to replace Ricky on the top of the berm. Then naturally, our soldier's dark humour kicked in and we all, including Ricky, began to heckle Pez.

What goes around comes around and, the following day, it would be my turn to be ridiculed. I remember that we had identified a building on the outskirts of the city that the Fedayeen were operating out of. Additionally, we had also observed that the RPG teams had been mounting attacks from this building and my Warrior crew were trying to engage them, but their sight system was limited in range and this had prevented them from effectively doing so. I had suggested that I acted as a spotter and could guide them onto the target area. I borrowed one of the snipers' Sophie sights and then began to guide my Warrior gunner and his 30mm cannon onto the Fedayeen's command post. After about 10 attempts, we were finally on target in what can only be described as a spectacular lobbed shot. A Fedayeen fighter came to the window to jeer us, when boom; a 30mm high explosive round landed in his very window, killing him.

Unbeknown to me, as they were on a different radio frequency, the tanks also wanted to play this game as they had a significantly more superior range than our Warriors. I was oblivious to the tank that had rolled up behind me as I was committed to guiding my Warrior crew onto our target. By now, the tank had put its barrel over me to acquire the direction of the target building. BOOM! The tank fired a 120mm high explosive round right above me, collapsing the Fedayeen headquarters. The vacuum of the shot instantly lifted me up off the floor then promptly slammed me back down with thunderous force. I was winded and temporarily deaf as I jumped into the shell scrape yelling 'Incoming'! I was disorientated and confused, to say the least, as my men laughed their socks off. When my ears finally stopped ringing, Pez informed me that it was just the tank firing. From that day forth, whenever a tank fired close by, my men would reassure me that there was no need to panic and that it was just a friendly tank and not incoming artillery fire.

In the build-up to the all-out assault on Basra, the infantry attacks from Iraqi forces intensified. Yet again, from Ski's very open honest letter, he states:

'Once we got to the outskirts of Basra, we went firm and put a ring of steel around it. No one could come out. It was like the wild west. The enemy were constantly trying to have a pop but they never had a chance. I was watching them get cut down by our tank shells, cut in half by our machine guns. I was next to my best mate, (Mac), who was on the machine gun when he shot an Iraqi in half. Chris is now being treated for PTSD [post-traumatic stress disorder] as well.'

I do recall Mac repelling a heavy enemy assault with the Gympie and he was an exceptional shot with this machine gun as he was engaging targets up to 800 metres away. This was generally followed with the usual bravado and we gave no thought to the fact that these were fathers, brothers, husbands, and sons. These were brave men that were outgunned, and they still advanced towards us knowing that they possessed inferior weapons that had less range and accuracy. At the time, I didn't care who they were but after the war, it dawned on me how courageous these Iraqi soldiers actually were.

I now have the utmost respect for all of the Iraqi Army, even those who bombarded me with artillery fire.

The battlefield trauma from this early period in the war would further exacerbate Ski's deteriorating mental health. I often think about these incidents and, although I respected the Iraqi forces, I have never felt any guilt or remorse towards those that were killed. The civilians, however, that's where my own trauma lies, and I can only suspect that this was the same for the rest of my men. Ski continues:

'I look back on these incidents a lot. Some of them haunt me and have ruined my life. I get bad flashbacks and nightmares. It makes everyday life very difficult for me.'

Ski would later be told that he did not, in fact, have PTSD but instead, he was diagnosed with a 'personality disorder.' This was 2005, and if the British Army admitted that Ski had PTSD from his battlefield exploits and experiences, then the Ministry of Defence would be accountable for his poor mental health and criminal actions. Yet, due to the negative national media coverage that surrounded his court case, it was easier for the top brass to separate and isolate Ski to avoid any further bad press. This raises many questions, especially as I shared all of the same symptoms as Ski, yet why was I not diagnosed with the same personality disorder?

Fundamentally, the Ministry of Defence would abandon and distance themselves as far as possible from Ski when it was obvious that he needed help and was in pain. His poor mental health would evolve into an irrational thought process that would convince Ski that he needed an assault rifle for the protection of his family. So, as a result, he stole one from Wellington Barracks. Subsequently, he was arrested and jailed for seven years and was disregarded by the very institution that had trained him, reprogrammed his psyche, and ultimately sent him to war.

Ski would not be the only soldier to be diagnosed with a 'personality disorder' in this period and I genuinely believe that this was a result of all of the bad press that was targeted towards the British Army. Let us not forget that the Blair Government blamed the 'illegal war' in Iraq on the British Armed Forces in what can only be classed as a political masterstroke. By no means am I vindicating Ski's actions, but it was blatantly clear that he was suffering from PTSD, a direct consequence of his battlefield trauma.

The day would finally come for our assault on Basra to take place. We had been gradually wearing down the Iraqi forces over the past week and now it was time to conduct the break-in. We were all solely focused on the mission and none of my men showed any signs of their deteriorating mental health; or maybe they did, but I was oblivious to it. On the morning of 6th April, we stormed the city after a series of airstrikes. I remember listening to the thunderous roar from the explosions taking place from the seclusion of the cave in the back of our armoured fighting vehicle as we approached the outskirts of the city. I recall that I was eagerly listening to the battlefield reports coming through on the radio and was trying to pass on the information to my men as we were literally kept in the dark as we approached!

My first mission was to clear an Iraqi RPG training barracks a few blocks into the city. Dicky, the Warrior vehicle commander, began the countdown and we exited, spread out and got into all-round defence. I reminded my men to watch the rooftops and the windows for snipers and RPGs as this was now a three-dimensional environment. Everything was quiet; too quiet. I then requested that the Warrior blew the wooden gates off the barracks to our front and to my disappointment, the 30mm high explosive rounds didn't explode but went straight through. I guess the gates would have to be opened the old-fashioned way! Our Warrior revved its engine and easily smashed through the gates and our Infantry assault could now commence.

I can recollect that the barracks consisted of a two-tier structure set out in a rectangular courtyard with a veranda and pillars on the right-hand side. As we approached, I ordered my men to immediately clear the ground floor as we could utilise the cover of this veranda and pillars to our advantage. As we moved forward, for some bizarre reason, I was treating this like a training exercise and was providing instruction to my men. I remember walking past my men whilst critiquing them! 'Mac, cover the window, Pez, watch the second tier, Dave, use that pillar as a better firing position,' then an RPG whizzed by and exploded to our rear! This was followed by a burst of small arms fire that was close enough to feel and I was fortunate to avoid!

My training instantly kicked in, and I dropped to my knee and took some cover next to Dave. The penny had finally dropped that I was in an urban firefight and I could feel my adrenaline take effect. My right elbow was stiff, and I could feel a warm damp feeling running down my right leg. Had I been shot? Regardless, this would have to wait as we had a job to do. We methodically and mechanically then cleared the barracks in a fluid-like motion. I remember hearing the shouts of 'room clear, floor clear' and it wasn't long before the barracks were cleared and deemed safe. The Iraqi soldiers had evacuated and had put up little resistance as we were entering. The job was complete; it was time to check my injuries.

I nervously put my hand on the back of my thigh and felt a warm wetness, but oddly, when I looked at it, there was no blood and it was clear! My initial thoughts were, 'Have I pissed myself?' I checked again and smelt my hand and it wasn't piss; this was water. The burst of rounds that had narrowly missed me on our entry had ricocheted off the nearby wall and smashed my water bottle as well as hitting my elbow. I was fine but realised how lucky I had been. There would be no more live instructional lessons in combat from now on. I had learned my lesson the hard way. I never mentioned this to any of my team, as I am certain that they would have mocked me for it, especially Pez! My elbow still aggravates me from time to time, but this is a welcome reminder of how fortunate I had been.

When we returned to our vehicle, a mob was gathering. I had been in civilian-led riots in Kosovo and was aware of how quickly they could escalate. These non-combatants appeared agitated, yet their anger wasn't directed at us. The mob was centred around a young woman who was waving her bloodied hajib in the air. The mob started to chant, 'Saddam Jundi! Saddam Jundi!' We had learnt basic Arabic and knew that they were trying to tell us about Iraqi soldiers, but we had to regroup with our platoon for new orders. The distressed woman then raised her arm in a chopping motion to her own arm and yelled, 'Baby!' The mob had just informed us that the Iraqi soldiers had chopped her baby's arm off to keep them quiet. I had just received my new orders and it was to kill these bastards that had mutilated this baby!

I immediately commanded my men to close in and issued some quick battle orders. I was aware that this could be a trap but that this was doubtful as the civilian population of Basra hated Saddam Hussein. Regardless, we had to be careful and expect an ambush. My mind, yet again, raced back to Kosovo, the morgue and all of those dead civilians. I had just been gifted an opportunity to do some good and to prevent any more harm to future non-combatants at the hands of these cruel soldiers. I thought about the infamous phrase 'evil triumphs when good men do nothing'. I desperately wanted to repent and be a good man and this was my opportunity. As one can imagine, my vehicle crew were not too pleased as this action would leave them vulnerable and this was not part of our mission. Plans often changed in combat and my mind was set; it was time to move out but quietly, in stealth, without the support of my armoured fighting vehicle.

The mob had pointed us in the direction of the compound of a large upper-class building and we halted the crowd as we began our stealthy assault. We didn't know what we were up against and had to carry out some reconnaissance before we could strike. Stevie took my delta fire team around the back of the structure as an initial cut off and my fire team observed from the front. I identified two sets of military-grade boots at the front door and gave the commands to conduct a simultaneous breach. I ordered my men to use lethal force if necessary but, if possible, they should be taken alive. I began a five-second countdown on the radio and my heart began to race; '5,4,3,2,1, GO! GO! GO!'

We breached both the front and back simultaneously. I booted the front door off its hinges and led my team in. It was an open area and we swept immediately to the left to a kitchen where an Iraqi Jundi was washing the blood off his arms and clothes. There was a large bloodied machete next to him, but before he could reach for it, I headbutted him and he fell to the floor. Concurrently, my delta fire team had also breached, also sweeping to their left and had captured another Iraqi Jundi. Both these Iraqi soldiers resisted capture and lethal force could have been used but I wanted them to pay for their crimes; I wanted them alive. We restrained our prisoners and I told the lads to search the building for evidence. This place was a gold mine and we bagged their uniforms, weapons, papers, and a computer. These were two high-ranking Iraqi officers and we found vast amounts of intelligence and treasures including captured loot from the 1990 Iraqi invasion of Kuwait. This intelligence coup would prove vital in the coming weeks and these Jundi would be later interrogated by special forces, which we had the opportunity to observe.

Returning to our vehicle was a difficult task as the crowd demanded mob justice. The woman with the bloodied hijab was now parading her limbless 'baby' who was actually about 7 or eight years old. This poor kid was screaming and was inciting the mob even further. It would have been an easy decision to leave these two scumbags to the mercy of the mob and I did consider it as the mob was now becoming hostile towards us. However, I was aware of the bigger picture and what intelligence could be extracted out of these two high-ranking officers. We fought our way through the mob as the captured Jundi were relentlessly beaten and managed to link up with our vehicle and then eventually, the rest of the platoon.

Then, we somehow managed to cram these two into our Warrior despite them fighting us at every opportunity. I can only imagine what the shock of capture actually feels like and they may have believed that we were going to execute them. This was no different from what I had taught my men - always fight, never give up and escape and evade where possible - and I could respect their guile. When we arrived at our Platoon's location and the Warrior's back door opened, we all spilt out onto the floor and a scuffle broke out. One of the Iraqi officers was reaching for a weapon and yet again, lethal force could have been used, but instead, Dave used his less-lethal right fist. We then handed these prisoners over to our Platoon Sergeant and that was the last we saw of them until their interrogation. This was conducted in a warehouse at night with a sole light above the Jundi as they were asked questions, reminiscent of a Hollywood movie.

The intelligence that was gained from these two Iraqi Officers would later be used to conduct a city-wide manhunt for the Iraqi general and war criminal, Ali Hassan Abd al-Majid, also known as 'Chemical Ali'. Blair was desperate to find evidence of WMDs and this had become one of our main efforts once the city of Basra was captured. Chemical Ali had been rumoured to be hiding out in the area of Basra to the north, by the port, but he was able to evade us. He would be captured later that year and sentenced to death for war crimes including genocide. As the war progressed, more emphasis was put onto us to find evidence of WMDs. From a discussion with President Bush on 24 March, Mr Blair underlined the importance of Coalition Forces finding Saddam's WMDs.[xix] It is evident that Blair was already aware of the growing anti-war movement back home and the prospect of answering to the people for the invasion and his 'illegal war'.

It was around this time that Fusilier Turrington was killed.[xx] My memory is very vague about this incident but what I do remember is how badly this affected his section commander and his friends and how hard they fought to save his life.

Ski wrote:

'*About two weeks into the battle, Fusilier [Kelan] Turrington was shot in the neck by a sniper and died there and then on the spot. He was just lying there because no one would go near him because of sniper fire. It seemed like he was there for hours. It was like time stopped, not nice at all.*'[xxi]

Tommy recalls our Platoon commander crying uncontrollably shortly after this incident and having to tell him to 'get his shit together!' Our Platoon commander was young and inexperienced, and this death had occurred on his watch, but Tommy was right! His job was to lead, and the mourning of Turrington would have to wait. Tommy went on to explain how badly this had shaken all of the commanders apart from himself and that he felt nothing on an emotional level. All that concerned him was the death and destruction of the enemy and that he had hoped to go out in a blaze of glory. Tommy had yearned to become a regimental history question through his battlefield exploits which implied a brave and honourable death, with medals, of course. He also remembers my section casualty evacuating a young girl who had been shot and, yet again, this didn't alarm him in any way. Tommy is by no means a sociopath, but this is the mindset that some soldiers revert to in combat; emotionless pragmatic killing machines. We suppress our feelings and emotions, and this allows us to function, to do our jobs and to stay alive. Fortunately for Tommy, his military mindset would revert back to a more socially acceptable one once he had settled down and started a family.

Following the tragic death of Turrington, I volunteered my men to double up on patrols to give the other section time to grieve and process his death. I didn't know Turrington and his death didn't affect me as much as maybe it should have, however, the reaction of watching what his death did to his section, especially his commander, had a more significant impact on me. We would later be informed that two of our own, Irish Guardsmen Lance Corporal Ian 'Molly' Malone and Piper Christopher Muzvuru were killed on the same day in a different part of the city. I didn't know Muzvuru, but I had been out drinking with Molly before the war. I didn't know Molly that well, just enough to have a few beers and a chat with at our local watering hole in Munster, yet, I felt nothing. I was emotionless.

That night, we were tasked with clearing a main supply route in the north of the city and the patrol consisted of two Warriors and two sections of Infantry. I had volunteered to satellite around the vehicles in the side streets on foot whilst the other Fusilier section patrolled, side by side, the accompanying armour. There was no power and limited sanitation, and wild dogs roamed the alleyways. These side streets were the perfect place for an ambush and the whole patrol had an eerie feel about it. I had the feeling that something bad was about to happen. Then, I heard a fierce growing mumble that quickly grew into a growl. The largest wild dog that I have ever seen was blocking our path. I contemplated shouting for the Gympie but opted to backtrack and return to our vehicles when the city lit up. The vehicles had driven into an ambush and they were taking incoming fire.

I could hear my radio buzzing the words, 'contact wait out!' We tactically but rapidly returned to the main road only to find that our two-vehicle convoy had departed. We had been abandoned, forsaken on the streets of Basra, and had just patrolled into an ambush. I yelled at my men to keep to the shadows and to observe the rooftops as this was not the remnants of the Iraqi army but the Fedayeen, a fanatical militia. The British Army was currently using an outdated and unreliable clansman radio series and I was carrying the inconsistent model 349 at the time. The only reliable feature of the 349 was that it was unreliable when you needed it most and I was now left with no communications. I didn't have a map, and I didn't even know exactly where we were. My men looked at me for direction and I had to do something as we were under effective enemy fire.

I informed my men that we would conduct a hard extraction under fire but not in the conventional sense where we would peel in past each other. This was far too slow; we needed to extract as quickly as possible if we were to make it out of this ambush alive. I quickly briefed my men that Stevie would lead and head in the direction of the vehicles and that myself and Ski would cover their extraction from the rear. This is when I made a hard tactical decision. I didn't tell my men, but this extraction would not stop even if we had a casualty. I had seven guns and it would take two more guns to carry that casualty, reducing my firepower to four and slowing our extraction, which would ultimately lead to more casualties. This decision still troubles me, and I do not know if I would have been able to see it through. Thankfully though, we successfully extracted.

I vividly recall that as the rest of the section extracted, Ski and I struggled to keep up. We were both very fit but covering the team under effective enemy fire whilst manoeuvring ourselves was mentally and physically exhausting. I was yelling, 'prepare to move'....'move!' Ski would scream his reply, 'moving!' The green tracer rounds were lighting up our rear and Ski was performing admirably. Then, my radio began to get a signal. I angrily shouted '23, this is 23/C, stop your extraction, you have left us behind, and we are in contact!' The armoured vehicles finally stopped and began to reverse towards us, and we eventually caught up after what felt like an eternity and when we opened the back door of our Warrior, we were met with a surprise.

When the vehicles had initially come under heavy fire, half of the section patrolling next to them had climbed into my vehicle and had shut the door for protection. Once the door was shut, the crew had anticipated that we were all in safely and shot off out of the ambush, breaking contact. There was no time for explanations as we were still in contact and we couldn't all fit in one vehicle. I furiously yelled, 'Delta fire team you get in our vehicle, my fireteam will get in the other vehicle.' I was beyond angry at the Warrior crew and the Fusiliers that had hijacked my vehicle, but more so with myself. I had never thought that I would ever be in a position where I would essentially condemn one of my men and, despite the fact that this was a conscious decision that was never acted on, it still plays on my mind to this day.

During the next few days, our mission was to secure all of the key objectives in Basra, such as power plants, hospitals, sewage works and the docks. Mass looting by the local population was well underway and we seemed to secure facility after facility before being moved on. Eventually, we would find a short-lived home in a scrapyard and this would provide us with some stability and routine. We would rotate through a cycle of patrols to guard duty then rest/quick reaction force, similar to what I had experienced in Kosovo.

I recall that on one such patrol cycle, we did a snap visit to an ice cream parlour and I treated my lads to some special Basra ice creams. The Iraqi Army had been defeated but the Fedayeen-inspired militia was still at large. By now, we had our own area of the city and we were familiar with our northern area of responsibility when we came under contact from small arms fire. Pez screamed out in pain and I seriously thought that he had been shot. He yelled, 'I need to shit!' But it was too late; the special Basra ice cream had given us all a serious case of 'Delhi belly,' and Pez was its first victim. We were all in cover on either side of the road as small arms fire passed between us when I saw Pez shuffle towards me with his combat trousers dropped down by his ankles, dripping with diarrhoea. For the second time in as many months, he was yelling, 'Somebody please shoot me!' It's a miracle that the insurgents never did, and it wasn't through the lack of trying. Pez continued to shout and moan as he made his way to some bushes to empty what was left of his bowels. The insurgents eventually withdrew once we returned effective fire and the men of 23/C awkwardly made our way back to our patrol base with our butt cheeks tightly clenched.

We eventually deescalated our aggressive patrol patterns, removed our camouflage cream and swapped our helmets for berets and became more of a peace-keeping force rather than a fighting one. The majority of the population were happy to have been liberated from the iron fist of Saddam Hussein and initially, we were greeted like heroes. There was secular religious division between the Sunni and Shia Muslims in Iraq and the population of Basra was mostly Shia. The former ruling Ba'ath party had favoured the Sunni population, and this had led to the Basra uprising in the aftermath of the 1991 Gulf War.

The following is an extract from a BBC news article that highlights how Saddam Hussein (a Sunni Muslim) dealt with this Shia uprising and highlights the depth of the religious divide.

'Some were shot in their homes and houses, others - young men especially - were rounded up from the streets and later executed en masse. Others still were gunned down by helicopter gunships piloted by Saddam Hussein's Republican Guards as they tried to flee. Women and children were among the targets of the violent crackdown.'[xxii]

Saddam Hussein would also order the bombing of Shia religious sites and temples in Basra and the surrounding area as further punishment. Basra had been governed through fear and violence and now there was a power vacuum.

Along with the Fedayeen and the Ba'ath Party, other militias were beginning to form and stake a claim to the city. We were now acting as peacekeepers and had reverted to a humanitarian role and this would involve water, food and medical distribution as well as maintaining law and order. Early one morning, when returning from a night patrol, we received orders that the central bank was being robbed. We were aware that Saddam had kept cash and gold reserves there and, if acquired by any of these militias, they would be able to fund a devastating counter-insurgency campaign against us.

We were on foot but that didn't matter as my section of men were exceptionally fit and robust and we ran to the bank and breached without even pausing to take in a breath. To our amazement, the vault was open but there was nobody else around. Once we had secured the building, we entered the vault and my eyes lit up. There were several pallets of U.S. $100 bills, stacked up to at least five feet high, wrapped in cellophane. There were millions of dollars right in front of us and suddenly I felt like Scrooge McDuck! The conversation immediately began about whether or not we should help ourselves to the 'spoils of war.' One must not be too quick to judge as we were all from lower working-class families; well, let's be honest, we were poor.

I have never been motivated by money, but this opportunity was too good to overlook. Then I thought about the airstrike and the persecution of the people of Basra at the hands of the malicious Saddam Hussein. This was blood money and stunk of death. I told my men that this money belonged to the people of Basra, that it was dirty and contaminated and had an immeasurable amount of unjust deaths associated with it. Therefore, as a result of this, I would categorically not be taking any of the nicely stacked wedges of $100 bills home with me. However, if they chose to, I would turn a blind eye. Despite everything that I had put them through, they still continued to make me proud as they all chose to leave Saddam's blood money in that vault. In hindsight, now that I have a mortgage and a family, I look back at this decision and often wonder if we all made the correct choices, as I could now have been mortgage-free.

My section had been given the nickname of 'the suicide seven' due to the simple fact that I would volunteer us for every dangerous mission. Our young Platoon Commander was at times indecisive and would rarely delegate, then again, I don't think that any of the other section commanders, including myself, made his job any easier. Besides, there was an unspoken inter- regiment rivalry between 1RRF and the Irish Guards to bear in mind as well. I remember our Platoon Commander briefing us on some recent intelligence that a newly established Royal Military Police station was going to be targeted by insurgents that very evening. He was fishing for volunteers and, like clockwork, and to the dismay of my men, 23/C would yet again offer our services. This was the beginning of May; the war had officially ended and some of us just wanted to return home safely. Personally, I don't think that I ever wanted to return home. I wanted to remain numb and to forget the darker side of warfare that I had witnessed and, more pertinently, been part of.

That same afternoon, we arrived at a medium-sized two-tier building set on a cross junction with a canal to its rear. I approached these four Royal Military Police (RMPs) stationed there and asked who was in command. A Sergeant informed me that he was and despite still only being a Lance Corporal at this point, and two ranks his junior, I cockily replied, 'Not anymore.' The RMP Sergeant didn't take this very well and in hindsight, maybe I could have explained the situation better. This wasn't about rank but about protecting my fellow British soldiers; so, I promptly reminded him why we were there. I bluntly informed him that we were here to fend off an attack directed at his four-man team by between 10-20 insurgents that evening. These police officers were poorly equipped with low levels of ammunition, they did have a medium machine gun but with only 100 rounds of ammunition.

Once our battle of egos had finished, I instructed my men to deploy claymores and trip flares to the rear and the flanks for protection. We even managed to hide our Warrior in the garage of the building. My plan was to defend this building from the roof as this gave us an excellent line of sight for our weapons with its clear fields of view and good all-round defence. We then smashed a hole in the roof and opened the mortar hatches on top of the back of the Warrior so that we could jump into it from our defensive position on the roof if needed. This would enable us to quickly extract if we were overrun, or alternatively, to conduct an offensive manoeuvre.

Once on the roof, I observed that the RMPs were in poor defensive positions. It was not their primary role to fight, after all, as they were policemen with limited combat training and experience, however, they even had their main weapon, the Gympie, facing the canal. This canal was over 5 metres wide and was not crossable and the Gympie was poorly positioned there. I was more than happy with the trip flare that I had positioned there as it was very unlikely that the attack would come from the rear due to this water obstacle. I repositioned them all and doubled them up with my men and, to their surprise, once in position, some of my lads got their sleeping bags out and attempted to get some rest. None of the RMPs rested that evening, whereas my men rotated their sleep and would be fresh for the impending attack.

I was woken by the familiar sound of the Gympie singing. Dave was covering the road junction and was already engaging a large crowd. I had doubled him up with two GPMGs so that he could switch guns quickly to prevent them from overheating. I approached his position to get eyes on the advancing militia in order to formulate a defensive plan. Concurrently, Mac jumped onto the 51mm light mortar and fired an illumination bomb that provided us with some much-needed visibility. I remember being slightly confused as the militia's assault had stopped and they were being engaged by another mob! Instinctively, I checked my battlefield radio just to make sure that there weren't any friendly units in the area and once this was confirmed, my quick battle orders would entail a full-frontal assault.

I signalled for Pez and Ricky to follow me into the Warrior and informed them that we would assault the militia. Stevie was to coordinate and provide covering fire from the rooftop with Ski and Dave. Mac would continue to use the 51mm mortar to illuminate the enemy and that the RMPs should cover our rear and flanks (do nothing). No sooner had we jumped in through the roof of the

Warrior and fired up the engine than it burst through the garage doors collapsing the front of the structure's wall. As the Warrior advanced towards this chaos, the three of us deployed out of the back to get a better view from the ground. It soon became evident that there were two different militias fighting each other and I didn't want to get involved in a Mexican stand-off. I decided to withdraw my men to the RMP station and let these two warring factions shoot it out. For the remainder of the night, we observed just that, and the following morning we were relieved of our RMP protection duties.

This would be our last engagement as a section. The insurgents that were approaching our location on the previous night had been engaged by an Iraqi security team assigned to protect a former local politician. They believed that the insurgents had come for them and had initiated the firefight and, in doing so, repelled the attack that was meant for us. Regardless, our deployment orders had come in and we would be returning home... as 'heroes?' Our time in Iraq and our war was over, but for some of the men from 23/C, a hidden war, the war from within, had just begun.

23/C The night we crossed into Iraq. Note the explosion in the background.

Myself, Stevie, Ski, Unknown sniper. Outskirts of Basra, 2003.

Pez and I, moments before being under IDF near the Basra Canal, 2003.

Pez testing his desert loo!

Ricky spotting whilst Mac is reloading the GPMG.

Riding a rocket at Basra docks. 2003

Chapter 8.
The Real War Begins

No serious consideration was given towards the mental health and wellbeing of any of the soldiers who participated in the vigorous ground campaign of the 2003 Iraq War. Before our return to Germany, I can recall that we were reunited with the rest of the Irish Guards in a temporary Camp named Matilda, and that there was a mobile shower facility there. This would be our first shower in months and that's all that I can really remember about this place. This camp was a movement control checkpoint, and, in good old-fashioned military manner, we had to be processed and all weapons and equipment had to be accounted for. The final checkpoint we had to enter was with the doctor and this would be the only post-operational stress assessment that we would receive, and it was conducted in the open without any confidentiality whatsoever.

Soldier 'G" recalls that we were all lined up outside a small 9x9 tent, and as we passed through, the doctor would ask us if we were feeling ok. There was no privacy and on the other side of the tent, (once you had signed off on your own self-certified mental health evaluation, of course), there were beers and a party waiting for us. Naturally, everyone said that they were ok as we all wanted to relax and to get drunk. One must not dismiss the fact that we were all trained, conditioned even, to ignore and suppress our emotions, our feelings. What soldier would ever admit to being 'weak' after what we had just experienced, especially in the company of their comrades? I often look back and question the strategic thinking of this and what could have, or should have, been in place. I ask the unproductive question of 'What if more emphasis was targeted towards the mental wellbeing of these soldiers, particularly my men, the men of 23/C?' Maybe, with adequate mental health aftercare, we could have managed our battlefield trauma before it spiralled out of control into something far worse.

When I passed through this psychological operational stress checkpoint, I thought that it would be funny to joke about my own mental health. When the doctor asked me if I was feeling ok, I replied with, 'Absolutely fine apart from the constant bed-wetting and nightmares!' I could hear my men laugh but the doctor didn't see the funny side. He then persisted with further questions and asked me to elaborate. Maybe this was a subconscious cry for help, but I was holding up the line and was getting booed by the rest of the lads who just wanted a beer. I informed the doctor that it was just a badly timed prank, signed my own mental health evaluation and got blind drunk with the rest of the Battalion. This was just a paper exercise and even back then, it felt like a token gesture.

When reflecting back on the operational stress and pressures that were put on all of us and what we had endured, it is no surprise that we would all eventually suffer with poor mental health. From the very beginning, soldiers accept the very real danger of death and injury. Then, add into the equation the imminent risks of biological and chemical weapons being deployed against us, which of course escalated to the retaliatory threat of nuclear weapons by George W. Bush, the fierce fighting that we had witnessed and, of course, the darker side of warfare...the civilians, the acceptable collateral damage! The majority of 23/C were teenagers, and this was their first operational tour; we were thrown into a hard-fought attrition ground campaign that saw the most intense fighting of our generation. In the First World War, it was referred to as 'shell shock', in the Second World War it was referred to as 'battlefield fatigue,' and in more modern times, PTSD. One would rightly imagine that we would receive adequate mental health training after self-certifying ourselves in Iraq, however, regrettably, we would be mistaken.

On return to our barracks in Munster, no sooner had we departed the coaches on the drill square than the party continued. That night, Dave informed me that after I had deployed early to Kuwait, some of the Northern Irish lads from the Drums and Pipes Platoon had conducted some kind of Ulster initiation on him and a few of the other new lads prior to their deployment. This consisted of being blindfolded and swearing allegiance to the orange men of Ulster. Both Tommy and Pez recall that we had all been drinking heavily and made our way to the lines of the Drums and Pipes Platoon for vengeance. Rather than having an all-out inter-platoon brawl, it was decided that Dave would fight in a bare-knuckle boxing match with Jimmy, the Guardsman who had prepared his Ulster initiation before the war. In the five months that I had known Dave, he had grown from a quiet, shy young man into someone who had reverted to what could only be described as a primaeval state of mind.

Dave had never boxed before, and it was pretty evident from the start of the bout that Jimmy had done quite a bit. Dave couldn't land a single blow and was repeatedly punched to the ground. This wasn't a traditional bout; there weren't any rules, no points or even a towel; it was simply last man standing. Dave was getting hit with combination after combination of punches yet continued to drive forward without even putting his guard up. With his face bloodied and bruised, Dave was knocked down again, but yet again though, he rose to his feet and let out a loud primal howl, at which the men of 10 Platoon all cheered in encouragement. Maybe Jimmy was tiring, but Dave managed to get in close and grab him in a bear hug-type grip, then, like a barbarian, proceeded to bite a huge chunk of flesh out of his shoulder! Jimmy screamed in agonising pain as Dave spat his flesh out, but Dave was by no means finished with him yet. Dave then lifted Jimmy off the ground and rammed both of them through a wardrobe. Jimmy screeched out in pain again and was the first to rise but it was evident that he had badly broken his arm and was unable to continue. Dave was triumphant by default. We raised Dave above our shoulders and paraded him round the Company lines as he was our new champion, our hero.

Retrospective analysis can be very dangerous and unproductive as this incident alone should have set off dozens of red flags. Initially, Dave's whole character had changed, and he was becoming a heavy drinker and would continue to use violence as a coping mechanism to deny his deteriorating mental health. Before Iraq, Ski was tee-total, but like Dave, after the war, he also turned to alcohol to help him process, then suppress his battlefield trauma. I was also struggling to process our battlefield experiences and was not adequately trained to identify or even be aware of the signs of PTSD in my men or myself, for that matter. This is a burden that I still carry with me as in hindsight, all of the signs were there in plain sight, yet I couldn't or didn't want to acknowledge them at the time.

In further reflection, Pez, who, at the start of the war, had a personality that was the polar opposite to Dave's, gradually withdrew to a more dormant temperament. Initially, he was upbeat and excited about the conflict but as the war progressed, he slowly became withdrawn and even reverted to referring to myself by my rank which I was totally against. Before the War in Iraq, Pez had been one of my good friends and I should have identified this change in his character as a significant consequence of his own battlefield trauma. Yet, no training was available at the time and the generic solution to mental health problems was to 'man up.' This toxic alpha-male culture of denying the existence of poor mental health of the British Army at this time was institutionally instilled into us, and as a result, some of us (myself included) would become ticking time bombs.

Trauma risk management training would be introduced for my final operational tour in Afghanistan in 2010, but this was 2003, and a million miles away. It is far too obvious when conducting retrospective analysis that we needed counselling or group therapy to help aid us in processing and accepting our battlefield trauma and I believe that this would have been beneficial. Nevertheless, we had beer and each other and that was the best practice and only available treatment at the time. Then there are the men of the Drums and Pipes to consider. Let us not forget that they were mourning the death of two of their brothers. We didn't even stop to think about how the war had affected them, and in hindsight, I am appalled by this. However, due to our numb emotionless mindset at that time, frankly, we didn't care.

No disciplinary action or charges were ever pursued over this illegal bout. This was just our way, the traditional Army way of managing post-operational stress in that period. I am not a therapist but getting blind drunk and brawling may feel like it releases stress at the time, but this never actually deals with the real issues and the basis of the underlying trauma. In my case, I would continue to use work as a coping mechanism along with alcohol as a tool to suppress my own inner suffering. I would not be able to just have a couple of drinks; I would have to get blind drunk at every opportunity.

At the beginning of the 21st century, the British Army had a detrimental drinking culture, and like many others of my generation, I hid my internal pain at the bottom of an empty glass, and this was particularly bad within the Sergeants' Mess. This culture would continue to be accepted especially as the high-intensity counter-insurgency operations in Iraq and Afghanistan gathered pace. Furthermore, it was not uncommon for Sergeants' Mess members to be late for work or fail outright to turn up, yet this was accepted despite being thoroughly unprofessional at the time.

Consideration must also be given to the increase in the operational tempo that had occurred after the events of 9/11. The British Army had global operational commitments in Northern Ireland, Afghanistan, Iraq, and the Balkans as well as humanitarian and diplomatic commitments to uphold. Then, on top of this, 'The Queen's Guards' were also responsible for conducting ceremonial duties at the Royal Palaces and residences in between these deployments. For the Irish Guards, we completed a unit move to London in the weeks after returning from Iraq, where we would be hurled into the stressful environment of public duties. I have never particularly enjoyed donning on the iconic scarlet tunic and bearskin due to the simple fact that it was manpower-intensive and highly stressful. Additionally, the Battalion had been stationed in Germany for five years where foot drill was considered a prohibited and dirty word as our focus was exclusively orientated towards combat operations.

On our return to the UK, we all imagined that we would be welcomed back as heroes, however, our delusions of grandeur were a far cry from the truth. The anti-war movement was at its peak in the summer of 2003 and we were now public enemy number one as we had just returned from the war. Let us not forget that we were conducting the Changing of the Guard on a daily basis and were an easy target for the press and these anti-war campaigners. There was public outrage at the lack of evidence of WMDs as this had been the main justification for Britain's participation in the war to begin with. We were frequently abused by the public and extra police protection was required when we conducted our ceremonial duties.

The chants of 'baby killers' were frequently screamed at us by these activists and for some of us including myself, this felt just. This would further exacerbate my deteriorating mood and it wasn't just limited to London. I can even recall being up north in Manchester at a friend's house when as soon as a mutual friend discovered that I had returned from Iraq, the 'baby killer' chants started. I was overwhelmed with guilt from my part in the war and was still traumatised by that airstrike. I would argue with myself and conclude that maybe I was a baby killer after all, but then I would get blind drunk and this would help me forget. I would proceed to shut myself off from the outside world and concentrate on my job as my own coping mechanism.

In the investigation that followed the War in Iraq, Mr Blair stated in the 2016 Chilcot inquiry that:

He believed the "assessed intelligence" had "established beyond doubt" that Saddam Hussein had "continued to produce chemical and biological weapons, that he continues in his efforts to develop nuclear weapons, and that he had been able to extend the range of his ballistic missile programme".[xxiii]

The keyword here is 'believed' and being the very astute politician that he is, yet again, Blair directed the responsibility of blame towards the intelligence community. As a result, the British Army were thrown to the will of the mob as scapegoats in a political masterclass by Blair to avoid all personal accountability for the perceived 'illegal war.' In the years that followed, all British soldiers were vilified by the public and the media. For soldiers such as myself, we continued to question our actions during the war and although I consciously accept that we were acting on behalf of the British people through Blair, this doubt, to a certain degree, still remains.

That September, I was promoted to the rank of Lance Sergeant and became an established member of the Sergeants' Mess. This fast track into the Sergeants' Mess gave me such pride and, let us not forget, a new status and identity. Once part of the Sergeants' Mess, your whole perception changes within the Battalion. One day, I was eating my lunch with my men from Iraq in the cookhouse, the next I was sitting opposite the Regimental Sergeant Major having breakfast in his Mess. I was now in the big leagues. It is within the confines of the Sergeants' Mess where most of the inner working problems of the Battalion are resolved. I had worked hard in Iraq and had earned my reward and I wanted more. I justified the horrors of war, many that still haunt me to this day, through that extra chevron and that promotion to the Mess. At the time, I genuinely believed that it had all been worth it; now, however, not so much.

It wasn't long after my promotion when I experienced my first panic attack but as a new member of the Sergeants' Mess, I was too afraid to seek help; too ashamed! To this day, I still do not understand why this panic attack occurred as I was not in any immediate danger and I was never afraid of a fight. Still, observing that brawl from the other side of the street and in the confines of my moving car was significantly painful. I experienced a tightness of the chest and had trouble breathing, my vision became blurred and I was struggling to drive my car. I was a brave, courageous soldier who insisted on leading his men from the front. I would always be the first one to run directly into a firefight, the first to lead my men when breaching compounds and now I was experiencing genuine fear, the type that completely overwhelms you, then shuts your body down. I needed help; I needed the men of 23/C. Without them, I felt naked and vulnerable...weak! All I could do was fight this head-on and told myself to 'man the fuck up' and once I made it to the confines of the Sergeants' Mess in Wellington Barracks, I finally felt safe and began to relax.

Besides, Sergeants were not 'weak,' and I was a war hero, wasn't I? I would use this new identity as a false persona to hide my own battlefield pain and lied to myself to convince my subconscious that my new identity was different from my previous rank and, therefore, I was not accountable for what had happened in Iraq at the hands of Lance Corporal Watson. Being stationed in central London also aided me in masking my pain as, in this vibrant city, you can party and drink 24/7 and that is exactly what we all did. It then became routine to party in the Sergeants' Mess bar afterwards as it was open all hours. This was a standard and acceptable practice at the time and, in hindsight, was very unproductive.

The bar would also be open from 12-1400hrs throughout the working day and it was not uncommon for members to have a couple of pints over lunch before returning to work. There was no evening cut-off time for last orders and the bar would stay open until the last member was finished drinking. For those of us who had witnessed the darker side of warfare, the accepted drinking culture of the Sergeants' Mess would provide us with an outlet to suppress our battlefield trauma. No matter how drunk we were or how much trouble we got into, not once was the question asked as to why? Years later, when I was the Battalion Welfare Officer, this would be my first question when soldiers were sent to me with alcohol-related issues. Back then though, there was an unwritten rule of 'what happens in the Sergeants' Mess, stays in the Mess,' and this acceptance of drunken antics was detrimental to the long-term mental health of my generation of soldiers.

My section second in command, Stevie, would be assigned to the Regimental Recruiting Team on return to London and that was the last that I ever saw of him. In a recent interview, he stated that he felt alone and isolated once he had left 10 Platoon and didn't know why. On leaving the Army, there was no interview with a doctor; in fact, the doctor was sick that day, so one of the medics processed him and that was that. No questions were ever asked concerning his mental wellbeing or about his time in Iraq. Stevie then informed me that he had a panic attack soon after leaving the Army when applying for a mortgage. He said that the whole experience was overwhelming, and he didn't know how to cope with life outside of the military.

He went on to tell me how angry and violent he felt after his service as this was not in his character before he had joined the ranks of the British Army. In the years that followed, Stevie gradually shut down socially and began to blame everyone else for all of his issues. Unfortunately, he would end up being arrested after an altercation with his boss at work. He regrettably explained that he had blacked out with rage and went into full combat mode, that if he hadn't been stopped, he may have killed his boss. This was his new mentality and he couldn't understand why. Veterans for Peace UK argue that most military personnel and veterans are not habitually violent, but, as a result of their training and experiences, they are more likely than civilians to behave violently in daily life.[xxiv] Stevie is an excellent example of this.

Fortunately, Stevie was saved by a local veteran who ran a boxing gym. Boxing, and then later, weight training would allow him to exhaust his anger and then vent his 'controlled aggression' through intensive exercise. Sadly, even to this day, Stevie is still angry and doesn't know why. He says that when it comes on, he has to withdraw from people and only feels better once he has lifted excessively large weights. I spoke to him about my own experiences and urged him to seek professional help only to be informed that he did reach out many years ago to a local charity, but they didn't pursue it. I am hopeful that he will engage with some professional therapist in the near future as I believe that he needs to resolve the battlefield trauma that we all experienced during our time in Iraq.

Furthermore, in 2013, Stevie collapsed after losing a substantial amount of weight. He was relieved to be diagnosed with type 1 diabetes as he had suspected the worst and thought that it may have been cancer. He was 29 years old at the time and in good health. This was not the usual age bracket to be diagnosed with type 1 diabetes; something was off. Besides, he was fit and healthy with no family history of diabetes. Further research would conclude that the onset of type 1 diabetes was a side effect of the anthrax injections that we had all received prior to the war in 2003. After an eighteen-month court battle, the Ministry of Defence would accept liability and award Stevie with a 40% medical pension. In a U.S. study of anthrax vaccinations that were given to American soldiers from 2008, it was found that there were 1,074 related side effects of type 1 diabetes. [xxv] No warning was ever given to us before these injections and, as a direct consequence, Stevie now has to manage his life around his medical condition.

Stevie then asked about the men of 23/C, particularly Dave. He then informed me that when looking back at our time in Iraq, there were times when he felt genuinely afraid of Dave. He mentioned how Dave 'would stare right through you, like he wanted to kill you,' and had genuine concerns about his state of mind in retrospect when discussing the war. I explained that we had lost contact, but in hindsight, that I had failed him as a commander, as the signs of battlefield trauma were staring me in the face. He then asked about whether an incident had actually occurred where a little girl had come to us with severe gunshot injuries for medical attention. Once I confirmed this, Stevie was relieved. He mentioned how his time in Iraq had become vague and that over the years, he had questioned his memories and had suppressed them. He was having trouble differentiating flashbacks from the truth, and as a result, he had forgotten about his own battlefield exploits.

He continued to tell me that his only real memories were before and after the war and that he vividly remembers the Irish Guards Commanding Officer chatting to us both after the war at Camp Matilda. Knaggsy, as we referred to him, had previously been my Company Commander and was without doubt the best officer that I knew. He genuinely cared about the men and could really inspire you; he was a true leader. Stevie recalls how he spoke proudly about our section's actions during the war and that we had been at the forefront of some of the most intense fighting. I can recall most of our combat experiences in Iraq but had mentally shut down once we had arrived at Camp Matilda in Kuwait. Maybe this was battlefield fatigue setting in or the start of my own PTSD. I didn't want to return home, I didn't feel like I was a hero. I fundamentally believed that I deserved to die on that battlefield for my hand in that airstrike. The death and mutilation of those innocent families that we had witnessed would haunt the men of 23/C after the war and, in some cases, completely ruin their lives.

On return from Iraq, I explicitly recommended that Ski should attend a junior non-commissioned officer cadre. He was an excellent soldier, and I had every confidence in his ability to lead, and he passed with ease; I was proud. Ski was promoted to the rank of Lance Corporal but would regrettably be reassigned to Number 1 Company. This was a new policy that was introduced to help freshly promoted junior commanders adapt to their new role in management. It was thought that their friends within their previous platoons would be too familiar with them, thus, on promotion, Ski was forced out of 4 Company. This was not always the case as I was fortunate enough to rise through the ranks of 10 Platoon and would complete five of my six operational tours with the fine men of 4 Company. I also believe that this familiarity aided me along the way. Sadly, Ski would be traumatised by the events that we had all encountered in Iraq, particularly, the darker side of warfare. Ski wrote:

"Because we were the initial fighting force, we didn't stop to mess around with dead bodies [Iraqis]. There was a little girl clinging on to her dead dad screaming her eyes out. We never had time to stop. We just pushed on past as the next line of soldiers behind us would sort it out."[xxvi]

On 30th November 2004, police in Birmingham would arrest Ski on suspicion of stealing an SA-80 assault rifle from Wellington Barracks in London.[xxvii] Ski's mental health had deteriorated to such a degree that he was living off Pro Plus caffeine pills to keep him awake. He refused to sleep as this kept him from his nightmares. He was suffering flashbacks from the trauma that we all had witnessed and didn't know how to process or even manage this internal pain. Ski would be diagnosed with a 'personality disorder' and thrown to the wolves due to the negative national press that had surrounded his court case. Regrettably, I wasn't there to help Ski at a time when he could only feel safe by having a rifle by his side. I can relate to this mentality as when I had my first panic attack the previous year, I needed my section, the men of 23/C around me to keep me safe from my own irrational thoughts.

A Parliamentary report from 1st Sept 2004 would conclude that of all the soldiers who had served in Iraq in its initial year, only 52 had suffered from PTSD. The report states:

"Over the period January 2003 to February 2004, the latest dates for which figures are available, 461 military personnel who served in Iraq were recorded as having experienced mental health problems. This represents 0.7 per cent. of those who had returned from deployment to Iraq at that time. Of these, 52 personnel were codified, under the International Codification of Disease system, as having Post Traumatic Stress Disorder."[xxviii]

I find these figures baffling, to say the least, as PTSD does not go away and cannot be miraculously cured. I cannot help but assume that these figures of a mere 52 personnel diagnosed with PTSD were set aside to appease the politicians; maybe it was to help Mr Blair sleep at night. These figures would only account for onset battlefield trauma that, if treated immediately, can offset the lasting damage of PTSD, but this treatment or policy simply did not exist in 2003. Then, there is the medium-term and then, finally, the more damaging long-term effects of battlefield trauma which are not even considered in this report. It affects every soldier differently and is unique to their life experiences and operational deployments. As for the remaining 409 personnel who had experienced poor mental health in this period, were they just sad, stressed or had anxiety? Maybe, like Ski, they had a 'personality disorder' and if that is the case, why are recruits not psychologically tested before they are allowed to join the British Army?

In an interview with the BBC in 2018, Prof Simon Wessely, Regius Professor of Psychiatry at King's College London, pointed out that there was now less stigma attached to poor mental health and PTSD and that, "It used to take people maybe 10-13 years to come forward for treatment; now that's down to around 2-3 years."[xxix]

I am pleased to hear that the stigma and shame regarding mental health and PTSD is now on the decline, but even 2-3 years is not acceptable. My generation, as Wessely rightly alludes to, would not openly admit to themselves or others that they were struggling with their mental health, especially PTSD, and as a result, suffered in silence. Maybe this was an issue within society as there was a changing of the guard in how the British Army operated in the following years. It gradually became more professional and acknowledged the impact that warfare has on our mental health. The chain of command, including medical personnel, was about to enter a ten-year period of high-intensity operational deployments where boots on the ground were often prioritised over the mental health of its soldiers. For the men of 10 Platoon, and the Irish Guards in general, our feet were yet to touch the ground for a split second in this 12-month period. No sooner had we returned from Iraq than we would find ourselves deploying on another operational tour that very same year.

Before the War in Iraq, the Battalion was scheduled to deploy on an operational tour to Northern Ireland in the September of 2003. This had been put back to the October as a consequence and now we had to rush through our pre-deployment training. Five months after returning from war, I would be deployed to South Armagh again. In the six years since I was last in South Armagh, the Irish Guards had drastically changed. Junior commanders such as Frank, Soldier 'G', and myself, were battle-hardened and the old ways of gaining forced respect through bullying, fear, and violence were being gradually weeded out. We were approachable, and valued and respected the Guardsmen.

During our Northern Ireland training, it was mandatory to complete a judgmental exercise with the Royal Military Police (RMPs). This was essentially a huge arcade game with converted SA-80 rifles, and I remember that none of my men were taking it seriously. The concept is quite simple; different video scenarios are played out on a huge screen to your front and two soldiers at a time react as they would if deployed on operations. Then the RMP would play back the scenario and point out all (if any) of their mistakes. Pez and Greeny were rolling around on the floor and attempting to shoot the tyres of a terrorist's vehicle, by which the RMP were not impressed. For argument's sake, and to wind up the RMP, I supported my Guardsmen's decision. The rules of engagement are completely different in Northern Ireland than in times of war and it was obvious that we were all a little trigger-happy and not taking our training seriously. This juvenile approach would stay with us throughout the tour and I can look back at this time with fond memories.

Our brief training package was intense but fun. In fact, the whole tour to Northern Ireland was extremely enjoyable and was a lifetime away from my first deployment to South Armagh in 1997. Yes, the same operational demands and stresses were there, but these were minuscule compared to what we had experienced in Iraq earlier on in that year. Plus, all of the terror organisations had almost ceased all aggressive activities since the events of 9/11 after the U.S. had declared its War on Terror.

Once deployed, 10 Platoon were stationed at a patrol base in a small border town called Forkhill. I would be working closely with Wade again as he was now my logistics manager or Company Quartermaster Sergeant (CQMS). As expected, Wade was still diligent and professional, and I thoroughly respected him. When we initially arrived at our new home in Forkhill, I remember him being specifically astonished and taken back about how expensive some of the large salient cameras cost, as several of these would be on his logistics account. Me being me, I joked about how I didn't want to be him, with that amount of responsibility, how £4 million per camera was a lot and that he better not lose one. To my surprise, Wade was smiling. This wasn't good! I knew that smile. Wade then kindly informed me that I would be responsible for four of the six of these cameras at the huge observation post called Romeo Tower number 21 (R-21). Suddenly, with my new-found £16 million worth of responsibility, I wasn't joking anymore. He then continued that I would also be R-21's tower commander and as such, I would be a smaller logistical manager on this small observation base. I wasn't happy!

I remember noticing there was a distinct difference in command styles on this Christmas operational tour of South Armagh. There were those who had been previously deployed to Iraq or Kosovo and, let's just say, were more relaxed about being in Forkhill. Then there were the traditional commanders who had only experienced tours of Northern Ireland and found themselves being overly stressed at every opportunity. This was by no fault of their own, but how they believed low-level commanders should act from their previous experiences. This outlook had been inherited from their previous commanders and it was obvious that times were changing, and for the better.

10 Platoon would spend two to three weeks at a time at the patrol base in Forkhill before rotating to the solitude of the watchtowers at R-21. This small observation base consisted of ISO containers that had been linked together almost like giant Lego blocks. It had two helipads and was located on top of Slieve Gullion, a steep-sided mountain with an impressive height of 1,880 ft. The naturally occurring flat top on this mountain would provide us with excellent fields of observation, and with the use of the Salient cameras, would allow us to see for miles around in all weather conditions. These huge cameras were motion activated and were state of the art for 2003. Our job was simple when stationed in R-21; gain intelligence of suspected 'players' (terrorists), observe and report.

We were always professional but had fun at the same time and may or may not have misused some of this high-tech multimillion-pound equipment for our own amusement in the process. My best friend Frank had missed the war as he was still instructing recruits at ATR Pirbright but was now back in 4 Company in 11 Platoon. Frank would be doing the same job as myself but at a smaller observation patrol base called Golf 40 (G-40). As always, we were in competition and his responsibilities were less than mine and I frequently enjoyed reminding him of this. He had just the one helipad, whereas I had two, he had one observation tower, whereas I had four and it didn't stop there. The shenanigans were coming in thick and fast and from all directions; no one was safe! The chief instigator was usually my good friend John Corcoran, he would have a hand in all of the mischievous activity that would occur. He had been assigned to 10 Platoon as a multiple commander for the deployment and I was glad as, like Frank, I thought of him as a brother.

My beloved MCFC mug was initially 'mug-napped' and I would receive ransom notes and pictures of it in different locations around South Armagh. Furthermore, my office phone in my bunk would ring at all hours with prank phone calls. This was generally Ski, Mac, Pez, and Ricky or at least, I suspected it was them, as I never really found out. The pranks were so bad that even when the Commanding Officer called the main sanger of R-21 to congratulate us on doing such a great job, Pez didn't believe him and rudely hung up. Knaggsy then rang my office/bunk phone and asked me to thank the team and thankfully saw the funny side. Besides the shenanigans, we had the right balance of professionalism, a diligent work ethic and a better working environment. In fact, this operational deployment felt more like a holiday with your mates and looking back, it was some of the best times in my career.

The only way to access these observation patrol bases was by helicopter and as such we would be required to return our waste and food swill once a fortnight. Frank and I were responsible for packaging this waste into cargo nets for the helicopters to remove as underslung loads. We would often use the salient cameras to stalk each other on the helipads, either receiving supplies or returning them. These helicopters were like our very own Amazon Prime and we would utilise them for our own amusement. On one such sortie, I had 'accidentally' left R21's waste for a week on the helipad in the rain. This was generally packed in plastic bags in an outer cardboard box, then wrapped in a cargo net. I had requested that the helicopter drop it at Frank's location at G-40, knowing full well that the cardboard would collapse and the swill from the kitchen would burst all over Frank and it didn't disappoint.

Myself, John and Frankie were the three amigos, good friends who were as thick as thieves. I remember that John in particular was overly excited as we observed our prank unfold on one of the salient cameras from miles away. The plan worked perfectly and as the helicopter dropped the underslung load on Franks' helipad, it collapsed, covering Frank with food waste. As one could imagine, Frank was not impressed and was out for revenge, but he never found out who sent him that underslung load, well, at least until now, that is.

We secretly fed John with protein powder and as there were no mirrors in the gym, we convinced him that he was bulking up with muscle when in fact he was just getting fat. John's wife, Sarah, didn't see the funny side when her husband returned home with excessive lard and we would continue to laugh and joke about this in the years that followed! Forkhill had a tiny sauna in a broom cupboard, and this is where I had my biggest victory over Frank to date. Several of us overcrowded ourselves into the sauna and decided to put the heat up in an attempt to see who was the toughest; this was a game of last man standing. It was no surprise that Frank, John, and I were the last three and we were all literally feeling the heat! Then out of nowhere, John pulled out a bottle of vodka and poured it on the rocks! This instantaneously burnt our eyes and airways and John exited the sauna realising that he had made a mistake. It was down to the last two and I was feeling the pressure. I began to play mind games with Frank and told him that I would rather pass out than admit defeat to him and that I was fine. This was far from the truth as I was just about to quit when Frank exited the sauna, so I was victorious and promptly followed him out almost on his back!

I was generally disappointed when this operational tour came to an end as it never felt like actual work. I have fond memories of our time in Forkhill and I believe that this was a welcomed distraction from our experiences in the War in Iraq. Whilst deployed to South Armagh, I was able to mask my pain by focusing solely on my duties and would continue to do this for the rest of my career. On my return to the mainland, I would be assigned to the Infantry Training Centre Catterick as a recruit instructor for the following two years. For the men that I had commanded in Iraq, this would be the last time that I would see Ski, Pez, Mac, and let us not forget that Stevie had already transitioned into civvy street.

Pez would go absent without leave whilst on a sailing expedition from Argentina to Australia. He would be arrested in 2010 and given an immediate discharge without serving any jail time. Mac would unfortunately be a casualty in a severe road traffic accident in Kenya which resulted in a medical discharge, and as for Ski... I believe that if he had been kept with the men of 10 Platoon for that tour, we could have helped him, but maybe that's the optimist in me. Regardless, no decompression or mental health evaluations or awareness training, for that matter, was conducted despite us deploying twice on operations within a twelve-month period. In hindsight, this is an institutional failure and would be justified by the operational intensity over the coming years. The Ministry of Defence would prioritise the operational needs over that of the individual soldiers and disregard their mental health and overall wellbeing in the process. The British Army's needs were always the priority and, as the indoctrinated soldiers that we were, we unconditionally bought into this rhetoric as the Army's needs became our own... we were selfless.

Chapter 9.
The Circle of Infantry Life

I was not at all nervous about returning to the Infantry Training Centre Catterick as a recruit instructor despite the harsh treatment that I had received there as a trainee. In fact, I was quite optimistic as I would be avoiding the stressful work environment of ceremonial duties in London. What was disturbing, though, was that I was joining a training team which had just witnessed another recruit suicide. Trainee Guardsman Brown had planned and successfully shot himself in the platoon lines a few weeks prior to my arrival and no counselling was offered to either the training team or the recruits. Surprisingly, I didn't even think about the suicide that I had witnessed nine years earlier on the drill square when I was myself a trainee. In hindsight, I was suppressing all of my emotions and experiences due to my ongoing deteriorating mental health and, if I'm being completely honest, I don't think that I was in the right frame of mind to be instructing the next generation of Infantrymen.

Brown's would be the seventh recruit suicide that had happened at Catterick since Isherwood in 1996. The inquest that followed acknowledged a severe failing throughout the whole recruiting process as Brown had a history of depression and had previously attempted suicide. xxx Brown should not have been able to progress through the British Army selection process to begin recruit training, let alone firearms training, as he was evidently mentally unstable to begin with. Despite the fact that this recruit was unstable and even wrote his name on the bullet that he had used to kill himself, the training team were vilified during the investigation by the Royal Military Police. At the inquest that followed, they would be vindicated but this suicide had happened on their watch and they will always ask themselves the unproductive retrospective question of, 'Could I have done more?'

Yet again, no consideration toward the mental health or wellbeing of the training team or the soldiers was ever provided. Furthermore, the British Army would continue to target recruits who were mentally unsuitable to be entrusted with lethal weapons and this would lead to more suicides in the years that followed. One can't help but wonder why, after so many public inquiries, there is no psychological assessment as part of the British Army selection process. Then again, if such a test was introduced, how many candidates would actually pass it and make it through to recruit training? This raises many questions, specifically regarding the type of person the military attracts. Personally, due to my upbringing, I seriously doubt that I would have been passed 'mentally fit' if such a test had existed when I applied to join. Maybe that's why this test is still aloof despite being much needed?

As a recruit instructor, you inevitably become a role model to the trainees, and, in some cases, a big brother or father figure. All soldiers remember their section commanders from training and often share their experiences of these perceived 'god-like' influential figures. My generation was trained by mainly Northern Ireland veterans with the occasional Gulf War Veteran and at times were violent bullies. Now, I was appointed this 'god-like' status and would I, a Veteran to Kosovo, Iraq and two tours of Northern Ireland, be any different? Would my generation of battle-hardened war fighters continue to be bullies, or would we, with our ongoing mental health battles, be any different?

I could not honestly answer this question due to the lack of objectivity involved but I can provide proof of several important incidents where change was being implemented. Personally, I was never exploitative of my position as a recruit trainer. I never took money or sold my recruits anything and even refused the encouraged 'thank you' gifts at their pass out parades. I wasn't doing this for free; it was my job and I was getting paid to do it! I was never physically violent when training recruits and if recruits made mistakes, I never got angry or lost my temper. There was no phase 1 and phase 2 training anymore and we had these guys for six months which allowed ample time to correct simple mistakes. However, I would use exercises such as press-ups or burpees as small punishments as this would also improve the physical fitness of the trainee.

Protocols would later come into place to restrict the amount that we could hand out, so we got creative to abide by these new rules by adding Regimental variations to each exercise. I can recall catching two trainees asleep on stag (guard duty) on a tactical exercise, and in the field army, this is punishable by 28 days in military jail, but as these were trainees, I decided that I would have them crawl around our Platoon location in the mud for 10 minutes as punishment instead. I remember that my training Captain pulled me to one side and told me that this was inappropriate behaviour and that times were changing. I respected this Captain and he was only looking out for all of our best interests and I never conducted this type of punishment again. I would later strike a trainee, but I still believe that this was just, as he almost killed me!

As part of their final weeks at Catterick, all recruits must complete an arduous live firing range package at the Warcop Ranges. All the ammunition used is real and this included medium machine guns, mortars, anti-tank weapons, demolitions, and grenades. Training was still focused on the attrition battles of the Falklands War and I vividly remember leading my men into a position to grenade a bunker. As we approached the enemy position, I broke away with one of the trainees - the grenadier! We crawled forward whilst the others provided creeping fire and mortar support until we came to our designated individual pens set adjacent to each other. These pens were designed to provide sufficient cover from the imminent live grenade blast to our front and I had completed this range on many occasions and felt safe. That was, until this nervous trainee scooped the grenade, and, in a bizarre and unpredictable throw, it landed an inch before my eyes as I was still firing at the target.

Time appeared to stand still as I heard this trainee scream, 'grenade!' The L109 fragmentation grenade has a 3-5 second fuse burn time until detonation, and I was now face to face with one. Everyone around me panicked and had taken cover and if I didn't act fast, I knew that I was toast! I have always been terrible at pool and snooker, but something inspired me to use my rifle as a pool cue to gently pot this grenade away from the top of my pen and towards the safe area for detonation. I quickly produced this 'trick shot' and waited for the explosion. Then, there was the anticipated horrendously loud bang and immediately afterwards, my 'controlled aggression' kicked in, yet I wasn't in control!

Even before the dirt had landed around me, I was up and out of my safe pen and running toward the trainee who had thrown this grenade that had almost killed me. I remember the fear in his eyes as I steamed towards him as I was probably frothing at the mouth in a fit of rage at the time. He was repeatedly screaming, 'Sorry, sergeant!' as I launched myself on him and threw several blows. Luckily, the range safety restrained me and as he was wearing his helmet and body armour, fortunately, he was not hurt. Once I had calmed down and noticed that this young trainee was in tears, I suggested that he should complete the range again. Everyone was confused as to why I had suggested this. More so, who would be willing to risk their life with this dangerous recruit? The common practice for a mistake such as this was for the recruit to be 'back-squadded' for remedial training; after all, he was dangerous and had almost killed his section commander! However, he was my responsibility and I would risk death to take him on this range for a second time.

I had personally trained this recruit for almost six months and this was the first time that he had made a mistake. Yes, an almost fatal one, but I would like to think that he didn't aim for me with the grenade and that it was just a bad throw, a freak training accident due to nerves. I pulled the recruit to one side and we practised some remedial grenade- throwing until I was confident enough to take him down the range again. We repeated the range and as we crawled to our designated pens for the second time, we were joking about his previous scooped throw and how I would throw the grenade back to him if he repeated himself (I think that I was joking?). Now more relaxed, this recruit successfully threw this grenade and completed his training.

Looking back on not just this incident, but on all of my experiences as a recruit trainer, I do not believe that I was in a sound enough mental state of mind to be allowed to train recruits. I had been deployed on two operational tours in the eighteen months prior to my posting to the Infantry Training Centre and no psychological assessment was ever conducted on me beforehand. I was aware that I was struggling with my own mental health as I had already experienced a panic attack and I was having weird dreams throughout my time there. Additional instructors would come and go with some even being posted in immediately from the high-intensity operations in Iraq and Afghanistan, yet again, with no mental health assessment before being allowed to teach the next generation of soldiers. This raises many questions regarding our suitability to train these recruits in this period.

I fundamentally believe that because of the amount of high-intensity warfare that my generation had experienced, we were more relaxed and approachable as recruit trainers. We didn't need to gain respect through fear, violence and intimidation as our battlefield exploits and medals were enough for us. We had witnessed great feats and acts of bravery from young trained soldiers and had a respect for them which was the polar opposite of the British Army of the late 1990s. Niall, now a tailor, having been posted to Catterick between 2000-2002, and now 2005-2007, had observed a seismic shift in how the recruits were trained during this two-year period.

Niall had witnessed how recruits were no longer beaten into submission but rather trained to be soldiers - good Infantrymen. We knew that once trained, they would be deployed to either Iraq or Afghanistan and they had to be prepared. As recruit trainers, we had a completely different outlook to those who had previously 'taught us'. The British Army was currently fighting a counter-insurgency war on two fronts and we were aware that in order to fulfil the

British Army's needs, we needed good capable soldiers, not the scared, uncertain ones that the previous generation had trained. Our approach to how we trained these young men may have changed but unfortunately, the harmful training methods remained the same. We would still refer to pain, and more pertinently emotions, as weakness and continue the detrimental process of creating a military mindset in our soldiers that would allow poor mental health to thrive through the established behavioural training methods.

As a training team, we would always look forward to the bayonet fighting lessons and this was where we all could go a little crazy and let off some steam! It was not uncommon for trainees to break down emotionally and cry throughout this process. I can shamefully recollect reducing a trainee to tears through such proven relentless physical and psychological training exercises. This so-called 'controlled aggression' had broken this particular trainee and whilst on his knees, mentally broken, bayonet in hand, he cried, 'I cannot kill.' It would come as no surprise that after this mental torment, this recruit would eventually decide to leave the Army at the next available opportunity. I believe that due to our own battlefield experiences and expectations, when we conducted all training under 'controlled aggression', that we were far more intense than what we had previously experienced as trainees. Maybe at times we did cross the line and were too intense, but one must bear in mind that we were all struggling with our own mental health and no support was ever offered or even available to us, for that matter.

When interviewing my Platoon Sergeant, Paul, from the Infantry Training Centre Catterick, he informed me that when I joined his training team, he was envious of my battlefield exploits and medals, as, like me, he had joined the Army to deploy on operations but was unfortunate to have only deployed to Northern Ireland in his career at this point. Paul was a fantastic soldier and an even better administrator; he was the complete package. Plus, he was a nice guy, which was a rarity. I found this envy hard to stomach because there were many men more capable than me and I was haunted by my experiences in Kosovo and Iraq. I often thought about why anyone would want this burden, this guilt and was gradually becoming disillusioned with military life as a result. Paul would be thirty-eight years old before he would experience his own high-intensity combat deployment in Afghanistan some years later. He would discover the reality of warfare, especially in the casualty intensive counter-insurgency fighting that occurred in Helmand Province. This would be an ocean apart from his romantic expectations and would leave him with his own personal trauma and guilt to live with.

When I asked him the difficult question of whether he knew that I was struggling with my own mental health whilst under his command, he reluctantly replied, 'yes.' He then went on to add that we were all under pressure from work to train the recruits and that was all that mattered. The mental health of the training team was an afterthought. Furthermore, the 'man up' military culture also played a serious part in ignoring my pain and let us not forget that mental health or awareness training was non-existent in the mid-2000s. Paul believes that he failed me not only as a commander but also as a friend and this is far from the case. This was institutional failure and unfortunately, we were part of that institution and would continue to play our roles. Regrettably, this was to the detriment of the recruits as we continued to train them in the ways of 'controlled aggression' and instilled into them that they had to suppress their emotions as they were a form of 'weakness.'

It was during my time at Catterick where I met Soldier 'S' and we soon became very good friends. Soldier 'S' would go on to have a very successful career and would reach the rank of Warrant Officer Class 2. With 8 years left on his service, he was destined for great things until he started to suffer from alopecia due to the high demands and stress of the job. Soldier 'S' had repeatedly informed his Regiment that he was suffering with his own mental health but was essentially told to 'man up', despite the obvious and visible hair loss now beginning to show. Furthermore, he was suffering from insomnia and was constantly retching and vomiting as a result of acid reflux. Subconsciously, Soldier 'S' was haunted by the death of several children that he had witnessed whilst in Afghanistan and this had laid the foundations for his mental health to gradually deteriorate over time. Despite the fact that he had courageously sought out help as a senior commander, which is a feat within itself, he was despicably let down as a result of the institutional failure regarding mental health within the Infantry. Even in 2014, emotions were still classed as weakness and this can only be a direct consequence of all of our behavioural training.

In the years that followed, Soldier 'S' would endure several personal tragedies in his home life and was denied compassionate leave due to his rank and status within his Battalion. This additional domestic pressure would culminate in Soldier 'S' going for a drive in the middle of the night with the intention of killing himself. The pressure of his battlefield trauma, work, and personal heartbreak had overwhelmed him and, in his mind, his only escape was through suicide. Fortunately, Soldier 'S' came to his senses and decided to seek help from the doctor. It was at this point that his Battalion pulled out all of the stops, but it was too late, the damage was already done.

Soldier 'S' had personally witnessed the British Army's disregard towards the mental wellbeing of its soldiers and after sacrificing so much, he felt betrayed. He had gone through the correct channels and been ignored, and it was only when he was at his phycological end of the road that he was hypocritically offered help after he had been asking for it for years! Soldier 'S' has now left the Army and, unfortunately, the leadership failing of a few have left him bitter towards his Regiment and his service to his country. He was unquestionably loyal to his Regiment and they showed him very little in return. He had always prioritised the job above all else, including his family, and had even missed my wedding! Soldier 'S' is just another example of how little consideration was given to the welfare of its soldiers by the Army after the events of 9/11. All that mattered to the Ministry of Defence was the mission, whether it be Iraq/ Afghanistan or the training of recruits, and the welfare of the individual became a sacrificial lamb as a result.

I was intrigued to challenge my own perceptions of being a recruit instructor and was lucky enough to be able to interview one of my former recruits to analyse his views. Johno, like myself, was 17 years old when he arrived at Catterick. He came from a military family and has a remarkable story to share. I was initially interested in Johno's training experience and what his perception was of me as his recruit instructor. I told him about my own struggles with PTSD, poor mental health and he just opened up and told me about his own battles and his many suicide attempts. This shocked me to my very core. I had trained this soldier; I was suddenly overwhelmed with guilt as I believed that I had a hand in establishing the conditions for his poor mental health through the behavioural training methods that I instilled into him. I understand that I was part of the indoctrination machine but cannot help but think about how hard we psychologically pushed the trainees.

Johno informed me that I was always good with the recruits but pushed them hard on their fitness. I would hand out press-ups for fun, but the trainees could have a laugh with me and that I was firm but fair. He also mentioned that one of the training team scared him because of his 'thousand-yard stare', a Military Cross recipient called Anton. When asked if I was ever a bully, his reply was no but there were some bullies in the Platoon, but they were the other recruits. I was oblivious to this at the time, as, from my experience of going through training, we had gelled as a team as we all despised our instructors. I was pleased that Johno's feedback was positive but was distraught about how far his mental health had deteriorated since leaving the Army.

The last time that I physically saw Johno was in the winter of 2010 in Afghanistan. He had re-cap-badged from the Irish Guards to the Royal Irish Regiment and was operating out of patrol base Pimom in Helmand Province. Once I knew he was there, I found my way to the sanger where he was on guard and we had a good chat. In the months that followed, a serious incident would occur that would change his life forever. His mental health would deteriorate so badly that at his lowest point, in over a three-year period, he would carry around a noose in a backpack, just looking, wanting an excuse to end his own life.

Johno had deployed to Afghanistan one month later than everyone else as a battlefield casualty reserve and said that it was the proudest day of his life when he was informed that he would be deploying that very same day. Coming from a military family, this is what he had always dreamed of and when he landed at Kandahar, he was listening to the theme tune from the film, 'The Good, the Bad, and The Ugly,' for inspiration. After all, Nad'Ali South, where Johno would be stationed, was the wild west! It wouldn't be long before Johno was engaged by the enemy whilst on a foot patrol and he immediately hit the deck whilst the other members of the team took a knee. He recalls that he was ridiculed for getting onto his belly, but this is what soldiers are taught to do in conventional warfare. However, in the Green Zone of Helmand, there were improvised explosive devices (IED'S) everywhere, so you took a knee to avoid less contact with the ground, thus, reducing the risk of detonating a bomb in the process.

After several patrols and contacts with the enemy, this was the norm and Johno was part of his team of gunslingers. Then, after one particular contact with the Taliban, Johno and his team were on a particular high! This is a unique buzz that only soldiers experience from their close encounters of near death. It is hard to explain what this is, but I suspect that it has something to do with an overload of adrenaline and Johno was toying around with his pistol, a Sig Sauer P226. This particular model has no safety catch, only a double pressure trigger. Hence, it is always loaded and ready to fire and Johno in his euphoria was waving it around when the pistol accidentally went off. There was the pop of the round being fired then a frightful silence. Panic began to set in as Johno had just set off his pistol unintentionally and shot one of his team, his military brother, in the chest.

Johno still has nightmares about this incident especially as he attempted first aid on his brother, a fellow gunslinger, who was now bleeding out in his arms. Fortunately, this was not a fatal wound, yet the look on Johno's mate's face still haunts him as there was no denying that this was Johno's fault. Soldiers use lethal weapons on a daily basis and freak accidents often occur, but some can be avoided with good practices. Like the grenade that had almost killed me whilst training recruits, accidents happen. They happen so frequently that we give them official names. In Johno's case, this was referred to as a 'Negligent Discharge' and many of my colleagues have had them in the past. The trauma from this incident would initiate a chain of events that would almost destroy Johno's life and the lives of those around him.

Johno was sent on R'n'R immediately for fourteen days leave to help him deal with this tragic accident. Like most soldiers returning home from war zones for leave, no mental health awareness training was provided. On returning to his home and already in despair, Johno would discover that his partner was cheating on him and completely lost it. He was then charged with assault and battery and given 200 hours of community service and two years' probation after beating up the other guy. The rest of his leave was spent in a drunken haze, and, as a consequence of his aggressive behaviour, he also now had a restraining order against his daughter. Johno would try to keep this incident a secret from the Army but they always find out...always!

On his return to Afghanistan, Johno underwent a psychological evaluation but stormed out after telling the captain conducting his assessment to 'fuck off!' Johno spoke about this officer with loathing as he would purposely antagonise him by saying 'two cm's to the left and your mate would have died, and I'm going to make sure that you get charged with attempted murder!' I suspect that this medical officer may have just been a doctor with limited mental health training; regardless, Johno was grounded and not allowed out of the main camp in Bastion. For the remainder of the tour, Johno would sleep throughout the day and be responsible for the guarding of prisoners throughout the night. He was burdened with guilt and had nothing to go home to. In fact, he didn't want to go home at all, which is a mindset that I can relate to.

Johno would inevitably experience an emotional breakdown during his two days decompression in Cyprus and his life would only get much worse in the years to come. Once home, he was quickly sectioned after a string of drug and alcohol-fuelled nights out. He had been spotted trying to hang himself from a tree with the cord of a phone charger and was held under the Mental Health Act, yet, Somehow, in less than four months, Johno was deemed fit to attend his military Court Martial with no consideration given towards his poor and waning mental health. Johno would be sentenced to 16 months imprisonment at the Military Corrective Training Centre at Colchester. The charge was 'negligent discharge with no intention to harm,' with the option to remain in service. Johno was delighted with the charge but not so much with the sentence as, for the past six months, he had convinced himself that maybe he had meant to shoot his mate! This was on the basis of what that Army doctor had said to him in Afghanistan and had laid the negative foundations and prejudice against all future therapists.

Johno would be released into the civilian world after eleven months and would move to his 'happy place,' Burnley. His extended family had set up a flat, furniture, clothes, food and even put beer in the fridge for him, yet he felt lost and abandoned; he had no identity. He was twenty-three years old and all he had ever known, or been part of, was the military environment. He would get a job at a local factory but would lose this after a fellow worker deliberately ripped his poppy off his shirt, so instinctively, Johno punched him; he was now in trouble with the police again. Johno had forcefully tucked away his emotions as indoctrinated by his training but was being consumed by his guilt. This guilt would manifest into anger and the only outlet was violence. He would later turn to class A drugs as these were the only things that helped him forget his nightmares, that look on his mate's face after he had been accidentally shot by him.

Johno was now having trouble paying for the drugs, his only respite from his inner demons, and was now working as a debt collector for a drug dealer. His mental health was so bad that he was now carrying a noose around in a backpack and on the days when he didn't have any respite, any drugs, he would attempt to hang himself to escape, to be happy. Eventually, Johno would find himself living on the streets and after painfully admitting that he didn't have 'the strength' to take his own life, Johno would start self-harming.

Luckily, Johno would in the end find his way to the charity SHAID. SHAID or the Single Homeless Action Inactive Durham would be a charity that would turn things around for Johno and put him on a different path, but through a strange intervention - the arts! I have tried not to mention soldiers' and veterans' true names in this book as many of them are ashamed or embarrassed about their stories, but this superstar, Tony Hammond, deserves an honourable mention. Tony is one of the volunteers at SHAID and was instrumental in saving Johno's life. Tony would encourage Johno to box to gain confidence and to get rid of his anger, then to perform on stage to tell his own story which, in turn, helped Johno release all of his suppressed emotions and self-loathing.

SHAID would work with the Royal British Legion and the B22 veteran performance company and Johno would find the confidence to perform at a celebrity-filled theatre at Western-super-Mare. This was in 2016, and since then, Johno has remarkably turned his life around. He has steady employment and a loving partner with two kids. I truly find Johno's journey inspiring. At his lowest, he was contemplating suicide on a daily basis, yet he somehow found the courage to fight off his inner demons and to finally make a happy life for himself. Then he was brave enough to share his shameful and embarrassing life experiences with me, to be used as an example to others that it **can** and **will** get better. Johno is undoubtedly brave and I only hope that he will continue to be courageous and to seek out professional help in the near future as he still carries around the psychological scars of his past.

It is obvious to me that Johno has been traumatised by his own reckless and negligent actions with his pistol. Ninety-nine times out of a hundred, the bullet misses everyone, but I genuinely believe that it was the first doctor that he spoke to regarding this incident who tipped him into the abyss. I am flabbergasted that in such a short space of time from being sectioned under the Mental Health Act, to his Court Martial, that no mental health support was made available to him. What is alarming though, is the long-term impact that this atrocious Army doctor had on Johno's trust in therapy and willingness to engage. He has overcome so much, and I am hopeful that he will seek out further therapy in the near future that will enable him to learn how to manage and cope with his inner demons; he is an inspiration.

After listening to Johno's journey, I began to wonder what had happened to Anton. Anton was assigned to our training team and I was asked to keep an eye on him as he had had a bit of a 'wobble' in Battalion life. The training team had been made aware of the fact that Anton had been suffering with his mental health and we either just paid lip service to this or just didn't care. Remember, emotions are weakness, and this is what we were teaching on a daily basis at the time. Anton was a fellow Irish Guardsman and was the youngest recipient of the Military Cross in the 2003 Iraq War. He had stopped an Iraqi soldier from throwing a grenade on his team through his quick actions by shooting him dead. He was a hero but was also struggling with his own inner demons; the unwanted psychological scars that somehow always seem to remain.

When I spoke to Anton about his experiences of joining our training team, his reply stunned me. Anton was relieved that he was just accepted for who he was and liked the fact that I never asked him about Iraq or how he had won his Military Cross. Previously, the Battalion had been parading him around as if he was a trophy and Anton didn't really feel he was worth such accolades. From his own perspective, he was only doing the job that he was trained to do. Anton explained to me that before being awarded his Military Cross, he was just an average Guardsman and that post-Iraq, there was immense pressure and unwanted expectations put on him. Officers would expect him to be the best at everything from fitness to marksmanship and he was always treated differently than his fellow Guardsmen.

I only worked with Anton for a short period of time, but I can vividly remember him physically shaking when I had put a weapon in his hands when asking him to simulate an enemy soldier for a lesson. Anton then shut down and was unable to function and I immediately removed the weapon from him and told him to take five. This was yet another red flag that I had chosen to ignore. Anton, like Ski, would be diagnosed with a personality disorder rather than a psychological disorder associated with combat. Let us not forget that this was a period when the British Army was under scrutiny due to the lack of WMDs found in Iraq. The Army didn't need any more bad press and God forbid that one of their trophies (Anton) now had poor mental health as a result of his bravery.

I cannot help but feel responsible for having a hand in both Anton and Johno's poor mental health despite them both stating the contrary. I had totally ignored the fact that Anton had poor mental health to which he kindly highlighted that I was also suffering with my own. However, what is deeply concerning is how I blindly followed the well-polished military training methods that had once been used to brainwash me. I would regularly yell 'pain is weakness' and 'emotions are weakness' and 'that they should be ignored.' I would go over the top and push recruits to their psychological limits without a single thought or regard to their long-term mental health. The British Army required its current batch of soldiers to be operationally ready, with many deploying to Iraq and Afghanistan in the coming months, once they had passed out. As a training team, we had fulfilled the Army's needs, regardless of the cost to our recruits' long-term psychological wellbeing. We categorically followed the previous generation in forging a military mindset that would allow poor mental health to thrive and this is something that I often regret.

It was during my time at Catterick that I began to receive phone calls about the whereabouts of one of my former lads from the War in Iraq, James Piotrowski. Ski had gone AWOL and was suspected of taking an assault rifle with him. From the tone of these phone calls, I couldn't help but get the impression from the 'top brass' that the Army wanted to throw him to the wolves. Ski was one of my lads and I always believed that I had a duty of care for all of them, more so the ones who entrusted me with their lives when we went to war. We wouldn't have hesitated to sacrifice our lives to save the other's and were bound by an unspoken bond that was forged on the battlefield. Ski's battlefield trauma wouldn't be taken into consideration despite the fact that all of the incidents that caused his deteriorating mental health genuinely occurred. [xxxi]

Ski, would eventually be arrested, 'but gave police the slip twice more in two months until he gave himself up at a hospital in Wales in January 2005'.[xxxii] In a strange kind of way, I was proud of Ski. I had trained him for war and had rammed into him that if caught, he must always escape and evade, and to always fight and never give up. Maybe this was my own way of hiding the same trauma that we shared throughout the early weeks of the war. In the months before his trial, I was interviewed several times by the Royal Military Police (RMP), then later the Special Investigation Branch (SIB), and these 'policemen' were completely biased. In the Army you were always deemed guilty until proven innocent!

These interviews were a complete joke and lacked objectivity and were more like interrogations. Initially, I was dragged by the RMPs out of a skill-at-arms lesson with my recruits without any warning. Immediately, this felt like a shakedown and I knew why they were here. The questions that they were asking were about Ski's battlefield experiences and particularly if he had experienced any traumatic events. 'What the fuck?' I thought to myself! 'Have these clowns ever seen combat or even deployed on operations? What a stupid question.' I couldn't take these RMPs seriously and began to toy with them due to their lack of operational experience, and they were failing to coerce me into painting a bad character reference about Ski when all I was doing was praising him. Looking back, I actually enjoyed this failed attempt by these monkeys to interrogate me. I was team Piotrowski and that was that, or so I thought.

The following week and again without warning, I was pulled out of another lesson with my recruits for a second interview with the military police, this time by the SIB. These guys were more experienced, older and in plain clothes. They outranked me, and, from the beginning, attempted to intimidate me. The shock and awe tactics yet again didn't work on me and I was in quite the pleasant mood until they suggested that I was accountable for Ski's actions and that I may also be investigated. If I am being completely honest, this did frighten me a little, but I wasn't going to abandon one of my men. One in, all in! Let's talk about the war, shall we?!

I answered honestly all of the SIBs questions about Ski's operational performance and was adamant that out of all of the Guardsmen I had commanded in Iraq; he was the best. Like their younger less experienced colleagues, they were probing about the very nature of warfare, asking stupid questions about whether Ski was ever in danger in Iraq, did he ever engage the enemy or was he ever engaged directly by enemy fire? Bloody hell, where do I start?

I condescendingly explained that in the early weeks of our time in Iraq, we were at WAR and that we exchanged fire with the enemy on a daily basis! I emphasised how it was the pair of us who had covered my section's extraction under heavy fire, after being forsaken on the streets of Basra after an ambush. Maybe Ski should have been decorated for his actions, but I always thought that we were just doing our jobs and Ski was exceptional at doing his. They seemed disappointed at listening about his feats of bravery and professionalism, then began to ask questions about the darker side of warfare, the civilians.

I could almost smell the desert again and taste the combat. I thought about that little girl, the pregnant woman with shrapnel injuries and those burnt kids. I composed myself and spoke about how I had instigated the airstrike, how I had reported the enemy fire from the village and how this was passed up the chain of command. If anyone was responsible or accountable for Ski's actions, then I was. What I refused to mention was my own deteriorating mental health, my own struggles with what we had experienced, and my own internal pain, particularly the harsh panic attack that had occurred after the war. Maybe if I had been brave enough to mention my own inner demons, then this could have helped Ski, but I was too ashamed. (Even writing this, I have a severe tightness in my chest just from recollecting this incident).

I explained how we came under heavy artillery fire on the outskirts of Basra and how later, we would pick off enemy targets for fun in the investment phase of the siege of the city. The SIB officers didn't seem too pleased with the character reference that I was creating and then asked whether or not Ski had conducted any war crimes or if he had disobeyed any of my orders or showed signs of cowardice. Wow; just wow! I now lost it as this wasn't an interview - this was a witch hunt! I told these two pricks that we were done and that next time they came back, I would be contacting a solicitor, but I was more than happy to testify under oath in a court of law.

That call never came and Lance Corporal James Piotrowski was sentenced to seven years and four months in prison.

Ski's father, Mark Piotrowski, would later state his son 'was suffering post-traumatic stress disorder after serving in Iraq and that he should have got better support after returning from duty in the Middle East'.[xxxiii] I genuinely feel that none of the front-line infantry soldiers who bore the brunt of the fighting in the 2003 War in Iraq received any mental health support. Dave, Mac, Pez, Stevie, Ski and myself have all since suffered with poor mental health from our experience of warfare. This raises many questions as to the root of our trauma; was this how we were trained, events from the battlefield, lack of aftercare or was it the consequences of how I led these men in difficult and demanding circumstances? In the years following my time in Iraq, I was always proud and took comfort in telling myself that I brought all of my men home, when the harsh reality is that this is, in fact, a lie! A lie that I can no longer take comfort in because the truth is, I actually left some of my men there.

After these interviews, I threw myself into work even further. I would get my reward and be given a temporary rank of Colour Sergeant (two ranks up) to go and teach a group of Iraqi Officers at the Infantry Battle School in Brecon. I was apprehensive as some of these Iraqis had fought against me in and around Basra during the war and my interpreter, Wahid, was a former Iraqi Republican Guard. This was just two years after the war in 2003, and, in hindsight, it may have been a bad idea. However, this was a fantastic career opportunity and not to be missed. So, I suppressed my emotions even further as my priority was solely focused on my career.

Before the course had started, the other instructors leant heavily on me due to my battlefield experience in Iraq, despite the fact that I was two ranks their junior. I didn't want this added pressure and had made it clear from the start that I was a section commander and not a Colour Sergeant. I wasn't even qualified to wear the rank, but this was a requirement to instruct at the Infantry Battle School. In the evenings, I had to pre-learn the instructional syllabus before I taught it the following day and found myself drinking heavily again. I was yet to complete the Platoon Sergeants' Battle Course which the course was mirrored around, and this would provide me with an advantage when I attended this course the following year.

It was on this course that I really got to know some of the Iraqi students and, despite my increased anxiety when around them, they were not bad guys. Of course, there were cultural differences, but at the end of the day, we were all soldiers and wanted what was best for our respective countries. Wahid, in particular, was quite opinionated, especially regarding the outcome of the war. He was adamant that if more qualified high-ranking Iraqi officers had led the Iraqi forces instead of the weak 'yes men' and friends of Saddam, then the outcome may have been different. I fundamentally disagreed, and we had many debates regarding this subject.

In the final weeks of instructing on this course, I received a letter from my Commanding Officer praising me for my hard work and, in doing so, representing and solidifying the Irish Guards as a fantastic Regiment. In the following days, I would receive a second invitation to transfer to the Small Arms School Corps (SASC). This is a small unit of soldiers who govern the safety aspect of all weapons training. I laughed this off as I was a dedicated Infantry soldier, or at least that is the image that I enjoyed projecting. I was always looking ahead, and this meant my next operational deployment to Iraq in 2007 as a Platoon Sergeant. I had convinced myself that I was destined to die on the battlefield and welcomed this; it was my destiny to die in Iraq from my part in that airstrike. This was my punishment and I accepted my impending death!

Chapter 10.
This is Sparta!

In the early summer of 2006, I successfully completed the Platoon Sergeants' Battle Course (PSBC) in Brecon achieving a below-average grade. I had clashed with my instructors throughout the duration of the tactics phase on this promotional course as I would challenge their theory against the group's experience. One must not forget that the majority of these students had current war-fighting knowledge from Iraq and Afghanistan and the syllabus was outdated as it was primarily derived from the Falklands War. I had also taught this syllabus the year prior and had an in-depth understanding of the advanced tactics and best practices that were being taught. Furthermore, the instructors delivering this course had just missed out on deploying to these war zones and, as a result, were a little envious of this current batch of students. Then there was my Marmite outspoken character to contemplate, so overall, I was satisfied with the grade.

In the last days of the final exercise, which was held in Malawi, (a small country in East Africa), I was informed that my grandfather had days to live and that arrangements were being made for me to return home. My immediate thought was that I would fail the course and, therefore, not be promoted! I was totally focused on passing this course and deploying to Iraq the following year as a Platoon Sergeant and, as such, I wanted to complete the final few days of the course. No thought whatsoever was given to my family as fulfilling the Army's needs was exclusively my priority at this point in my life. Thankfully, the Company Sergeant Major pulled me to one side and informed me that I had already easily passed the course before we had deployed on this final exercise in Malawi. Now I was interested. He went on to tell me that this was one of the few times where the British Army's welfare system worked well because it was a training exercise and not an operational deployment. I was then flown to what can only be described as a chicken freighter to South Africa before a connecting flight to London and I cannot fault the welfare team for their rapid response and sound planning. They were second to none and in retrospect, I would like to thank them.

However, when I landed in London, I received a voicemail that my grandfather had already passed; I was too late. My mind raced over this unproductive journey as all I could think about was how this would affect my course grade. For the past decade, my grandfather had become the stable father figure that I had always craved and now I was more concerned about a course grade than his grieving widow, my nana, and other family members. My grandfather had requested to be buried in Milford, a small town in Cork, Ireland and as my nana didn't want to fly, I drove her there. I carried the coffin at the funeral and didn't even shed a single tear. At the wake, I recall some bartender giving me a drink on behalf of some 'suspicious' men hiding away in the secluded corner of the pub. I was informed that they knew I was part of the British Army, so not to leave this bar and was advised to return to the UK the following day; and that is exactly what I did. I had clashed with similar 'suspicious' men in Sligo three years prior at my nana's 70th birthday party. This was weeks before I had deployed to South Armagh and, as a result, I had vowed to never return to Ireland again. I wasn't afraid of death, in fact, at times I sought it, but this was my grandfather's dying wish and I wasn't going to let him down.

Reflecting back on my grandfather's death, I am saddened by my lack of emotional reaction. I was far more concerned with my own selfish career needs, the British Army's needs and my focus, which was evidently on the next deployment to Iraq. My memories of the 2003 War had been firmly suppressed and ignored, but something deep down in my conscience was telling me that I deserved to die for my actions in the war and that I was going to die on this next operational tour. I accepted this as my fate and had shut down emotionally as a result. I came to loathe myself and shut out the outside world, which included friends and family. Drinking again became my coping mechanism and not once was this ever questioned. Maybe this was because I was not the only one feeling and acting like this at that time?

After the funeral, I would return to my Battalion and be given the position of Platoon Sergeant of my beloved 10 Platoon. This was a dream come true as the men of 10 Platoon had always been my family; however, none of my men from 23/C now remained. I recall that it wasn't long after I had returned to the Battalion when a recruitment team from the Defence Human Intelligence Unit or 'Op Samson' gave us a presentation and asked if anyone was interested in joining their organisation. I put my hand up and asked when the next selection course was and was pleasantly informed that there were some places available on the following Sunday. This was the Thursday and the recruiter then went on to inform us that it was normal protocol for students to prepare themselves from between 3-6 months to be physically and mentally prepared for the course. I had two mundane Barrack Guard duties the following week, so I blindly threw my name into the hat and volunteered, to the recruiter's bewilderment. Surely this arduous selection course would be more exciting than guarding our camp?

Three days later, I turned up at Chicksands, home of the Intelligence Corps, and after a quick orientation brief, it was time for a fitness test. At this stage, I had serious doubts about being there as all of the other students had been training for at least six months, whereas I had spent my two days of preparation in the bars in and around Aldershot. Regardless, 'this was better than being on guard duty so I might as well give this a go,' I thought to myself. To my amazement, myself and a Lance Corporal from the Irish Guards finished the fitness test in first and second place despite having no preparation time whatsoever, but he dropped out as the course intensified. I am still governed by the Official Secrets Act so am not permitted to discuss the selection process but what I will say was that I enjoyed it. Towards the end of the selection, I was given a very uncomfortable psychological assessment, and this was the only one that I ever had during my 20-year career. I failed this test and, as a result, was not selected but was advised to return for the next course as I had passed everything else.

During my debrief, I was informed that I would have done my utmost to achieve the mission and this was not how human intelligence worked, which still confuses me. I was a conditioned Infantry soldier and mission success was always the priority for me. Apparently, it was assessed that I would have sent all of my recruited assets to their deaths in order to achieve my mission. Seemingly, this was not accepted as the Ministry of Defence had a legal duty of care towards all recruited intelligence assets. I was later approached by a member of the Intelligence Corps to consider transferring across, but it soon became apparent that they were just after my range qualifications. They had taken casualties the previous year[xxxiv] and desired experienced Infantry soldiers to transfer across to help them train for the current operational climate. This intrigued me but was something that I would never consider and turned down as I was blindly loyal to my Regiment. Besides, I resolutely believed that I was facing my impending death in Iraq and that this was my destiny, my penance.

No sooner had I returned from this selection process than I was called in front of my Commanding Officer to discuss my PSBC course report. He was slightly disappointed with the grade as I had a reputation as a competent junior commander, but I had other strong reports that conflicted with it. The report stated that I didn't belong in the field and was more suited to the drill square. I recall that on hearing this, the Regimental Sergeant Major interrupted and highlighted the fact that this was quite personal, and that there must have been a clash of personalities. He wasn't wrong about the clash of personalities either, as the instructors from Brecon were of the generation that had instructed us as recruits and were generally bullies. They loathed our operational experience and, of course, our medals. On two occasions, I can recall instructors threatening me with violence for challenging their theories on low-level tactics, and of course, they had backed down when I had taken them up on their offer of settling our differences the old-fashioned way.

The Commanding Officer then referred to me as an enigma. He read out quotes from my outstanding reports from the Infantry Training Centre then looked at me with a smile and said, 'Now we have your course report from special forces selection to consider. This report recommends that you should return to Op Samson selection in six months' time, as you currently have no signs of empathy, and it also recommends that you would be an excellent candidate for the SAS.' He went on to tell me that he didn't know what to make of me and joked about the welfare of my men as 'I lacked empathy,' as we were due to be deployed to Belize in central America for some jungle warfare training.

It may seem odd that a Battalion that is training for a desert tour in Iraq would conduct training in the jungle. The logic behind this was that if you can operate in the unforgiving jungle climate, then you can operate anywhere in the world. Besides, the British Army at this time was constantly deployed and was limited to where they could conduct large scale exercises. What would make this exercise interesting was that Frank was now appointed as the temporary Platoon Sergeant of 11 Platoon and our friendly rivalry could continue. Once the exercise had ended, I flew straight to France to spend the Christmas leave period adventure training with the Battalion ski team. I was completely shut off from the civilian world and all relationships outside of the military. Only by keeping busy and focused on the Army's needs was I able to keep my inner demons at bay, so this is what I did.

In that new year, I was disappointed to hear that Frank had already handed in his notice to leave the Army and I was saddened to see him go. He had deployed to Iraq in 2005 with the Coldstream Guards and was part of the Basra riots alongside Soldier 'B'. He had a tough time adapting when he had returned home and had received no support for his deteriorating mental health. Frank had witnessed his Platoon Sergeant being killed[xxxv] by a roadside bomb and had almost been overrun by the mob in the horrendous Basra riots in that same year. He had failed PSBC, was in the middle of a divorce and wasn't receiving any help for his battlefield trauma and was told to 'man up'. Then, on one fateful afternoon in the Sergeants' Mess, Ireland would play England in an epic clash and his future fate would be decided by the score line. The majority of the Sergeants' Mess had donned their Ireland shirts and there must have only been three of us wearing England's colours and after a few drinks, I suggested that we raised the stakes. It was decided that when the opposite team scored any points, through a try, conversion, or penalty, that the other person had to do a shot of tequila.

The game would finish 43-13 in England's favour and one must not forget that at the Sergeants' Mess Bar, all singles are automatically upgraded to doubles. Furthermore, the sitting bartender was Butch, a good friend of both of ours and made sure that we both received good portions of tequila. Frank would get so drunk that he would throw up in the Sergeants' Mess but not before he had informed the Regimental Sergeant Major that he was going to withdraw his termination papers. Not only that but he outrageously claimed that we were both going to win Victoria Crosses in the impending deployment to Iraq. I was overjoyed that Frank would honour his drunken decision and he withdrew his termination papers. This would mean we could selfishly spend some more time together; besides, he was an exceptional soldier and my best friend; my brother.

Yet again, through the luxury of hindsight, it was obvious that my best friend was suffering with his mental health from his 2005 tour in Iraq and no help was made available for his deterioration, nor was it even acknowledged, for that matter. This was just the 'man up' culture at that time and one must not forget that the military was under insane operational commitments in 2007. The mental wellbeing of its soldiers was not a priority or even an afterthought. The senior commanders were the junior commanders of the mid 90s and, as such, the British Army had a detrimental philosophy towards mental health. i.e., it was ignored.

Our Op Telic 10 pre-deployment training would be the polar opposite to our previous tour and would be fundamentally different to what we had experienced prior to the 2003 War. All of our training was now prioritised around the concept of de-escalation and avoiding the fight. It was made evidently clear to us that we were no longer at war with a conventional army but with an insurgency in an asymmetric conflict. Since the end of the Second World War, British Forces had gained a vast amount of experience in counter-insurgency operations (COIN). As a result, the British Army have continuously built on their successes and failures from their COIN lessons learnt from Palestine, Malaya, and Kenya, and let us not forget about the 30 years of insurgency of Northern Ireland by the IRA. Ever since General Sir Gerald Templer applied his successful hearts and minds policy in Malaya in 1952, the principle of 'minimum force' has been identified as a crucial component in COIN strategic planning.[xxxvi] This policy would be effectively implemented for the British withdrawal of Basra but was not instilled or effectively enforced by the low-level commanders at the lesser tactical level during the summer of 2007.

In the weeks prior to the Battalion's deployment to Iraq on Op Telic 10, I had been handpicked to work with the Americans in Baghdad as part of a joint task force. The aim was to use our combined best practices to help get the insurgency under control in rural Baghdad. Our team consisted of a Captain, James, Shaun, who was a Colour Sergeant and Jim who, like myself, was a Sergeant. We were all Irish Guardsmen apart from James who was a Royal Marine Commando and together we were a professional and experienced team. Our job was to train and integrate an Iraqi Shia Infantry Battalion from the Basra area to operate in a Sunni-dominated area of rural Baghdad. We formed a part of a U.S.-led Military Transition Team (MiTT), and despite handing over the reins of 10 Platoon, I was optimistic about the forthcoming experience.

Our four-man team was one of the first of our Battalion to arrive at the Contingency Operating Base, or the COB for short. The COB was built around the Airport and within hours of returning to Basra, we were under enemy fire. These were generally Chinese 105mm rockets and were not very accurate. The camp was tented but within each tent, there were pens made out of breeze blocks into which, for our protection, we were required to jump into when hearing the mortar alarm. On this such occasion, the four of us did just that. I remember sharing a nervous laugh with the other lads as this was a lottery and the protection on these fabric tents was minimal, to say the least. I couldn't help but think back to my previous time in Iraq and wished that I was in my trench again as this would offer far better protection and safety!

These indirect fire (IDF)attacks would intensify throughout the Irish Guards' deployment on Op Telic 10. These constant IDF attacks would result in five deaths of British personnel at the COB, and would be responsible for a further 127 British casualties in that same year.[xxxvii]A Counter-Rocket Artillery and Mortar (C-RAM) Phalanx would be installed in the May as the indirect fire intensified, but unfortunately, some would inevitably always get through.[xxxviii] The increase in attacks was a political strategy from the local insurgents known as the Mahdi Army. It had previously been agreed at the political level for British troops to withdraw from their security duties in the city area of Basra and hand over the responsibility to Iraqi Forces. As such, the Mahdi Army would politicize this to support the narrative that they had forced the British out. This would solidify their claim to the city, and one must not forget that they had already infiltrated the Iraqi security forces as well.

After a few days, we were flown to Baghdad to liaise with our U.S. counterparts. On arrival at Camp Victory, we were all in awe of the sheer scale of everything, from the cookhouse to the number of troops and equipment that was on display. We would be joining the 10th Mountain Division, more specifically, 2nd Battalion of the 14 Infantry Regiment, the Golden Dragons. These were some battle-hardened and experienced soldiers with some already on their third 12-month deployment in four years. I was intrigued to learn that a member of the MiTT had previously been part of Operation Gothic Serpent in Somalia in 1993, (best known by the movie 'Black Hawk Down'), yet Smithy looked nothing like his chiselled Hollywood persona.

Our American cousins were a mixed bunch with the stand-out soldier being a British Platoon Sergeant equivalent named Sergeant 1st Class Scott Madden. Scott was extremely competent and more than capable of holding his own in the ranks of the British Army and we became good friends. Integration was effortless due to a shared mutual respect through our shared military history and of course, there was no language barrier to overcome. The perk of being attached to the U.S. was that we could pick our own personal call signs. *Big Guns* was our Apache air cover and our Company Commander was called *Terminator Tango,* so we chose to use the call sign *Spartans* after the popular Zack Snyder film 300! In Baghdad and whilst on the radio, I would be known as *Spartan 4*!

Our combined mission was to integrate and train our Iraqi Battalion of soldiers to competently operate independently in rural Baghdad which seemed near impossible at first. We would be given an abandoned Iraqi army patrol base called Lion's Den from which to train and deploy our Iraqi battalion. The U.S. had been forced out of Lion's Den the previous year as it was an outstation with only one sandy road in and out, just off Route Aeros, probably the most dangerous road in Baghdad. Route Irish got all of the media attention because this was the only route that reporters generally travelled on to and from their hotels and the Airport, and as such, it was greatly exaggerated, however, Aeros was the real dangerous road and we had to patrol this almost daily.

When interviewed by a U.S. Army reporter, James summed up our mission with the Iraqi Army perfectly:

'We're not trying to get them up to Western standards. We're trying to get them to Iraqi standards, so that the British and American Soldiers can go home, and they can have a functional Army of their own. We're not here to change their culture; we're just here to train them.'[xxxix]

It wasn't long before we would come under heavy fire at Lion's Den. James and I were in our makeshift gym at the time, working out, when there was a thunderous bang close by; we were under mortar fire! The rounds were close enough to be hit by ricocheting debris and to feel the heat from the impact of the blast; this was followed by immediate small arms fire. We were both in just tight shorts and flip flops but had our equipment close by and I quickly put on my body armour and helmet and grabbed my rifle and began to observe from our pre-determined defensive position whilst James was getting fully dressed. He looked up at me and said, 'You are actually enjoying this, aren't you?' I may or may not have been smiling but the rush that you get whilst in combat cannot be explained to those who have not witnessed it. The Iraqi soldiers that we were training repelled the attack sustaining only one casualty with a non-fatal gunshot wound, which was reassuring for everyone at Lion's Den, but more attacks would follow.

After a few months of training from patrol lessons derived from Northern Ireland, our Iraqi unit were patrolling confidently, and we were able to take a back seat. They would do things their own way, which was appropriate for their own culture, but to which we sometimes had to turn a blind eye; besides, it was their country and who were we to tell them to be less aggressive? They would still require coalition soldiers to support them with intelligence, air support or artillery, but for Iraqi standards, they were exceptional. Initially, the U.S. were reluctant to patrol on foot due to the IED threat, but we gradually persuaded them that the best way to dominate the ground was through deception and quiet stealth-like patrolling. Maybe they had been spoiled with their seamlessly unlimited resources and equipment, but you cannot win over the hearts and minds of the local population by destroying their crops with huge armoured vehicles on a daily basis.

Looking back, we were trying to change their patrolling outlook to fit the more reserved British mindset and, at times, this was a battle in itself due to the cultural differences. Many of the commanders foresaw foot patrols as needless risk and when considering the high fatality rates that summer, I can understand why. Furthermore, these guys were on a twelve-month patrol cycle with only a singular two-week slot of R'n'R in between. As such, the divorce rate among the U.S. soldiers was astronomical! This would probably explain the exceptional welfare packages that were available for the Americans to help alleviate the operational stress. In comparison with British standards, we had the equivalent of a company's worth of welfare support for just twelve of us.

They were also completely dry which was something that we could help with as beer was readily available from the British Embassy in Baghdad. I remember acquiring a crate of beer and stashing it in Lion's Den as a surprise for my American cousins. I had planned for all of us to share a few beers that evening but I still had two more patrols to complete that day. Finally, when I had finished, I was mortified that Smithy had drunk the whole crate by himself. These were only 330ml small cans, but Smithy had reverted to full-on 'red neck' and drank the lot! Smithy was a huge well-built soldier but was very softly spoken, a gentle giant and we would joke about his ability to guzzle beer in the coming months. There is a myth that American soldiers cannot hold their ale; Smithy is the exception to the rule and is in a league of his own.

I recall being the watchkeeper in our control room in Lion's Den when the MiTT team were on a particular patrol to inspect an Iraqi permanent checkpoint on Route Aeros when they came under indirect and small arms fire. The quick reaction force was already deployed, and *Terminator Tango* had advised me to call in the *Big Guns*, the Apache Gunships helicopters. Even in 2007, the technology that the U.S. Army possessed was out of this world. They had their own version of google maps called the *Blue Force Tracker* which was useful in identifying friendly positions on the battlefield in real time. I requested immediate support from the Apache Gunship helicopters, who by now were already hovering above the MiTT team. I called it in, 'Big Guns 66, this is Spartan 4, fire mission, over' only to be told by the Apache pilot, 'Don't give me any of that Brit bullshit voice procedure, just tell me where they are,' so, I reviewed the Blue Force Tracker and responded, 'Multiple insurgents in the wood line to the north, engage!'

Big Guns 66 emptied his entire payload of ammunition then returned to base and it was rumoured that the Apache Gunship pilots would be teased if they had any of their payload left on return to base, but it was job done, the insurgents had been eliminated and the MiTT patrol saved. When they returned to Lion's Den, they were euphoric and were all giddy about their firefight and of course, I was ridiculed for missing out. I let them have their moment as the jokes came in thick and fast about how I was apparently cowering under the desk when I had called in the airstrike. This somehow even made it into the Regimental Journal that year and I was teased even more but this was good old military banter! The main thing is that none of our team was injured, yet, I couldn't help but think about that American airstrike from 2003. That night, I remember being very withdrawn as I was conflicted about what had occurred. I wasn't on the ground and my mind raced, contemplating whether or not I had made the right decision! I wondered whether or not there had been any civilian casualties as a consequence of my actions and still do. Regardless of how I felt, we still had a job to do, so I would have to 'man up', as the mission was the only thing that mattered.

After a few months, it became very evident that we were the poor cousins in every aspect. The U.S. war budget appeared to be endless and it was clear that they were here for the long term. An example of this was their enormous US Embassy which was under ongoing construction at the time. This had a vast substructure which was rumoured to have twenty sub levels. The airspace was dominated by attack helicopters, all of their personal protection equipment was regularly updated to counter the IED threat, the food was fantastic, the dining facilities were of restaurant quality, and the sheer number of troops was overwhelming, however, this came at a cost. There was a noticeable disparity between the more competent professional soldiers and their Army Reserve counterparts, yet each respected the other as they understood that they were symbiont.

In my last week in Baghdad, we were all on edge as the U.S. were losing personnel at a rate of three soldiers a day. Things were tense, to say the least. In between training the Iraqis, we would also be required to conduct a combination of foot and vehicle patrols for our own base protection. Whilst on vehicle patrols, I always opted to be the Browning .50 calibre gunner on one of our three Humvees convoys. Our rules of engagement were different from the Americans as they were permitted to use lethal force more frequently, whereas we had more restricted guidelines, derived from Templer's model of prioritising winning over the hearts and minds of the population. This, at times, made it problematic as the U.S. were very trigger-happy and it is understandable as Baghdad was a completely different insurgency when compared to Basra. However, we were still accountable by British law, so we had to remain diligent and accountable for our battlefield decisions.

On one such patrol, we had stopped to conduct a snap vehicle check when a loaded minivan rapidly screeched around the corner towards us. All of the Americans screamed at me to engage with the .50 calibre machine gun and I would have been well within my rules of engagement to do so. The Browning .50 calibre is designed to shoot through engine blocks and is a tremendously destructive heavy machine gun that is utterly overpowering. This vehicle had all the signs of a vehicle bomb and was heading towards us at some speed. I instantly conducted a tactical analysis of the situation and prepared my heavy machine gun. It didn't stop when asked, the driver was erratic, and, from the struggling suspension, it was clearly overloaded (possibly with explosives).

I removed the safety and fired half a magazine into the engine of the minivan, then continued to observe as it crashed into a ditch at the side of the road; there was a sudden onset of silence! My American cousins then aggressively surrounded the minivan with their weapons raised and to their horror, this was not a vehicle bomb, just a minivan full of kids on their way to school. Fortunately, I had opted to use my own low-calibre assault rifle to shoot the engine of this incoming vehicle. If I had opted for the .50 calibre, it would have shredded the car and killed all those inside, including the children. We were all relieved, more so my American cousins. I had made a lifesaving decision and I deeply believe that this was a result of witnessing those civilian vehicles being engaged on the outskirts of Basra throughout the 2003 War. I fundamentally accept that over the years, my battlefield experiences had changed my trained perception of warfare and although at the time I didn't think too much about this incident, in hindsight, I am proud that I didn't destroy that minivan with the Browning .50 calibre as I would also have these deaths on my conscience.

When reflecting on my time with the U.S. MiTT team, it was thoroughly enjoyable and a fantastic experience to work with some extremely talented and knowledgeable soldiers from the 10th Mountain Division. What I found odd though, was how American Officers could transfer to Infantry units from logistical roles without undertaking any specialist training whatsoever. I don't think that this would necessarily work within the British Army as many of the senior non-commissioned officers like myself were far too outspoken. Besides, at Platoon level, both the Platoon Sergeant and Platoon Commander had to pass a similar arduous tactical course which formed the foundation of mutual respect. This enabled the British Platoon Sergeant to heavily influence tactical decisions whereas this was absent within the U.S. rank system with the American junior officers having complete operational freedom.

Although we shared the same language and, arguably, the same history, there was a noticeably huge cultural divide which affected how we operated tactically. The Americans had become so reliant on technology and urban operations that some of their basic rural soldiering had been neglected as a trade-off and this is where we could help balance the MiTT. We both knew our strengths and weaknesses and by being open about them, this made us a stronger team. Collectively, our American cousins were far more relaxed despite continuing to suffer immense casualties throughout that summer. Maybe this was down to how they had identified the importance of maintaining the morale of the troops throughout a twelve-month deployment. The investment in the welfare of the operational soldiers was a world away from what I would ever experience as a British soldier. This was probably due to our limited six-month deployment cycle which came with its own additional pressures as senior commanders always attempted to make a significant impact in such a limited time frame. Furthermore, on British deployments, we were always pushed to our physical and mental limits with no consideration given to the welfare of the men which often led to operational burnout. We were always undermanned and ill-equipped and pushed to our limits, which was the polar opposite to our American cousins, but at least we occasionally had alcohol to help alleviate the operational pressures.

In terms of welfare, the U.S. (even in 2007) were years ahead of the British Army and understood how maintaining the morale of the troops increased battlefield efficiency. The American Government has since been recording the harmful psychological effects of warfare and currently openly advertise this on their own recruiting web pages. In 2021, in the U.S., 17 veterans commit suicide daily. In fact, the suicide rate for veterans who have deployed is 1.5 times higher than civilians.[xl] Although this is staggering in terms of numbers, the U.S. government has acknowledged that there is a correlation between veterans and suicide, which is a welcomed start. This is an ocean apart from the Ministry of Defence as we have to rely on a veteran support group for these numbers and the British Government still refuses to document the suicide rates of our own veterans. This raises many questions about the cause of the high rate of suicides amongst the Armed Forces, especially the argument for liability concerning the psychological damage from the British Army's harsh behavioural training methods or the battlefield trauma from our operational experiences, or maybe both?

Chapter 11.
The Political Betrayal

O n my return to Basra, I was full of beans and was looking forward to meeting up with all of my pals. However, on arrival at the COB, it soon became apparent that there was a distinct lack of morale within the Battalion and I naively found this quite bewildering. I was optimistic about returning to 10 Platoon and would be surprised to be informed by the Adjutant that I would be commanding the Reconnaissance and Snipers as their new Platoon Sergeant. I wasn't qualified for this position but was told that I was more than capable of doing a good job, but I had serious doubts as they didn't even have a Platoon commander. Thankfully, the interim Platoon Sergeant was an exceptional soldier called Johnny. He was also the lead sniper within the Battalion and was referred to as the 'Master Sniper.'

Johnny was all about soldiering and I had the utmost respect for him and would depend heavily on making the most of his knowledge and experience in the coming months when planning and conducting our missions. I would take over the role of the Platoon Commander and Johnny would continue to be the Platoon Sergeant. We had a good understanding of each other's strengths and weaknesses and made a good team. Looking back, I was initially too harsh on the men of the recce/snipers because I didn't show them any respect. I thought of them like junior soldiers that one would find in a rifle company and these were far from that. The best out of the bunch was a chap named Sam, a solid all-rounder who was more competent than most of the junior non-commissioned officers at that time. I would have to adapt my command style to get the most out of these soldiers and mistakes were made along the way.

I decided that all of our patrol planning would be incorporated around the long-range assets of the snipers and the remaining recce soldiers would be re-employed as heavy support gun groups; this worked quite well for us. Most of our patrols began once nightfall was upon us, then we would be dropped off by helicopter, but the choppers would perform 6-7 dummy drops so that the insurgents would not know exactly where we were. Deception was key as we were always being watched. Next, we would lay firm for fifteen minutes before continuing on foot to our desired target area before generally liaising with Warriors to be returned to our base the following day. Some patrols would be longer, and this depended on what operational intelligence was available at the time. However, we didn't need any intelligence reports to know that we never could trust the Iraqi Police Force, and, on one patrol, this was more than evident.

Our helicopter was on its second or third dummy drop when I had noticed that an Iraqi Police car had put on its emergency lights in our previous dummy drop-off location. We were the next drop, so I asked the pilot to delay as we observed from above. Yet again, this police car followed the helicopter and yet again, set off its emergency lights. It was immediately obvious that these police officers were signalling the insurgents in the city about our patrol location as we were only a few miles from the outskirts, vulnerable in the middle of the open desert. I gave the signal to the pilot to land in a new location and we all went firm in all-round defence. I called Sam to my position and told him to put a belt of 200 rounds on his machine gun and if the police car approached or if it put on its emergency lights, that he was to treat it as hostile and engage with all of those rounds. Additionally, if we were to come under mortar fire, he was to engage the police car. Fortunately, the car never pursued us, and an international incident was avoided.

I was not the only commander in Basra that summer who had identified how critically important snipers were for success in urban operations. As such, the snipers were often in high demand and would be loaned out to the 'hotspots' such as Basra Palace. The palace had taken the brunt of the fighting that summer and was home to the men of 1 Company amongst others, which was hit with a staggering 135 projectiles in just one nightmare 36-hour period.[xli] Basra Palace would significantly benefit from having these snipers assigned especially as they were armed with a powerful new .338 rifle. However, due to the increase in lethality and damage by this new sniper rifle, new tactics evolved. One such practice was to fire through the structures of identified insurgent fire positions, such as the sides of windows or doors. The increase in bullet size allowed this new rifle to easily blast straight through walls and still continue to do lethal damage. This was successfully implemented on many occasions and was witnessed by a defence reporter who was at Basra Palace:

'Irish Guards sniper Cpl X, 23, also covered himself in glory by defeating a 100-strong enemy attack with a SINGLE shot. He saw a gunman scurrying behind a breeze block wall as British forces defended Basra's police HQ from attack. Armed with a powerful new .338 rifle, Sniper X decided to try firing a shot THROUGH the wall. It worked. The gunman was killed and all those around him were so terrified they took flight.'[xlii]

This was just one such incident and because of the high tempo and constant attacks, there was very little downtime. Whilst in the COB, I would spend my limited free evenings chatting with Niall in the welfare tent. The Recce/Sniper Platoon generally operated through the night, so this was a rarity. During the day, Niall would work as an equipment repair storeman and during the evenings, he was in charge of the welfare tent and shop. The service that Niall provided was pivotal as it provided the only available respite that some of the soldiers would receive throughout Op Telic 10. I had observed that as the tour progressed, the morale had decreased amongst the personnel who were somewhat logistical prisoners within the COB. This only further identified the importance of Niall's job in helping to maintain the morale of the troops.

Looking back, this low mood was a combination of both the derivative attitude towards their underappreciated but vital Infantry support roles from the soldiers who went out on patrols, accompanied by the constant bombardment of the indirect fire. In many ways, being under constant enemy fire for over six months would take its toll on the mental wellbeing of the best of us. In the years that followed, Niall would never refer to himself as a 'proper soldier' due to some of this belittling and I have always found this to be very untrue. Niall had patrolled South Armagh in the late 1990s, had been part of the Liberation of Kosovo in 1999 as well as the ground war in Iraq in 2003. Maybe now, he was taking a second-tier logistical role but none of us can be combat soldiers 100% of the time. Besides, he had a vital role that was appreciated by so many.

It may surprise people to know that even in 'war zones,' soldiers are still required to participate in mandatory educational courses. There was an education centre located at the COB, housed in mortar-hardened accommodation and I would have to complete a Senior Leadership and Management Course there. This was a ten-day course of group exercises, presentations, and written essays. I was chosen to write an essay on the British Army's recruitment policy which would result in a later posting to an Army Careers Office in Manchester. Even back then, I had identified that the British Army was failing to consider the soldiers' social and domestic needs which was quite the paradox as I was still unknowingly prioritising the Army's needs above my own. General Sir Richard Dannatt had even commented that the Army was at breaking point and that the tempo of life in the field army was intense and not sustainable.

Whilst on my education course, I was temporarily assigned to Headquarter Company which the Regimental Sergeant Major appeared to be quite disappointed with. I had a great relationship with Pearse, and we respected each other, and he was a good role model. He was fair, approachable, professional, but more importantly, he had a sense of humour. Whilst in Basra, he would terrorise the troops with his battery-operated hair clippers and if he deemed that your sideburns were too long, he would take it upon himself to trim them for you. This would more often than not leave many a victim with a 'Robocop' haircut. (It's probably worth a google).

He had always taken pride in his fitness and had organised a Headquarter Company fitness test for the following week, anticipating that he would easily finish first. Well, that was until I was encouraged to participate. I was ten years younger than Pearse, and he knew that I was faster over the 1.5miles so schemed a plan to thwart me. I always took pride in finishing ahead of Physical Training Instructors (PTIs), but I was unaware of the current abilities of this new one, Paddy. He was attached to us and asked if I wanted to race him so I naturally accepted, thinking that this would be another scalp for my collection.

All physical exercise had to be conducted at first light due to the immense heat and our race would commence on the airfield at dawn. As we warmed up, Pearse was sledging me and trying to get in my head. He was threatening me with endless duties if I beat him and telling me how fit he had become whilst in the COB. Then Paddy, without warning, set off like a sprinter and initially, I struggled to keep up. Every time I got close to him; he increased the pace. I had represented the Battalion in athletics, mainly middle-distance track events and was quick but this was a different level. I dug deep and overtook Paddy the PTI but found myself struggling to keep up the pace. We were only half a mile in, and my legs were feeling heavy and I was exhausted. Paddy then began to speak to me, and what was disheartening was that he wasn't even out of breath! We approached the mile marker at just over four minutes, and I had nothing left. Then the penny finally dropped. This was Pearse's plan all along!

Paddy then informed me that he was an elite runner, the Army marathon champion, in fact. He went on to tell me that Pearse had asked him to run me into the ground and I had arrogantly taken the bait. Still, on the plus side, I only had half a mile left to stagger and Pearse was nowhere in sight. I then heard the Regimental Sergeant Major shout my name; he was catching me up and fast. My stagger became a jog, then my jog became a run and to Pearse's disappointment, I somehow managed to cross the finish line barely before him. Pearse was disappointed that after all of his training, he would not hold the accolade of being the fastest man in his Company; well, technically, neither did I - that rightly went to Paddy.

Pearse took his defeat well and we laughed about how his plan had almost worked. Then his clippers came out and this was my signal to leave. I did not want to be Robocopped!

It was whilst on this education course that I bumped into Tommy. Tommy was now working within the logistical department of the Irish Guards after suffering a nasty leg break in 2004. He had struggled to return to full fitness and unfortunately never again regained the robust fitness that was required to lead men on the battlefield. He had been at the forefront of the battle of Basra four years earlier and had played a key role in Kosovo's liberation in 1999; now, he was struggling to accept his new identity as a second-tier support soldier. I wasn't aware of this at the time but after his leg break, Tommy had suffered with his own mental health as he gradually lost his identity as a warfighting Infantry Soldier.

Tommy had achieved Sergeants' Mess status in under five years and had gained a reputation as a competent fighting soldier and, as a result of his early success, had struggled to accept the limitations of his injury and now a lesser secondary status. This wasn't helped by the two-tier politics within the Battalion as those who had a more logistical role were belittled and referred to as 'in-camp commandos' or ICCs. This would later escalate in Afghanistan to the logistical support being referred to as 'leaf eaters' and the soldiers on patrol being called 'meat eaters.' Maybe this was a throwback to the primitive hunters and gatherers where the alphas went out hunting. This toxic alpha-male atmosphere was unproductive, yet I never prevented my Platoon from using this derogatory term at the time as it was classed as 'banter.'

When interviewed, Tommy informed me that after his leg break, all of the emphasis was focused on his physical recovery and after years of failing to return to full fitness, he would later become withdrawn. Tommy would miss meals and avoid all social interaction outside his work commitments and at the weekends, he wouldn't even get out of his bed in the Sergeants' Mess; maybe Tommy was depressed. When asked if he had sought any help for his low mood, he replied, 'No, as it was frowned on at that time'. A doctor would later question whether or not he had even broken his leg to begin with, as it was not recorded in his medical notes! Years later, a military physiotherapist would inform the Commanding Officer that Tommy was faking a back injury despite an MRI scan stating the contrary. It's no wonder that Tommy didn't reach out to his military doctor for help as he had no trust or faith in them.

When I asked him how he overcame his depression, he explained that once he had come to terms with the fact that nobody was going to help him, he had to be accountable and help himself. He accepted that he would never be that once-proud combat soldier who welcomed a glorious death on the battlefield and began to take personal responsibility for his new role. I also believe that the courtship of his now-wife also helped him escape this low mood.

Tommy despised his new role as a storeman as he had joined the infantry to fight! He would reluctantly watch the other soldiers leave the COB on aggressive operational patrols and felt inadequate as he was no longer able to join them. I would also feel the same way in Afghanistan when I also had a logistical support role. Personally, I felt like a coward as I was on an operational tour and I wasn't fighting! Then, when the casualties or fatalities would occur, I would be overwhelmed with guilt and self-loathing. This secondary trauma was never addressed, and I experienced many conversations between these tier-two logistical soldiers as they were told to 'man up!'

On his discharge in 2020, Tommy would transition well into the civilian world and would eventually find a decent job as a site manager through a military charity named Combat Recce. On his final medical before discharge, he had informed the doctor that he was always angry and asked for support for the future. The doctors, who had consistently failed Tommy, continued to do so, and responded by forwarding him a list of military charities. What is very saddening is that Tommy's two young boys now refer to him as 'angry dad.' I don't know whether his anger is a direct consequence of how he was trained or as a result of his operational experiences, but I am discovering that he is not alone with his post-service anger issues. This highlights, yet again, the better need for Governmental aftercare for our veterans, especially on discharge.

Once I had successfully completed my education course, I returned to my operational duties. I remember looking for the men of my platoon only to find them all in the ablutions, naked and rubbing foam over each other which was not something out of the ordinary for recce soldiers to do. They had somehow gotten their hands on some high-powered American bodily hair removal foam; however, this foam had a maximum application time of two minutes and they were having a 'foam off' to see who could last the longest with this now burning and painful beauty product. I must point out that his foam was primarily applied onto their genitals and bottoms and resembled a man nappy. So, I did what any respectable commander would do in this situation...I joined in and became hair-free, silky, and smooth! During that evening's pre-patrol brief, I recall that many of the men were sat on ice-cold cans of pop, regretting their poor life choices and throbbing genitalia! I could have screamed and shouted at my men, but I knew the importance of maintaining their morale and this was a little bit of necessary fun that was required and that we all still laugh about to this day.

In that September, I can remember returning from a patrol and being completely overcome with rage when informed about the death of two of our own, (again, from the Drums and Pipes Platoon). Lance Sergeant Chris Casey and Lance Corporal Kirk Redpath were killed by a roadside bomb that had ripped through their Armoured Snatch Land Rover.[xliii] In hindsight, when considering the increase in IEDs that year, these poorly armoured vehicles should not have been used as they were not fit for purpose and offered limited protection to their occupants.

In fact, they were relics from Op Banner and were designed for the streets of Northern Ireland and not the explosive power of the shaped charge IEDs that were commonly used in Iraq. In 2005, there was just 82 recorded IEDs in the Basra area; this would increase to 169 in 2006 and, in our time on Op Telic 10, an IED was recorded almost daily with 296 recorded in 2007.[xliv] Whilst I was in Baghdad, our U.S. Humvee vehicles had been up-armoured twice to counter the IED threat. Soldier 'G' would comment that the British Army was always under-sourced and poorly equipped and judging by the continued use of these poorly armoured vehicles, I completely agree with him. Furthermore, we were reactive rather than proactive to the perceived threat. In the 2003 War, we didn't even have desert clothing, sufficient weapons, or enough body armour, for that matter. Bearing this in mind, I cannot help but feel that these deaths should have been prevented and, as a result, these vehicles were retired shortly afterwards.

The Mahdi Army and other insurgent groups would get very creative with their IEDs. In Baghdad, suicide bombers and vehicle-borne improvised explosive devices (VBIED) were commonly used, but in Basra, they were more sophisticated and tended to stray away from suicide martyrdom and favoured victim-operated devices. Due to advances in technology, the traditional preferred method of triggering IEDs, such as command wires and mobile phones, would be refuted by British Electric Countermeasures (ECM) equipment. After all, the British had experience from their 30 years of counter-terrorism operations in Northern Ireland and had tactical protocols already in place to protect its soldiers. This would push the envelope farther and the insurgents would get even more creative by incorporating complex passive infra-red devices to detonate sophisticated explosive formed projectile shaped charges. The basic pressure pad would be rarely used in Iraq but would be utilised with deadly efficiency in the years to come in Afghanistan. In the months from March to August 2007, IEDs would be responsible for the 368 coalition deaths in Iraq, with 90 deaths in the May of that year alone.[xlv]

Soldier 'G' and the members of 4 Platoon were the quick reaction force and were the first on the scene after the IED had occurred. They had arrived in the heavily armoured Mastiff trucks that were purpose-built for the modern IED threat and these were almost indestructible. Soldier 'G' recalls that once they had dismounted, the casualties and bodies of our fallen brothers were being flown back to the COB by helicopter. It was their job to secure the site and relieve the men of the Drums and Pipes Platoon. At this stage, the patrol was barely functioning due to the loss of their command element including their Platoon Commander, with many of the Drums and Pipes going into shock. The men of 4 Platoon then secured the perimeter which would then allow the Drums and Pipes to safely return to the COB. They would later find the firing mechanism, and this was a basic command wire that was less than 200 metres away.

I recall angrily barging in to see the Commanding Officer in the aftermath of this event and in no uncertain terms told him, 'that we were fighting a defensive war and needed some offensive action to raise the morale of the troops.' We were all hurting and at this time and I wasn't really concerned about the larger political picture and the agreed handover from British Troops in Basra to a militia, the Mahdi Army. All I wanted was revenge and had suggested that my Recce/Sniper Platoon be allowed to aggressively hunt the insurgent IED teams who had killed my brothers. This was a turning point mentally for me as I had previously thought that I was returning to Iraq to die. However, I was now solely focused on hunting down those accountable for the death of my fellow Irish Guardsmen. I wanted vengeance!

Regrettably, my proposal was not welcomed, and I was referred to as a hooligan. Then, I was reminded that my request went totally against our mission and I did the rounds to be shouted at by everyone in a more senior position than myself. In reflection, I did have the audacity to attempt to advise the Commanding Officer on how to do his job, therefore, these rollockings were rightfully deserved. I had never stopped to think about how everyone else was feeling. I was fortunate to have been in Baghdad for almost four months, whereas the majority of the soldiers in the COB had been at the mercy of daily bombardments of rockets, artillery, and mortar fire. This had gradually taken its toll on everyone stationed there; everyone was on edge and the morale was non-existent.

In the week that followed, my Platoon was tasked with providing protection for a logistical resupply patrol to Kuwait. This was referred to as an 'Op Sheffield,' and not only would we be accompanied by some of the Drums and Pipes who were in the IED attack a week prior, but we would also be travelling along the same route. Furthermore, we would be travelling in the same Snatch Land Rovers and as we approached the location where the fatal IED attack had occurred, the scorch marks of the IED attack visibly remained. I can still recollect a fellow Sergeants' Mess member talking us through the incident in a complete ghost-like daze as we approached. One thing stood out though, and that was the courage and bravery of the men from the Drums and Pipes Platoon. I can only imagine how difficult this patrol would have been for them and in hindsight, they were grieving the loss of their brothers and should have never been put on this patrol to begin with; they were numb, empty vessels. No counselling or respite was ever conducted, and they would have to 'man up' and continue to soldier on.

Trauma Risk Management (TRiM), would be trialled by the Royal Marines in 2006/7. This scheme would allow low-level commanders to be trained to notice and manage the signs of battlefield trauma. This would include identifying and managing potentially traumatised soldiers after a battlefield incident had occurred; they would then be offered immediate support and treatment. The Ministry of Defence would describe this practice as being 'a tool to assist commanders in discharging their responsibilities for managing stress in traumatic circumstances.'[xlvi] This statement from JSP 770, which outlines the protocols for the operational welfare of Tri-Service personnel, comes across as callous. In my experience, TRiM was just a paper exercise that was never implemented or followed up correctly, or as Soldier 'G' blatantly put it, 'TRiM was an umbrella'.

In an article by the JR Army Med, it is stated that from an organisational perspective, there is also evidence that it may benefit organisation efficacy.[xlvii] In the same article, it is also concluded that 'the main aim of the TRiM project is not to prevent PTSD, which is probably impossible given the role of the Armed Forces.'[xlviii] After reading both JSP, articles and interviewing soldiers who have been through the TRiM process, it is evident that the Army's needs were always prioritised over the soldiers' mental wellbeing throughout the mid-2000s when our Armed Forces were overstretched. This is further supported by the leaked memo from General Lord Richard Dannatt when he warned that the Army had virtually all its units either mobilised or preparing for operations in Iraq and Afghanistan. Thus, by papering over the cracks and managing the effects of short-term trauma to its soldiers, the Army could still fulfil its needs and be combat effective.

Since I left the Armed Forces in 2015, I have been informed that the TRiM process and the management of these traumatised soldiers has drastically improved. I am pleased to hear this, and this is no doubt a reflection of the low operational tempo that the British Army are currently committed to, as this allows for a thorough TRiM process to be implemented. However, in the future, I genuinely hope that the lessons from my generation are taken into consideration, as a significant proportion of my brethren seem to struggle with their own mental health.

Some of the most intense ground fighting since the actual Iraq War would occur on the resupply runs to the British outposts in the city of Basra. These supply logistical runs to the Provincial Joint

Operations of Command (PJOC), Old State Building (OSB) and Basra Palace were easy pickings for the Mahdi Army according to Soldier 'G', as British troops found themselves under constant small arms and RPG fire. Then, if they were unfortunate to be held up and were static, the predictable IDF would commence and this would inevitably occur at the Palace Vehicle Park or in the tight confines at the PJOC. It was not uncommon for them to conduct a 'wagon train' ring of steel for protection; this really was the wild west!

Soldier' G' recalled an intense firefight on the handover of the Palace where the men of 4 Platoon were engaging insurgents at close quarters for sixteen hours as British Forces withdrew from the city. The fighting was so intense and ammunition exhaustive that the Platoon Sergeant would go on to lose the hearing in one of his ears as a result of continuously firing mortar bombs throughout this particular engagement. Soldier 'G' would be decorated for his actions and despite his section being resupplied three times with ammunition whilst in contact, his men were never relieved despite Platoons like my own being in reserve. He modestly believes that more decorations should have been awarded but reluctantly stated that the 'top brass' had concluded that they were just doing their jobs. On return to the COB, he wouldn't be praised for his courageous actions but inexplicably scrutinised for his ammunition expenditure.

Soldier 'G' had one priority, and that was ensuring the survival of the men under his command. Now, on returning to the safety of the COB, he found himself under scrutiny because his men required a full ammunition resupply, and this meant additional paperwork for the senior logistical managers. Soldier 'G' had to restrain himself; he had done his job to an exceptional standard in trying and demanding circumstances and, by some miracle, had survived. He was exhausted, frustrated, and angry, but was a soldier and told himself to respect the chain of command. On return to the COB, Soldier 'G' had just three rounds left in his magazine. From this day forward, Soldier 'G' despised all of those in logistical support roles and I believe that the operational stress from his 'ammunition trial,' from his perspective, was more traumatic than the actual sixteen-hour firefight.

Soldier 'G' was a skilled junior commander and in the 2003 War, he had gained vast combat experience and was highly respected by his peers. He has what he describes as 'a spartan mentality; you protect the man on your right.' No support towards 4 Platoon's mental health or wellbeing was given; in fact, scrutinising Soldier 'G's brave battlefield actions only further exacerbated the operational stress that all of the soldiers in the COB were under. It is evident that the senior logistical managers had failed Soldier 'G' and the men of 4 Platoon. One must not forget that these were some of the same junior commanders of the late 1990s and had a completely different mindset to our generation. We were no longer in Northern Ireland but for them, it was all they had known, and they treated it as such. This was a mistake and had a detrimental effect on the morale of all of the troops at the COB. Maybe they were envious of Soldier 'G's' actions, or maybe they were simply poor senior commanders, only they will ever know why they treated the men of 4 Platoon with such contempt.

Not long after the handover of Basra to the Mahdi Army, the Recce/Sniper Platoon was deployed to Shaibah Airfield to assist Number 4 Company with training the Iraqi security forces. Shaibah was a breath of fresh air compared to the COB and the morale-sucking senior logistical managers who reigned there. Shaibah was rarely attacked, and it was nice to see my old pals, such as Frank. For the rest of the tour, the majority of my Platoon would be stationed at Shaibah with the exception of the Snipers who would still be in high demand. Much to his disappointment, Frank would not actually win a Victoria Cross, but he did receive a commendation for his work in training the Iraqi Army and Police Force. We would quietly see out the final weeks of Op Telic 10 Training the Iraqi Security Forces in a stress-free environment despite coming under IDF on several occasions.

Once the tour was finally over, we would be flown to Cyprus for two days of decompression. This is essentially a couple of days of beach sports and, let us not forget, drinking. For the Recce/Sniper Platoon, we would make good use of our bed sheets and have a toga party. I remember that one of my lads was constantly picking fights with members from another Platoon and when I questioned him to seek out the root of his anger, he turned on me. After he was restrained, he burst into tears and informed us all that his fiancée had left him two months prior and that he had nothing to return home to. Yet again, no counselling or psychological assessments were ever even offered to us and we were left alone to simply get drunk and resolve our issues amongst ourselves. This policy was implemented to allow us to vent our frustrations on each other rather than on our wives, girlfriends, children, and society in general when we returned home. Did this work? I don't know, but it was a vast improvement from our previous tour in Iraq.

I fundamentally believe that the soldiers stationed in the COB also experienced a traumatic and difficult tour and their stories are often downplayed and overlooked. They may have not been engaging the insurgents like some of us, and at times, this can be perceived as much worse. For over six months, they would be on the receiving end of constant rockets, projectiles, and mortar fire in a tented camp, whereas the fighting elements were able to escape the IDF prison of the COB. At least whilst on patrol, you were the master of your own fate rather than waiting for a projectile to hit you at work, or even worse, in your sleep. The poor leadership from the senior logistical commanders combined with a lack of understanding about the high demands of modern warfare, particularly COIN operations, established the foundations for a two-tier split within the Battalion. This destroyed the morale of the men and would be harmful to the combat efficiency of the Regiment. It would plant the seeds for a distasteful relationship and lack of trust between the logistical and fighting units of the Irish Guards in the years to come.

In the 2003 War, the British Army had deployed 45,000 of its service personnel to Iraq, and now, four years later, only 5000 remained, the majority being in combat support roles. No foresight was given towards the British providing a long-term stabilization force and it was a huge mistake by coalition forces to disband the Iraqi Army after the 2003 War.[xlix] As a result of this very significant oversight, British and American forces would be bound to stay on as a stabilization force and this was something that the British Parliament had not foreseen. The insurgent groups were well aware of the dwindling support for the prolonged occupation of British troops in Iraq and capitalised on the lack of WMDs for their own propaganda. Their rhetoric was that they had successfully forced the British out of Basra and, from a certain point of view, this is correct.

I was deeply saddened once Basra was handed over to the Mahdi Army. I thought back to the scenes of jubilation when we had entered the city in 2003 and the sacrifices that we had all made. Then,

I recalled the pride that I had felt when returning to the same streets and witnessing how vibrant they were, and now, after our withdrawal, the city would gradually become a haven for militia and criminal activity. Rival militia, insurgent factions and criminal gangs would compete for control of Basra's lucrative infrastructure and resources.[1] This was mostly through oil and shipping and it would appear that my two tours of Iraq were a complete waste of time as we had defeated one dictator only to hand over the control of Basra to criminal elements, all because the British people lacked the resolve to see the mission through. We had been defeated by the political will of the British people and this, at the time, felt like a betrayal.

However, I had faced my own inner demons; moreover, I had survived my anticipated and accepted death and now lacked direction, I lacked purpose...

Children in rural Baghdad.

Above. Shaun patrolling and making friends.

Patrolling Lion's Den perimeter. I am bottom right.

Members of the Recce/Sniper Platoon, Basra, 2007.

Decompression, Cyprus 2007, Recce/Snipers' toga party.

Chapter 12.
The Queen's Personal Bodyguard

After some not very eventful leave, I was assigned to the Training Wing of the Irish Guards after a Battalion reshuffle. I was also waiting to be given my posting orders for my next job and my interview would be conducted in an unorthodox location. I recall being in the Sergeants' Mess one particular 'Happy Hour' when the Regimental Sergeant Major had unconventionally invited the Commanding Officer in for drinks. This was out of the ordinary and his presence in the Mess bar was killing the atmosphere. The Commanding Officer made a beeline towards myself and Frank, then, without any prompt, stated that he couldn't make his mind up whether he liked or disliked me because when he asked me a question, I gave him a direct and honest answer. By this stage in the afternoon, I was already a few beers in so replied with, 'I have the answer to your conundrum, Sir...Don't ask me any more questions then.' The Sergeants' Mess erupted with laughter and the tension then eased.

I didn't know this at the time, but I was being interviewed for my next job role. He went on to question me about why I had joined the Irish Guards and what the connection was to Manchester. I informed the Commanding Officer about my Irish lineage, then I explained about how the Manchester Ship Canal was built in the late 1900s with Irish labour and as a result, it had connected the Irish Sea directly to the Manchester docks, bypassing Liverpool in the process, thus, negating the historic Dublin – Liverpool connection and bringing Irish workers and settlers directly to Manchester. Furthermore, I reminded him that two of our Victoria Cross recipients were also from the Manchester area. In fact, our latest Military Cross recipient from Iraq was also a Mancunian! This conversation would go down in Sergeants' Mess folklore with some even citing (Patto) that I had handouts and even delivered a full PowerPoint presentation! The following week, I would be informed that I would be posted to my hometown of Manchester as a Recruiting Sergeant. This was a direct result of the essay that I had written on recruiting and retention whilst in Iraq, but everyone seamlessly forgets this fact.

I was happy with this two-year post as I had genuinely believed that I was destined to die on Op Telic 10. I was 28 years old and had completed five operational tours in my first ten years as a soldier and was psychologically burnt out. The high tempo of Army life was beginning to take its toll, both physically and mentally. Up until this point in my military career, I had never given a second thought to what comes after the rank of Platoon Sergeant. Now, it was clear that as my days of leading men on the battlefield were numbered, I would foreseeably become a second-tier logistical soldier which was the inevitable consequence of promotion. For the first time in my career, I began to think about life after the Army and what comes next? It was this realization and self-awareness of a future civilian life that would help me to gradually break free from my indoctrination and co-dependency on Army life and this was a deciding factor in accepting the recruiting position.

On my recruiting course, much of the emphasis was centred around political correctness and equality and diversity training which I found quite surprising. Sure, I had witnessed the ongoing sectarian racism within my Battalion but racism regarding skin colour was never an issue. Within the Infantry, you were merely judged on your character and soldiering ability; it was that simple. However, this racism awareness training was specifically targeted towards the British Muslim community. I can recollect that we were all informed by an external civilian speaker that we were all racists and that we had to adapt our outlook to recruit more ethnic minorities. As one can imagine, this opening statement didn't sit well with the military students as it had been delivered from an external civilian speaker and was possibly a reflection of society at that time. Furthermore, we couldn't understand why the recruiting emphasis was directed towards the Muslim community. Looking back, maybe this was Human Intelligence-led as they required more applicants from an Asian background to be able to effectively assimilate into the current Middle Eastern operational environment.

I was personally taken back by this as I had always taken pride in my small contribution to the liberation of the mainly Muslim Kosovar and Iraqi people, and in doing so, helping them to gain their independence. Then again, the British Army was always reactive, therefore I cannot help but wonder what incidents had occurred previously for such diversity training to be implemented in the first place. I do recall one such racist incident when I had thrown an association member out of the Irish Guards Sergeants' Mess. This was not the thing to do, as these members were guests and were treated like royalty, but after I had overheard him referring to the Iraqis as 'rag heads' and some other more derogatory words, he had to go. He was a former soldier from the 1970s where racism was rife and institutionally accepted. Looking back, he was no longer in the

British Army but reflected wider society, so maybe this training was actually needed despite not being welcomed.

From a 2003 research article, 42% of the ethnic minorities interviewed stated that racism and lack of equal opportunities had prevented them from joining the British Armed Forces. Furthermore, the Labour Government wanted all public services to reflect the wider society. In the Armed Forces, only 1.7% of personnel originated from an ethnic minority background despite making up 7% of the national population at the time of the study. Thus, this drive was solely political as the fire service at the time was less diverse with only 1.6% of its firefighters being from ethnic groups.[li] Identity politics are not necessarily a bad thing but I felt that this inclusion of ethnic minorities felt somewhat forced and lacked sincerity.

As the course progressed, we conducted role-playing exercises that all of the students, including myself, found odd. We were taught sales techniques used by car salesmen and how to subconsciously manipulate customers into buying needless products. I fundamentally disagreed with these training methods as we were not selling encyclopaedias, we were selling a hazardous lifestyle that could potentially be fatal. There are very few occupations where, on entry, you write a blank cheque for your life and I fundamentally believed that we had to be completely honest and transparent with the young men and women that were interested in joining the British Army. Yet, throughout this course, I kept my opinions to myself as these were requirements that had to be completed to pass the course; however, once in post, I could be honest and open using what I had seen from my own experiences.

I took over my post in the March and was very much learning the ropes, but by the end of June, there had already been twenty British soldiers killed in Afghanistan.[lii] I had been consciously noticing the increase in British fatalities in Afghanistan whilst on Op Telic 10 and it was strategically obvious that as combat operations in Iraq were drawing down, our commitment in Afghanistan would increase. Part of me felt guilty for not being over there as I was in a safe sedentary job but the other part of me felt a sense of relief. The news seemed to continually show clips of the Union Jack-draped coffins of my fallen brothers being repatriated at the small town of Wootton Bassett. I dealt with this as I had been previously accustomed to and it was not uncommon to finish the day's work at five o'clock and directly hit the town. After all, this was the city centre lifestyle of the single man and all of the other recruiters participated. Drinking your problems away was just how we dealt with our suppressed emotions and was still an accepted cultural practice.

Ironically, in the immediate aftermath of the death of British service personnel, we would be inundated with applicants wishing to sign up. I would personally provide these applicants with just information then turn them away, but not before asking them to complete some further research. These patriotic young people may have been joining for the wrong reasons and were a recruiter's dream, but I wanted to make sure that they knew exactly what they were getting into. I would always explain the risks, especially for those who desired a career in the Infantry, but like myself many years before, some kids just want to fight due to the unhealthy romantic nature that attracts certain people to military life. In my experience, these were from the more deprived areas of society and like myself, when I was in their position, they craved structure and stability.

Traditionally, those sent to recruiting offices were either injured or were seeing out their final few years of service. If a soldier was non-deployable due to medical reasons, then they may have found themselves stuck in a career's office indefinitely with minimal opportunity for promotion. As a result of this, I immediately stood out as I had recent combat experience, I had been a recruit instructor and could advise potential trainees on what to expect in training and I was young enough to build up a rapport with the potential recruits. I would keep myself fit and was able to play rugby at the weekends. It really was like having a civilian job - a civilian job with annual fitness tests.

I would always run the 1.5-mile fitness assessment with potential recruits and in those two years, I would never be beaten. Despite being almost thirty, I could still complete it in under eight and a half minutes. I recall being at Fulwood Barracks in Preston for our annual fitness test which was being supervised by a very young physical training instructor (PTI). He was quite abusive about us recruiters as some of them were slightly out of shape and didn't actually physically look like what one might expect of a soldier. I asked about the route and was rudely informed that all we were required to do was to follow him. This was a basic three-lap circuit and before long, I decided to increase the pace. I remembered what Paddy had done to me the previous year in Iraq and before long, this PTI couldn't keep up. He would later explain that I had an advantage as he was wearing trousers whereas I was wearing shorts. As excuses go, this one was the worst that I had ever heard as this PTI had dropped out of the race to avoid any further embarrassment. I was a hero amongst these out-of-shape recruiters and somehow everyone managed to pass the fitness test that day. Maybe this was because we had all finished before our PTI, who was timing us, as someone had run him into the ground!

I quickly became accustomed to the perks of the civilian world and was able to detach myself from the toxic alpha-male-orientated environment of 'Battalion life.' There was no rank in the office and for once, I was known simply as Paul, which I found quite refreshing. I enjoyed being able to plan my weekends and I could actually book future social events such as holidays. I enjoyed reconnecting with my school friends as, for the past decade, I had rarely been home. However, our social interests differed as many of them were secretly heavy recreational drug users and this had never interested me. This was part of the reason that I would mainly socialise with the other military personnel in the careers office as I was still disconnected from the civilian world.

Before Op Telic 10, I had become emotionally detached and consumed by survivors' guilt, which made me believe that I was unworthy to be loved or cared for by another person, especially a girlfriend or future wife. However, having survived my yearned-for death on my second tour of Iraq, towards the end of my time as a recruiter, I would buy my own home and move into it with my future wife, Jayne. We had been friends since school, and she made her move on me after a party that I had hosted, and I initially rejected her advances. I had become emotionally disconnected and genuinely believed that I wasn't worth loving and as such, I would avoid being in a relationship, or just blatantly sabotage them and would consistently purposely push people away. For some strange reason, Jayne stayed around despite my best efforts and this helped me to regain some of my lost humanity. It would be the love from Jayne that would gradually, over time, help me break the shackles of my military indoctrination and this would allow me to eventually prioritise my family over the mission. These days, my family is exclusively my mission!

At times, many soldiers can develop a narcissistic personality that feeds within the constructs of the military environment. I for one had always prioritised the needs of the British Army, the mission above all else. If this meant sacrificing a relationship, then so be it. I had returned to Iraq to die and now I was lost, and I felt that I lacked military purpose. Being in the recruiting world didn't help me either, as I was surrounded by second-tier logistical soldiers who lacked motivation and ambition, whereas I was very much the career soldier. Or at least, I told myself this as I was caught in the pension trap.

The daily working atmosphere in the career's office was different to what I had previously experienced as most of the other Sergeants were 'washed up' and wouldn't be eligible for further promotion. This established a pleasant work environment that was the polar opposite to what I had experienced in the Battalion, whereas, in the Irish Guards, it was very much a relentless pissing contest, dominated by over-inflated egos. This was very negative and was encouraged, which created a dog-eat-dog culture in the race for promotion, in which I seldomly participated. I naively thought that promotions were earned through hard work and it was only in my final years in the Army that I finally understood that promotions were awarded by successfully playing the political game.

Regardless of the workplace politics, I had easily established myself as a prolific recruiter, not only for the Irish Guards but also for the wider Army. What was alarming though was the minimal qualifications that were required to join the Infantry. Minors with no academic qualifications could join the Infantry at age 15 and 9 months with consent from their legal guardian. These boy soldiers in the infantry would amount to a third of all junior applications and just like myself at that age, they would fully buy into the British Army's values and standards, becoming easily indoctrinated in the process.

What even now still makes me chuckle to myself is that I would reel some of these potential recruits in with the 'Queen's personal bodyguard' line, which was still amazingly very effective in coercing young men into a life in 'The Guards.' I was always open and honest about the dangers of life in the Army and often spoke about my own battlefield exploits which, astonishingly, only further encouraged some applicants to pursue a career in the Infantry. Some young men and women will always be attracted by the ill-perceived romantic association to warfare regardless of the associated and very real risks.

However, there are times when I feel a tremendous amount of guilt for the soldiers that I recruited who were either injured or possibly killed on operational deployments, such as Nathan. Some young people would have joined the Armed Forces regardless of what was advised to them by their parents or a recruiter and Nathan was one such applicant. Nathan wanted to be just like me and, in a way, regarded me as a role model. He successfully passed recruit and Infantry training and even reached the dizzy heights of the Sergeants' Mess in the Irish Guards but was unfortunately medically discharged after 11 years' service. He is currently wheelchair-bound after sustaining a spinal injury in Afghanistan.

The increased dangers to the Infantry soldiers are highlighted in article 34 in the House of Commons' Defence Committee Future Army 2020 Ninth Report of Session 2013–14, in which it acknowledges the increased risk of fatality for the Infantry. It states the following:

"*Soldiers who enlist as minors are disproportionately likely to join the Army's front-line roles because these have the lowest age and qualification entry requirements. Consequently, they face the greatest risk of death or serious injury once they turn 18 and can be deployed. For example, the Infantry contains one third of all the Army's minors even though it comprises only one quarter of the Army overall; Infantry fatality and casualty rates in Afghanistan are five times those faced by soldiers in the rest of the Army.*"[liii]

Article 35 of the same review highlights the risk to those young infantry applicants from disadvantaged backgrounds with fewer qualifications than their adult equivalent as being in a greater risk category and that joining the Infantry is not in their best interest. Bearing in mind that a vast majority of career soldiers in my generation were boy soldiers from disadvantaged backgrounds and that we were five times more likely to be injured in Afghanistan, this begs the question as to accountability for the aftercare of these vulnerable soldiers. The upsetting truth is that on medical discharge, they often fall on hard times and are reliant on military charities for financial, physical, and psychological support.

The recruitment process has now completely changed as a result of austerity and manning reductions. It is now completely online with only one physical interaction with a serving soldier before attending a recruit development and selection centre.[liv] Yes, this is more cost-effective, but it has completely removed the nurturing element from the serving Army Recruiter. We were the ones who could identify the suitability of applicants, including any red flags, which was often the case. Effectively, we were responsible for screening the mental suitability of the applicants and advising them accordingly, which more often than not disappointed them. For example, a well-built tall chap of 6' 4" would not be suitable in one of the Cavalry Regiments as he wouldn't be comfortable within the tight confines of a tank and may be best suited in the Royal Artillery or Infantry Regiments. It was this personal rapport, nurturing, and knowledge that allowed us to successfully advise applicants as well as weeding out those who were not psychologically fit to join the ranks of the British Army.

It was whilst I was at the careers office that I was having concerns about my actions in Iraq in 2003, specifically, that airstrike on the village in the initial days of the war. Being alone without the high-tempo distractions and pace of normal military duties, I was finally allowed to reflect on my own memories from Iraq. Maybe this was brought on by the very public persecution of British soldiers by the Iraq Historic Allegations Team (IHAT). This would cost the British taxpayer £59.7 million, yet no British soldier would ever be convicted. However, it did ruin the lives of all of the soldiers involved as well as their families.

One such soldier who was illegally pursued was Guardsman Joseph McCleary from my own Regiment. He was one of four soldiers from the Household Division who were wrongfully hunted by the IHAT. McCleary was snatched from his Platoon lines in 2004 and intimidated by the Special Investigation Branch of the Royal Military Police. This was another attempted shakedown by using the shock of capture/arrest to coerce a confession out of McCleary, a betrayal by the very institution that he had given his life to. McCleary's story has many similarities to Piotrowski's regarding the lack of backing from the Ministry of Defence in supporting our soldiers; apart from the fact that McCleary was innocent and that there was no substantial evidence, whereas Piotrowski was guilty. The IHAT case was merely founded on allegations, yet, in the case of McCleary, he would undergo a traumatising eight-week trial.[lv]

McCleary had to wait two years for his trial and was segregated from this Battalion during that time. He was immediately deemed guilty by the senior commanders of the British Army even before the trial had begun and was offered no support; he was cast out. Whilst isolated and under the threat of a 15-year prison sentence, McCleary began to drink heavily and went to a dark place, and even tried to kill himself only to be fortunately saved by his brother. Then, after a second attempt to hang himself, he was sectioned under the Mental Health Act. It would appear that he was immediately deemed guilty by the Ministry of Defence as along with the IHAT, both these organisations represented the British Government and they could not support our soldiers due to the ongoing bad press surrounding the 'illegal war.'

McCleary states in a Leg-it podcast interview in January 2021, that whilst in the Army, he was not allowed to show emotional pain but whilst separated from his military brothers and under enormous stress and anxiety, his emotions overwhelmed him. McCleary found therapy difficult as he no longer wanted to live as a result of his own demons and his overwhelming anxiety. The Ministry of Defence was informed of his current situation, but he was abandoned, and no aftercare or assessments for his deteriorating mental health was ever provided by the Army. He had been cut off, abandoned, left to rot with his inner demons eating away at him.

McCleary was once a proud soldier with a bright career ahead of him. He had deployed on two operational tours and had been to War; he was willing to make the ultimate sacrifice for his country and now found himself isolated without any support. He was treated like he was guilty, and he couldn't understand why he was not getting any support from the institution that had sent him to war. He then spiralled out of control to drink and drug misuse and the suicide attempts continued, and at his lowest, he was borderline to almost becoming an addict due to this betrayal and being cast aside.

When the trial began and the Iraqi witnesses were questioned, they stated that they were promised compensation and that their only motivation was money. Phil Shiner, the solicitor responsible for pursuing British Soldiers, was struck off the Solicitors' Register in 2017 after being found guilty of telling blatant lies for his own financial gains and had 12 charges of misconduct proven against him.[lvi] In a time when the British Army was ill-equipped and soldiers were dying in Iraq and Afghanistan because of a lack of sufficient protective personal equipment, this highlights how little consideration was given to the safety of individual soldiers as almost £60 million was provided by the Government to pursue false claims against individuals. This money could have been better spent in providing better armoured vehicles for our deployed troops or even a substantially improved welfare support package at a time when we were over-stretched.

McCleary is just one example of a good man who lost everything as a result of the IHAT's illegal pursuit of British soldiers. Once found innocent, he was given the option to remain in the Army and he refused. Why would he soldier on after being thrown to the wolves, been deemed guilty from the start, abandoned, and offered no support? IHAT was set up by the Government but not one soldier was ever prosecuted. McCleary would continue to be investigated yet would continue to be found innocent every single time. He would be primarily informed by the press about future investigations and this traumatised him even further. The Government didn't even have the courtesy to inform him before the press which is appalling treatment of a patriot as he was continuously thrown under the bus. This raises so many questions but for me the one regarding loyalty springs to mind. We were taught to be loyal to the needs of the British Army yet as soon as there is an inkling of bad publicity, the loyalty is replaced by abandonment. McCleary still suffers from anxiety and low confidence and is still traumatised by the whole ordeal. Thankfully he has found stability, he has overcome his inner demons and has a loving family, but I cannot help but feel sorrow for him. I never knew McCleary when we served together, but his story is one of inspiration as he continues to overcome this horrendous treatment.

In January 2016, David Cameron announced a change to legal aid that would prevent *no win no fee* cases which included the banning of foreigners for the eligibility of seeking British tax-funded legal aid.[lvii][lviii] To this day, new legislation continues to be written to safeguard our soldiers but this political rhetoric is only as good as the Government of the day allows. I, for one, was often worried that the IHAT would come for me although, like McCleary, I knew that I didn't commit any war crimes, yet, the inner voice inside me was always saying that I needed to be punished. Maybe this was my own inner demons within my subconscious eating away at me from my battlefield experiences. Maybe being at the career's office in a non-military work environment had allowed some of my suppressed emotions to surface? Regardless, these emotions would have to be kept suppressed as my focus was now on my next deployment to Afghanistan.

For two years, I had enjoyed living like a civilian. I had my own house and commuted to my 9-5 job; I wore the uniform of a soldier, yet I was not a soldier; I was referred to by my Christian name rather than my military rank or nickname, and the soldier in me had become dormant and weak! Then towards the end of my time within the recruitment world, I would be brought back down to reality when Davey Walker was killed by enemy fire in the Nad' Ali district in Helmand Province in mid-February 2010.[lix] I had known Davey from my time at Catterick instructing recruits, as we had been part of the same Company as Lance Sergeants together and this was a stark realisation of what the job of an Infantry soldier really entailed. This rattled me as on return to my Battalion in the coming months, I was aware that The Irish Guards would be deploying to Afghanistan later that year; more specifically, to the Nad' Ali district in Helmand Province which, at that time, was the most dangerous combat zone on the planet. Over the summer of 2010, I was glued to the news as the fighting only intensified with British Forces being engaged in a casualty-intensive guerrilla war with the Taliban. I wasn't afraid of deploying to Afghanistan, but I was certainly apprehensive as a result of my two years in a civilian job.

My time in the career's office had provided me with a necessary break from the non-stop and relentless pace of 'Battalion life.' I was able to recharge my batteries, but, on the downside, I had finally allowed myself to pass through the looking glass and to experience a normal job. My love for the Army was now in the decline but my commitment remained steadfast. I was shaken by IHAT's persistent pursuit of British soldiers but all that I had known since I was a boy was the military way, and no matter how much I denied it, I was institutionalised, I was loyal. What is reassuring though, is that the

British Army has now changed its recruiting strategy regarding minors, as, under article 38 of the 2013 Future Army review, it has finally recognised the following:

Current recruitment policy does not respect "the best interests of the child" and puts minors at significantly increased risk of serious long-term physical and psychological harm compared to adult recruits.[lx]

Does this mean that boy soldiers such as those from my generation who endured so many operational deployments were at an increased danger to psychological risks? Maybe this is a combination of both the brutal instruction practices in recruit training and the inhumane lessons that we were reluctantly taught on the battlefields of Iraq and Afghanistan? The positive outcome of this is that the British Army has now reduced the percentage of minors that it annually recruits into the military and that will mean fewer of the 'Queen's Personal bodyguards!'

Chapter 13.
'The Dirty Dozen'

I n mid-2010, I would return to my Battalion and be thrown into the world of logistical support as the new Company Quartermaster Sergeant (CQMS) of Number 12 Company for our next deployment to Afghanistan. This Company was not a traditional Infantry fighting Company as it mainly consisted of a highly experienced team of both senior non-commissioned officers and officers. Our mission was to train and mentor the Afghan National Army (ANA), as Kandak advisory teams on Op Herrick 13. I would have a dual role in mentoring an ANA Battalion as well as providing logistical support for the men of 12 Company who were scattered out in six locations in Nad' Ali South in Helmand Province. During our pre-deployment training, the focus was on adapting to U.S. protocols and, at the time, I had no inclination of the political reasons behind this and, quite frankly, none of us really cared.

At international level, the Anglo-American 'special relationship' had been damaged when the British had withdrawn from Basra in 2007. The aftermath of this was that the U.S. were reluctantly required to commit further troops to the Iraqi southern city. Then, to regain American favour, the British would be coerced into increasing their troop numbers in Helmand Province, not under the autonomy of British command, but rather in line with U.S. foreign policy and under the guidelines set out within Operation Enduring Freedom. This would favour a more kinetic approach to the counter-insurgency and lacked the subtlety of British strategic thinking, especially the concept of hearts and minds.

However, this does not suggest that British forces did not have a COIN strategy in place as the 2006 Helmand Plan consisted of a policy of clear, hold and build, by initially securing the key towns of Lashkar Gah and Gereshk.[lxi] This was not successfully implemented due to the lack of troop numbers that were required to hold and dominate the ground as this strategy was manpower-intensive. This Helmand Plan would evolve into the Helmand Road Map in 2007 when Brigadier Andrew Mackay highlighted that the 'people were the prize, not ground or attrition'.[lxii] Minimum force was always a priority for British military commanders especially when fighting a guerrilla force such as the Taliban, as winning over the population was a key factor for strategic success.

It is evident that under British leadership, the principles of hearts and minds and winning over the population were at the very core of all military thinking, but this would change due to international pressure from Washington. British senior commanders would come under criticism from the U.S. because British forces were defending towns and cities from Taliban attacks and this did not comply with the narrative of Operation Enduring Freedom.[lxiii] British forces were becoming fixed in defensive positions in temporary 'platoon houses' whilst defending the towns in the north of Helmand Province. This favoured the insurgents and left the towns and the poppy fields in Nad' Ali in Taliban hands and this is where the Irish Guards would be deployed on Op Herrick 13.

The Taliban soon realised that they could not win a symmetrical war with the British in Helmand and had recognised that the key principles of COIN operations were vital for their own success. They understood that by forcing the British to rely on their core competencies, the high-intensity fighting in Helmand would destroy the Afghan towns and villages along with their inhabitants, thus, gaining political support and favour for the Taliban. Therefore, through a combination of a severe lack of military resources and U.S. political intervention, British forces were not able to successfully implement their planned hearts and minds campaign and resorted to a more kinetic approach that was primarily focused on defeating the Taliban militarily.

Winning over the hearts and minds of the population was crucial for success in Helmand and despite being part of our pre-deployment training, once we deployed, these lessons would be quickly forgotten. When we arrived in late September 2010, there had been 59 amputations and a staggering 92 deaths of British personnel already that year.[lxiv] Bearing these casualty rates in mind, we were all aware that British Forces could not successfully adhere to a policy of minimum force as Helmand Province had become the most dangerous combat zone in the world.

I would be stationed primarily at Camp Tombstone, which was part of the ANA camp, along with the rest of the Irish Guards Logistical Department. Camp Bastion was the main British Army base in Helmand and by 2010, it was the size of Reading. Then, there was Camp Leatherneck where the Americans were based which had its own bus network and even an allocation of highway police who would continuously pull me over for speeding. All three of these camps were secure and we very rarely came under indirect fire, or attack, for that matter. I would be given a quick orientation tour and my two main locations of interest were the hospital and the helipad.

I understood the importance of relationship-building and quickly made friends with the loaders on the helipad. I had previously been qualified to rig underslung loads for helicopters prior to my 2003 deployment to South Armagh and was aware that all six of my locations in Nad' Ali South would have to be re-supplied by air. I had noticed that the movers at the helipad were still in the old-style combats and their boots looked weathered and this gave me a way in. I introduced myself as just Paul, as there was no need for formalities with my soon-to-be new best friends. I came bearing gifts and provided them with shiny new uniforms, boots, and expensive Gerber multi-tools as I knew that throughout our deployment, I may need a favour from them, and it didn't take long for me to call it in.

I recall receiving news that some of the men in 12 Company had been in contact with the enemy and had luckily avoided taking any casualties. However, a vehicle had been damaged and they were combat ineffective until they could receive replacement parts. The main vehicles that we were using in 2010 were the Jackal lightly armoured vehicles. These offered excellent mobility but limited protection from small arms fire and IEDs and one of them required two new wheels to be flown to Shawqat, a Forward Operating Base (FOB) in Nad' Ali South. This was also home to the 1st Battalion Royal Irish Regiment with whom we had a friendly rivalry as we were the only two Irish Infantry Regiments left in the British Army. Getting hold of the wheels and replacement items was the easy part but once on the helipad, the loaders informed me that there was a two-week backlog on the flight manifest and that I would have to book my replacement vehicle parts through official channels. I took a quick look at the manifest and noticed that there was a sortie to Shawqat that very afternoon. A plan was forming!

There was already an underslung load of supplies for the Royal Irish waiting for collection on the helipad so I asked if I could add my wheels and replacement parts, only to be informed that this was not possible as there was a weight limit to consider. There was only one solution then; I would have to unload the Royal Irish supplies and load up the Irish Guards' vehicle parts and that is exactly what I did. This did come at a price as for the next six months, I had to avoid the senior logistical manager (the Quartermaster) from the Royal Irish as he was out for blood after not receiving his own supplies. This was made increasingly difficult on my frequent visits to his own FOB of Shawqat as I was on his most-wanted list but luckily, the cat never caught the mouse.

About a month into the tour, I was required to recalibrate all of the Company's electronic countermeasure equipment, and this had to be completed in person by a one for one exchange due to the sensitive nature of the equipment. I would load as many sets as possible into my large backpack and then fly by helicopter to the various patrol bases where my men were located before returning to Camp Tombstone with the outdated equipment. On one such flight, the helicopter loadmaster was struggling to move my excessively heavy backpack and asked for assistance. We were travelling in a large Chinook helicopter at the time, so I unstrapped my seatbelt and made my way over to him. As I picked up the heavy backpack, we must have come under enemy fire as the helicopter initiated some evasive manoeuvres and set off its chaff and flares. I lost my balance and attempted to steady myself but the weight of the equipment in the backpack caused my torso to sharply jilt in a pendulum motion but was restricted by my body armour plates just above the waist. I felt a pop in my lower back, dropped the heavy backpack and sat back down. I was in excruciating pain; I was hurt.

When we finally arrived at the patrol base, I was having cold pain sweats and had to ask two private soldiers to pull me to my feet and then to help me with my backpack. The average infantry soldier on Op Herrick regularly carried weights well in excess of 100 lbs and this was largely from the front and back body armour plates and ammunition which I was still carrying despite my debilitated state. I wasn't able to put on my backpack by myself and still needed additional help from these two private soldiers. I then made my way to the Irish Guards location and collapsed in a heap of pain. I knew that I had seriously injured myself, but I was stuck in a patrol base in the dangerous war zone for the next few days so I would have to 'man up.'

On return to Tombstone, I immediately sought out our Battalion doctor and was referred for physiotherapy at the hospital in Bastion. I would always make the effort to visit any Irish Guardsmen if they had been unfortunate enough to have been injured and I was a frequent visitor to the hospital. I would witness the medical staff often breaking down in tears as they were responsible for the medical care of not just the coalition soldiers in Helmand and the ANA, but also the Taliban fighters as well as the civilians who were frequently caught in the crossfire. The Taliban cared little for the safety of non-combatants and, if I'm being honest, by failing to adhere to a policy of hearts and minds, neither did we. You cannot successfully win over the political support of the local people when you are continually calling in Artillery, Apache Gunships and dropping 2000 lb bombs! The tempo of the fierce fighting would result in the emergency room being frequently inundated with complex casualties which was a battle within itself for the medical professionals at Bastion to deal with, and, at times, this took its toll on the medical staff.

My physiotherapist granted me four days of light duties and gave me some exercises to build up my core strength. When reviewing my own medical notes from Afghanistan, it is clear from my symptoms that I was suffering from a core instability that was originating from a herniated or bulging disc in my back. However, one must acknowledge that these medical personnel are soldiers first and have a chain of command to follow. As soldiers, there is always an underlying mission and theirs was to keep as many boots on the ground as possible and this was required to make Op Herrick a success. Let us not forget that the Army's needs are prioritised above the soldiers and my long-term physical welfare was a gamble that the Army was willing to take to fulfil its short-term goals. Personally, I was frequently witnessing soldiers being medically evacuated with gunshot wounds and with the loss of limbs from IED blasts and it didn't seem fair that I was complaining about a bad back. Besides, pain was weakness so I would rely on my training and just have to get on with it.

For the remainder of the tour, I would avoid where necessary lifting heavy items but could not avoid carrying the excessive weight of my body armour, radio, ammunition, medical kit, and water. I would be pulled to one side and informed by a senior commander that I was setting a bad example to the junior soldiers due to my 'bad back.' The same senior commander would also accuse John of faking a 'bad back' to avoid aggressive patrolling when he was in fact experiencing the onset of the early stages of cancer. All the command element cared about was amputees and if your injury was not visible, in their eyes it was non-existent, and you were classed as a malingerer and a coward. John and I were two respected battle-hardened soldiers and I am still saddened at how we were treated by a senior commander within our own Regiment throughout Op Herrick 13.

For the first time in my career, I was experiencing the unjust stigma attached with being a second-tier logistical support soldier and would attempt to shake this off by getting out on the ground as much as possible. Despite being in severe pain the whole time, I would volunteer to replace any members of 12 Company at every available opportunity, whether through an injury to a soldier, or simply covering whilst someone was on R'n'R. Every time there was a casualty, whether a gunshot wound, blast injury or amputation, I would feel guilty for being in the confines of a safe location. I didn't join the Infantry to provide logistical support, but my current job role was a prerequisite that all Infantry soldiers were required to accomplish for further promotion and I felt that I was unfortunate to have to fulfil this whilst on an operational deployment. In fact, throughout my whole deployment in Afghanistan, I only ever came in contact with the Taliban on one such occasion.

I was covering one of the other commanders whilst he was on R'n'R and I was the vehicle commander of a Jackal, which meant that I was the operator of the GPMG. We were part of an ANA convoy and whilst we were patrolling on a narrow dirt track that was parallel to a canal, we came under small arms fire. We were silhouetted and from the chatter on the ICOM scanner (a radio that scans the Taliban communications), the Taliban were specifically targeting our three-vehicle convoy rather than the ANA vehicles. In an ambush situation, we had taught the ANA to keep driving through and get out of the killing zone but for some reason, they just stopped. We were now trapped in between ANA vehicles to the front and rear on a single-vehicle track, silhouetted, with rounds ricocheting off the limited composite armour of our Jackals.

I instinctively screamed, 'Contact right,' but this wasn't necessary as everyone knew where we were being shot at from and were already engaging the firing point. I then swung my GMPG to the right to engage, only to find that I was unable to use my favoured machine gun due to the safety limitations of the way in which the gun was vehicle-mounted. I rapidly unclipped my seat harness whilst simultaneously grabbing my personal weapon and began to engage the firing point. We were trapped in the killing zone of an ambush with nowhere to go; this was surely the end as it was a pre-determined ambush and the Taliban had the advantage. To my bemusement, the ANA soldiers had debussed from their vehicles and were casually chatting away to themselves whilst the Taliban bullets rained in around them. What seemed like a lifetime was only minutes but eventually, the front vehicles mounted up and slowly began to continue on the patrol and we drove out of the killing zone to safety; it was a miracle that we didn't receive any casualties.

On return to the patrol base, I joked with the drivers of the Jackals that I would be billing them for the damage to my vehicles as 'bullet holes were not cheap to repair' and they didn't know if I was serious or not! By now, all of the British soldiers had been in several contacts with the Taliban and this was just a normal day for them, so maybe, like I had felt on my previous tours, they had become numb. What was surprising though, was how little regard the Afghan soldiers had towards their own safety. Their culture and religious values were completely different when comparing them to the Iraqi Army, let alone a western one. Shortly after this event and from my experience of mentoring my own Afghan logistical department, it became clear to me that our presence here was futile. We were forcing our western culture, western democracy and western values onto a people that didn't want or ask for it. We were only in Afghanistan because of 9/11 and the hunt for Bin Laden, but after almost a decade of fierce fighting and the enormous loss of human life, our mission had become diluted.

The British Army were now fully behind Operation Enduring Freedom which was part of the U.S. foreign policy and its War on Terror. Therefore, and not for the first time, British soldiers would help implement the U.S. global rhetoric. Then, we must look at the strategic locations of U.S. forces in the Middle East. American forces still continue to dominate the Middle East in 2020, with almost 70,000 soldiers stationed in Afghanistan, Iraq, Jordan, Bahrain, Saudi Arabia, Qatar, U.A.E., and Kuwait.[lxv] This raises many political questions as to why the British were still in Afghanistan in 2010 as Al-Qaeda had already been defeated and Bin Laden would be killed in the following May. Were we now just an extension of U.S. foreign policy as, geographically, we had surrounded the dangerous Islamic country of Iran? I cannot help but think that due to the vast riches that are obtained through liquid gold in the region and the unpredictability of Iran, that the War on Terror was a smokescreen for U.S. dominance for control of the region and to also put military pressure on the Iranian Government.

Looking back at my initial months in Afghanistan, I never really committed myself to the mission. I don't know whether this was because of my age and experience from previous tours or the fact that I was not primarily deployed in a combat role and leading men.

In Iraq, I had to convince myself that we were just, as if I had doubts then my men may have had doubts, and this may have led to indecision, hesitation and possibly the injury or death of one of us. As a battlefield commander, you have to inspire confidence in your men, and this is a prerequisite for leadership. In Afghanistan, however, I was no longer a commander but a logistical manager, and this afforded me the luxury of a more holistic outlook. I would observe the vast amounts of heavy ammunition being used against the Taliban with no consideration given towards its destructive power and the unavoidable damage to the local population. This went against the principles of my previous five operational tours where the proportionality of our weapon systems was always predetermined by the law of armed conflict.[lxvi] The high numbers of coalition casualties, and deaths, for that matter, would also have a harmful effect on the combat soldiers on the ground. As a result of this, they would disregard the more traditional and reserved British approach to counter-insurgency operations. This would result in British Forces being drawn into fighting an unwinnable symmetrical war against a well-organised and efficient guerrilla force as this supported the principles of Operation Enduring Freedom.

Soldier 'G' would be deployed on Op Herrick 13 as a Fire Support Group (FSG) commander. His primary job was to provide heavy supporting firepower in overwatch to the Infantry who were generally conducting foot patrols. At his disposal in his 4 Jackal vehicle convoy, he would have snipers, GPMGs, Browning .50 calibre heavy machine guns, 40mm Grenade Machine Guns (GMG) and Javelin anti-tank missiles. In one single engagement, when providing fire support for a Company of Infantry soldiers in contact with the Taliban, Soldier 'G' gave the orders to fire multiple Javelin missiles and almost depleted all of his GMG ammunition. Soldier 'G' stated that this was necessary as the Infantry he was overwatching had sustained several casualties in a fierce ten-minute firefight and that he was responsible for providing sufficient covering firepower for their tactical withdrawal. This was achieved by winning the firefight which meant using all of the overpowered and destructive weapons at his disposal. He emphasised that once he had asserted dominance and control of the battlespace, the Company of Infantry were able to tactically withdraw and the casualties were able to evacuate by helicopter back to Bastion.

On return to their patrol base, Soldier 'G' would be thanked by all of the junior commanders as they had been pinned down by Taliban fire in a designated killing zone. It was only because Soldier 'G's' sole concern was the safety of his comrades that he utilised the superior weapons systems of his FSG and they were able to break free with no fatalities. However, the senior commanders were not so content and would criticise Soldier 'G' for being far too aggressive. Soldier 'G' was doing his job effectively with the tools and training that had been authorised for use in this operational theatre. Helmand was no longer under British stewardship and we were becoming more in line with the U.S. approach to counter-insurgency operations which was directed towards defeating the Taliban militarily through dominating the ground.

Quite often, and from my own experience, once the bullets and bombs start flying, the political element of the operation is no longer significant and my only purpose at that immediate moment was the wellbeing and protection of my brothers. I, like Soldier 'G', was at times criticised for being overly aggressive but it is through aggression that battles are won and, in this instance, the Company of Infantry were able to withdraw without sustaining any further casualties. I acknowledge that at the tactical level, where the warfighting generally happens, the strategic mission is often lost, but one must understand that the junior commander is only focused on his tactical mission and may not necessarily understand or have any strategic insight into the long-term political goals.

Was Soldier 'G' in the wrong for using such devastating firepower? Absolutely not! He had used authorised weapons in the correct way and was able to win the firefight and, in doing so, saved the lives of his military brothers. He essentially did the job that he was trained to do but this did conflict with the preferred British approach to counter-insurgency operations in winning over the hearts and minds of the population. However, we were under the U.S.-led Operation Enduring Freedom as a consequence of our political failing in Iraq, much to the distaste of British High Command who often tried to strategically undermine our American cousins. It is no surprise that our mission had become confused and as a result of the intensity of the warfighting in Helmand, British Forces would continue to meet aggression with increased aggression which was detrimental to the principles of a successful counter-insurgency strategy.

Trauma risk management was supposed to have been successfully implemented by 2010 and even had its own designated page in the Sept 2009 edition of the Op Herrick Tactical Aide Memoire. From a management overview, it states that TRiM practitioners should intervene when personnel have been involved in a 'near miss,' or have sustained serious injuries to themselves or others or witnessed trauma involving death, particularly grotesque death. Furthermore, from a management perspective, initial interventions should be made within the first 24 hours of an incident, then followed up by a 72-hour assessment before ongoing support and monitoring.[lxvii] From the guidelines set out in this memoir, I should have been considered for trauma management due to my 'near miss'. Then there are the men of the Infantry fighting Companies to consider; they were constantly being engaged by the Taliban. According to Soldier 'G', not once were any of the soldiers at his patrol base offered any support under these guidelines for the management of battlefield trauma.

The men of Number 2 Company would have a difficult tour in Patrol base Knarnikah, particularly my friend Nathan. I had recruited Nathan into the Irish Guards in 2007 whilst I was a Recruiting Sergeant and he would be unfortunate to witness one of his brethren lose both legs and an arm when he stepped on a Taliban IED. Guardsman Manneh would survive, but only due to the quick actions of soldiers such as Nathan, who applied immediate first aid and tourniquets. On another occasion, Nathan witnessed the Taliban using children as human shields and these kids were regrettably killed in the crossfire by British Forces. Furthermore, he would be standing next to Liam, a dog handler from the Royal Army Veterinary Corps, who was shot in the face and killed instantly by Taliban fire despite Nathan's best attempts to apply immediate first aid.[lxviii] Then, there were the less traumatic patrols and near misses that often took place that would eventually take their toll on Nathan's mental health.

Nathan didn't receive any TRiM after any of these incidents despite several members of the Company being trained as TRiM practitioners. Nathan believes that the only person who was successfully managed for battlefield trauma was a Guardsman who stowed away on a supply helicopter back to Camp Bastion; unless you did something dramatic, then, as far as the command element was concerned, you were fine. Maybe these TRiM practitioners should not have been aggressively patrolling with the Company as they too had become emotionally detached and therefore not been able to identify the signs of battlefield trauma in others. After the tour, Nathan would turn to alcohol as a coping mechanism as he would be haunted by survivor's guilt. He would relive Guardsman Manneh being blown up in his nightmares, but in his dreams, Nathan would be the one to step on the IED. Survivor's guilt would gradually eat away at him from the inside and recently, he has been getting treatment from a local complex mental health team. He is aware that he will never be cured of his battlefield trauma, but at least he is now better able to manage it.

Nathan would be medically discharged from the Army in 2018 due to a deteriorating spinal injury as a result of being blown up in an IED blast that overturned his Jackal. He has since had multiple spinal fusions and has lost control of his bladder which now requires a catheter. Additionally, he is also wheelchair-bound if he wants to leave the house and is on constant morphine for pain management. Yet, Nathan rarely leaves the house as he is ashamed about his new identity as he is a shadow of his former self; the soldier, the PTI and the respected Sergeant that he once was. What has also exacerbated his PTSD is that the Armed Forces Compensation Scheme is yet to settle his claim. This claim has been ongoing for over three years and has led to several suicide attempts by Nathan as he is struggling financially due to the fact that he is not physically or mentally fit to work. This is shameful as Joint Service publication 770 clearly states that any ill-health pension benefits that soldiers are entitled to, normally should be settled no later than 6 weeks prior to their date of discharge.[lxix] Yet, in Nathan's circumstances, and like most spinal and musculoskeletal injuries, the aftercare and compensation for these injuries would be denied and contested for many years to come. This disloyalty by the Ministry of Defence would exacerbate Nathan's PTSD and he now feels abandoned and rejected by the very society that sent him to Afghanistan.

Survivors guilt was a frequent occurrence and can make returning home feel abnormal with many soldiers preferring to be re-deployed on operations, rather than facing their battlefield trauma. There are guidelines to prevent back-to-back tours, but these can be superseded by the soldiers signing individual waivers. Frank was one such soldier as he had to sign a waiver to deploy on Op Herrick 13 as he would deploy to Afghanistan three times in a four-year period. Some soldiers have said that they preferred the tempo of life of operations to the pressures of civilian life which is something that may be linked to institutionalisation and may have a similarity to career criminals and their preference for prison life. Maybe Frank enjoyed being deployed on operations as this kept his mind solely focused on the mission, or maybe, like myself years earlier, he believed and accepted that he deserved to die on the battlefield. I suppose only he will truly know why he opted to continually be deployed.

Due to spending the majority of my time on Op Herrick 13 in the confines of safe Camps and Patrol Bases, I would experience a different type of battlefield trauma - almost secondary. Initially, I would be upset at seeing one of the men I knew from 10 Platoon being medically evacuated on the same flight to the UK that I was on for my R'n'R. Banner had suffered severe blast injuries but at least he had all of his limbs. He had been very lucky to have stepped on a partially detonated IED which had fortunately only shattered the bones in his lower leg and ankle. After my R'n'R, I was devastated to hear that he had chosen to have his leg amputated to prevent infection and to get rid of the pain. The leg was damaged beyond repair and it was a tough decision but the right one. I don't know if I would have had the courage to make such a decision and this is a testament to Banner's courage.

Then, weeks later, another member of 10 Platoon, Spike, was blown up by another IED. Spike was even luckier than Banner and should have died as a large piece of shrapnel forced its way under his jawline through his teeth and wedged itself into the side of his skull. I remember visiting him at the hospital in Camp Bastion before he was about to have surgery to have the shrapnel removed. Spike was conscious but off his head on painkillers and seeing him like this completely devastated me. This was the first high-intensity deployment when I wasn't emotionally numb as a result of my combat support role. I no longer had the mindset of those soldiers out on the ground who were constantly witnessing their brothers being injured, disfigured, or killed. I was reacting like any rational human being would in seeing his mates injured. Maybe this was a consequence of spending the previous two years in a civilian work environment in the career's office or maybe my six operational tours had taken their toll on me, but seeing the young men of 10 Platoon, my Platoon, my family, being injured broke me. Then, things would go from bad to worse.

John had been ambushed by the Taliban by a multi-weapon shoot, including a medium machine gun, whilst on a foot patrol around Patrol Base Hazarat in the November, in which Guardsman

Davies was killed in action and pretty much everyone else in that section was shot or wounded, including some of my good friends. In the months afterwards, John was an empty vessel and he often linked the stress of being in that ambush to triggering his cancer. John was never the same again and he would only ever speak about this traumatic incident when blind drunk. However, we had been fortunate as the Battalion as we had only suffered one fatality at the hands of the Taliban throughout Op Herrick 13. Then, on their very last patrol before returning home, Major Collins and Lance Sergeant Burgan were killed by an IED on their way back to Camp Bastion. Soldier 'G' recalls listening to the incident over the radio and instantly gathered his men to deploy for immediate support, only to be told to stand down and return to base as they had died instantly in the explosion. He was helpless and there was nothing that he could have done to save them and like many soldiers of my generation, he feels guilty for not being able to have done more.

I recall being in a happy mood as more of my comrades were filtering through Camp Bastion and Tombstone and that we had all switched off as we were preparing to return home; our time in Afghanistan had come to an end. We were all summoned to the cookhouse and were sharing 'war stories' and were in high spirits when we were informed of this saddening news. This was a 9/11 moment for the Irish Guards as these were two very popular soldiers. Perhaps it was because it was their last patrol that it hit everyone so hard. The atmosphere within the room quickly changed to anger and rage with tables and chairs being thrown; some soldiers had tears in their eyes, whereas others were screaming and punching walls. This was the final nail in my emotional coffin. I was done. My second-tier logistical role had opened my eyes to the true cost and futility of warfare and thankfully, this would be my last operational deployment.

Our decompression was sombre due to the recent deaths of our two brothers and I do not recall too many soldiers getting totally wasted on beer or even fighting with each other. It was better organised with decent entertainment such as live bands and comedians, but this was not a party or fun atmosphere; it felt more like a wake. Yet again, there was nothing in place for confidential mental health support. Sure, we could talk to the Padre and this was the preferred approach, but the death of these two soldiers had rocked the whole Battalion and it was blatantly obvious that we all were collectively suffering and, like always, we would have to 'man up'!

Reflecting back on my time in Afghanistan, I genuinely believe that our presence there was a complete waste of time. This was a different kind of warfare than what we had previously experienced in Northern Ireland, Iraq and Kosovo and we were always destined to fail. This was a result of the lack of consideration that was given to the social, religious, and tribal elements of the Afghan culture and the simple fact that there was no coherent long-term strategy in place. Then there is the political dimension of the damaged Anglo-American 'special relationship' to consider, as British politicians foresaw Helmand as an opportunity to redeem their lost prestige over our withdrawal from Basra. As a consequence, the U.S. coerced us to support Operation Enduring Freedom, which focused on a policy that prioritised combat operations and, as a result, abandoned the British policy of minimum force and hearts and minds. This not only went against the ISAF mission but established the conditions for the Taliban to win over the political dimension of the Afghan people.

Then, there are the 454 British deaths to consider as well as all of the life-changing injuries and let us not forget the hidden wounds as a result of the darker side of warfare. Afghanistan opened my eyes to the futility of war, and this was because I was not warfighting or responsible for men in battle; I was able to see it for what it actually was; political failure. Our only presence in Afghanistan was an extension of U.S. foreign policy which saw the Irish Guards arguably experience more intense firefights than they had witnessed in the 2003 War in Iraq. However, the only positive I can take from our military failure in Afghanistan was that for over a decade, we kept the fundamental extremist fixed in this region, but we did also provide them with invaluable lessons in warfighting, which they would utilise in future terror attacks on the west such as the Charlie Hebdo incident in Paris in the January of 2015.

I still feel that we were politically abandoned by the British Government throughout my two tours of Iraq, but in Afghanistan, we militarily defeated ourselves by adopting the U.S. policy of militarily overpowering the Taliban on the battlefield. Counter-insurgency warfare is not a new concept and it saddens me that the vital lessons from previous conflicts were not consistently applied in Afghanistan. My experience and lasting memories of Op Herrick 13 are, unfortunately, bitter and full of regret, and, like many soldiers of my generation, our experiences of warfighting, especially the darker side of warfare, would take its toll on our mental health, an invisible burden that would stay with us for the rest of our lives.

Members of Number 12 Company, Shawqat FOB 2011.

On Patrol Nad' Ali South Winter 2010.

Chapter 14.
Sedentary Soldier

On return from Afghanistan, Number 12 Company was disbanded, and I was redeployed to the role of CQMS for Number 2 Company. These men, well, let's be fair, boys (as the majority of them were under the age of 21) were battle-hardened and a good bunch. However, we were thrown straight back into the stressful world of public duties but not before a medal parade. This would be conducted by the Duke and Duchess of Cambridge and would be their first official military engagement as a recently married couple. I had been asked if I had wanted to participate in the Royal Wedding as part of the Guard of Honour, but this was during my post-operational tour leave and I just wanted a break from all things military. In hindsight, I regret this as it was a once in a lifetime opportunity, but as a consolation, I would meet the future King and Queen when they would present us with our Afghanistan Medals.

To begin with, the Royals were late for the parade which was putting pressure on some of the single-leg amputees who had chosen to stand. Furthermore, many of the soldiers on parade, such as myself, were suffering from spinal and musculoskeletal injuries as a result of the horrendous weight that we had been hauling for the past six months in Afghanistan. Eventually, they arrived, and the parade began. I was responsible for holding the tray with the medals on it for Princess Catherine and as she presented the men with their medals, she would ask them questions about their experiences in

Afghanistan. To be fair to the lads, they were all very polite and respectful; well, that was until Prince William approached Guardsman Manneh!

Manneh was a Commonwealth soldier from The Gambia and was on parade in a wheelchair as a result of being a triple amputee from an IED blast. We were having some military banter beforehand but Manneh would eventually have the last laugh. He had just received his medal from Princess Catherine when Prince William joined us, and the two of them engaged in casual conversation. Prince William then mentioned to Manneh that if he needed any assistance, he should let him know as he was the Colonel of our Regiment, to which Manneh immediately replied, 'When I was blown up, I had $100 in my wallet and I never got it back from my CQMS!' Prince William and Catherine both looked directly at me in disgust and must have thought that I had stolen Manneh's wallet whilst he was dying on the battlefield. I wasn't even his CQMS in Afghanistan! Did Manneh really think that his wallet with $100 had survived an IED blast that blew his arm and legs off? Maybe this was his attempt at humour, but the future King and Queen didn't think so and I can still feel the shameful, chilling, and disappointed look that they gave me even though I had done nothing wrong! Maybe Manneh thought that this would be funny, but I certainly didn't think so.

In hindsight, it was obvious that many of the boys in Number 2 Company were suffering with their mental health and they were doing what was institutionally acceptable throughout the summer of 2011 and that was to get drunk. We all would often turn up late for duty and disciplinary action was still rarely implemented. The command element was aware of the tough fighting that had occurred during Op Herrick 13, and this was a cooling-off period for us all. I was still suffering with my back and was under a physio conducting rehabilitation, yet despite this, I was still required to perform ceremonial duties due to manning shortages. I was still being 'institutionally bullied' by a few bad apples from the previous generation of dinosaurs and because my injury wasn't visible, in their eyes, it didn't exist. In that October, I finally got the MRI scan that I had been requesting since I had originally pulled my back in Afghanistan 12 months prior. Finally, I have medical evidence that acknowledged that I was injured. I had a significant L4/5 protruding disc that was pushing on my spinal cord but what was more important to me was that I had a copy of the MRI images to visibly show people.

The Battalion doctor was the only one to apologise as he believed that I wasn't showing any medical symptoms from such a severe spinal injury due to the fact that I was still able to function in Afghanistan and continued to carry out my daily tasks including ceremonial duties. I had even taken part in Trooping the Colour, the Queen's birthday parade that year! Although I no longer desired to be deployed on operational tours, I was still institutionalised and therefore, the British Army's needs were always prioritised above my own, even if this was harmful to my own long-term physical health! I remember forwarding the images from my MRI to all of those who had insinuated that I was faking, setting a bad example, or who just blatantly called me a coward. Surprisingly, none of them ever replied, yet I felt a satisfying sense of vindication. Part of me had believed that I may have been faking my back injury as we were taught to follow orders and I was indoctrinated into military culture. Therefore, if someone above me in the chain of command said that I was faking injury, I was trained to accept their military diagnosis.

It soon became apparent that I would require surgery, and, at this point, it became clear that I was no longer useful to the Army as I was considered non-deployable on future operations. There are limited uses for a senior non-commissioned officer in an Infantry fighting unit so I was sent back to Manchester in the January of 2012 as a Recruiting Colour Sergeant and informed that I should use the time there to try and regain my full fitness. In 2012, the country was currently bankrupt as a result of the expensive prolonged conflicts in Iraq and Afghanistan and all areas of public services were being cut, including the Armed Forces. Redundancies were being offered initially to the civil servants at the Ministry of Defence with the average payoff being in the region of £30,000.[lxx] Unfortunately, this immediately impacted the civil servants at the Army Careers Office in Manchester as the clerical support staff would be reduced by 50% and even the office manager, a long service Warrant Officer, had been given his marching orders.

This would leave myself and a Staff Sergeant from the REME to pick up the pieces. He would run the administrational side and I would be responsible for the operational running of the Greater Manchester region which also included five smaller offices. I was now the boss of some of the same Sergeants whom I had known from my previous posting there but now, I wasn't even invited out on Friday drinks, which kind of hurt! Like the rest of the British Army, we were expected to keep up our same productivity with less manpower and resources. For the Sergeants in the recruiting environment, this meant weekend duties, which was not a popular decision and excluded me from all social gatherings. (Ouch!).

The careers office was the ideal place for me to recover from my injury as I had bought a house there before Op Herrick 13 and I had married Jayne on my return from Afghanistan. I had delayed my proposal until I had returned safely. Soldiers are superstitious since it always seemed to be the ones with the most to lose who were, more often than not, killed in action. I had always segregated Jayne from army life and was adamant that I never wanted her to live in army quarters due to the constant moving around which provided very little stability for her or any future family. The only positive of this posting was that it was the ideal opportunity to audition as a happy family in normal civilian life and I soon realised how lucky I was despite my agonising back injury. Yet, the Army was still my priority and I was convinced that I would make a full recovery, therefore, I was determined to make good use of my time as the office manager to put my back injury behind me and return to my Battalion as a potential Warrant Officer.

Once settled into my new job, I was quickly referred to an orthopaedic surgeon in Teesside as this was the nearest military facility and I was fast-tracked for a discectomy on my bulging disc in the March of 2012. My surgeon was overly confident and had convinced me that I would be running again in three months, which was reassuring and welcoming news. The L4/5 nerve root in my spine had suffered damage, and this was affecting my lower left leg and this operation was 18 months after the initial injury had been sustained in Afghanistan. Unfortunately, I would fall into the category of the 10% of discectomies where they immediately re-prolapse, which I fundamentally believe was due to my initial aftercare. The day after my spinal surgery, I was informed that the operation had been a success and I was discharged. I then had to wait for a military driver to collect me from Manchester and was placed in an uncomfortable upright chair for three hours whilst I waited. Then I had to undertake the painful two-hour drive back home to my house for a few weeks of bed rest before gradually returning to my sedentary duties in the career's office.

Later that year, I received a personal injury claim for £10,000 from the Armed Forces Compensation Scheme and this was welcomed as I had spent all of my savings from Afghanistan on my wedding to Jayne in Las Vegas. This compensation seemed fair, as at the time, I was convinced that I was going to make a full recovery and return to fitness. After the surgery, I was optimistic, and I was planning for my next promotion. I desperately wanted to be the Company Sergeant Major of Number 4 Company, and this was easily achievable as I was a Colour Sergeant with a maximum of eight years left on my contract - six if I wanted to be pensioned off early. I was ticking all of the boxes for promotion to Warrant Officer Class II. I had completed an operational tour as a CQMS, I had conducted a unit move and now, I had a strong external report which would further support my recommendations for promotion. The only thing that was holding me back was my medical fitness.

Subconsciously, I secretly knew that the operation had not been a success as I was still in a lot of pain, however, I have always been able to tolerate pain, but I was still unable to run. This was a combination of my weak left leg and the increased pain from the impact of running which is why I bought a cross-trainer exercise machine for my home. This allowed me to maintain my fitness levels without the added pain of impact exercises and I was still fit despite the lack of running. However, my two-year 'recovery' posting would be cut short when I received a phone call from Wade informing me that I was being recalled to my Battalion to replace him as both the

Welfare and the Recruiting Officer, despite not holding the rank of a Warrant Officer or a Captain.

I was disappointed as Jayne was pregnant with our first child and I had hoped to be around for the full pregnancy, and now, I was going to be married unaccompanied in Aldershot, 230 miles away. This did present a career opportunity though, as in the past we have had both a Welfare Warrant Officer and a recruiting Warrant Officer and if I was doing both these jobs, then it would almost guarantee my next promotion. So, rather than prioritising my family and the birth of my first child, I had selfishly prioritised my own needs which, of course, were the same as the British Army's above all else. When you are consumed within the military bubble, it is quite easy to justify putting the Army before your family as the rest of your colleagues are doing the exact same thing. I thought that through promotion, I could please everyone as it would provide financial rewards for my family as well as recognition from my military masters from whom I still sought approval. I had convinced myself that the ends justify the means and that I was fulfilling the British Army's needs as well as my own egotistical ones. I was selfless?

I remember that Jayne was naturally disappointed that I was called back to my Battalion after just 12 months, but I was a soldier and, as such, followed orders. Besides, I was terrified of being made redundant and didn't want to make any waves as we had a baby on the way, and I needed job security. I would be taking over from Wade and was looking forward to seeing him, but he was a shadow of his former self and it didn't take long to understand why. He had been the Welfare Officer for the Irish Guards on Op Herrick 13, and this had, in no uncertain terms, broken him. He had been responsible for the aftercare of the injured soldiers and the amputees and let's not forget that he had to link up with the families of those killed at the hands of the Taliban.

This was made even more difficult due to the fact that Wade often had a personal relationship with many of these soldiers and their families. He had in-depth battlefield experience from his deployments to Northern Ireland, Kosovo and Iraq and was an excellent career soldier who had gone from recruit to the rank of Captain, but his welfare support role had taken its toll and reduced him to an unrecognisable shell of his former self. Wade could no longer provide Welfare support for the families and soldiers of the Irish Guards, especially as 2 Company were due to deploy back to Afghanistan; he was emotionally exhausted!

Number 2 Company were training to deploy to Afghanistan in the coming months and Wade could not tolerate the emotional burden of providing welfare support for their pending deployment. Wade would take me to the recovery and rehabilitation wards at Headley Court, and it was no surprise that everyone knew him. He even drove me to Birmingham to walk me through the 24-hour casualty evacuation procedure from the time of the incident in Afghanistan to the injured soldier arriving at the Queen Elizabeth II Hospital. As always, Wade was thorough and professional, and I remember how difficult this was for him as all that he had from these locations were bad memories. It was upsetting to see Wade like this, and I am still disappointed that he didn't even receive a medal or any recognition for the important job that he did as he was very much part of Op Herrick 13.

Wade would leave the regular army shortly afterwards but would return on a short engagement detached from the Irish Guards at a local Personal Recovery Unit close to his family home. He would essentially be a civilian in a uniform under a 12-month renewable contract, but he would keep his rank and identity, and this is a path that many of my brethren would follow. Some would join the Army Reserves in a desperate attempt to hold on to their military identity as, after over two decades of service, you can quite often become the uniform; it defines you and is hard to let go of. Bearing in mind that most career soldiers like myself were recruited as teenagers and had only known military life as adults, this may explain why detaching themselves from their military identity is so difficult.

However, I was only concerned about my next promotion and was thriving in my new dual role despite the added pressure, but my physical health was suffering as a result. Most weekends, I would be stuck in the Friday rush-hour traffic heading home and, on one occasion, this took me nine hours. These long weekly drives were also harmful to my ongoing back issues and I was having a combination of steroid and facet joint injections in my spine to keep me going. The recruitment side was easy, and I formulated a completely fresh new marketing strategy for the Irish Guards that was aimed at the civilian sector and incorporated the use of social media. For some strange reason, the traditional Regimental marketing campaigns of the past had been targeted at the current military audience which made no sense to me as they were already recruited!

The welfare side was more complex as I was dealing with some very multifaceted and personal issues. On my Unit Welfare Officers Course, we were taught that the Army's needs were always the priority, followed closely by the soldiers, then their families and this was evident within the Battalion. I would witness Company Sergeant Majors blatantly ignoring young soldiers' injuries and I even witnessed one Company Sergeant Major ordering a soldier who was on crutches to deploy on a tactical exercise. Soldiers with drink-related issues couldn't hide anymore due to the added manning pressures of the redundancies and the accepted drinking culture, especially within the Sergeants' Mess, was gradually weeded out. These reduced levels of manning made all of our jobs incredibly difficult, with some, like me, having two roles, and this left little time for the welfare of the soldiers. This would result in the slightest issues being raised to my office. Whereas welfare was every commander's responsibility, yet, this had somehow been forgotten due to the busy schedule, reduced manning, and the high tempo of 'Battalion life'.

I remember that when my wife went into labour, I immediately downed tools and drove to Manchester in record time, overtaking a 1985 DeLorean along the way. Thankfully, Jayne's waters had broken on a midweek evening and I was able to arrive back home in sufficient time to witness the birth of my daughter. When Mara was born, I was completely overwhelmed and emotionally compromised and began to cry tears of happiness. All of the years of suppressed anger, trauma and emotion were suddenly released. The birth of my daughter would change my whole outlook as my loyalty was no longer to the British Army but to my family. However, I was still working from home on my paternity leave; in fact, I was always working on leave whilst I was in the Welfare Office so my loyalty and priorities would progressively take time to switch over during the following twelve months.

Maybe it was because I was no longer in combat roles, but I felt like I was becoming soft, more emotional and maybe this was the reason that I was struggling with my back and leg pain and was subsequently sent for another MRI scan. The scan clearly showed that my L4/5 disc had popped again, and I would need further spinal surgery, this time a revised discectomy. I was snowed under with work and was killing myself because I was due for promotion, but more importantly, I was terrified of being made redundant. I remember that on the day of my surgery, I was so focused on my work that I had to be forced out of the office. Then, whilst in my hospital bed in pre-op, I was still working on the laptop and taking phone calls and even tried to delay my operation to complete my duties. From my perspective, I would do whatever it took to salvage my career and to provide job security for my family. The operation in November 2013 initially appeared to be successful and I was sent home for six weeks to recover, but with my work phone and laptop, of course.

I would use what was left of 2013 to physically rest despite still working from home. The only advantage of this was that I could frequently see my good friend John who was losing his battle with cancer. John was like a big brother to me and was always there to guide me in times of hardship. We had similar experiences of childhood, from abusive Irish families, to being in the care of the state, and then had both excelled in the Irish Guards and this helped us forge a special bond. We had served closely together in Kosovo, Northern Ireland and Afghanistan and it was devastating to witness him deteriorate and waste away so quickly. John was convinced that the operational stress of fighting the Taliban in Helmand Province had triggered his cancer and he was tremendously angry with the way in which he had been treated by the Battalion when he had started to experience the early symptoms of this cruel illness. In hindsight, we were both failed by the medical personnel and our chain of command whilst we were deployed to Afghanistan as their only priority was the mission and we were disposable tools that could be cast aside once the mission was complete. Sadly, this was the unwelcomed truth as the strategic needs of operations always came before the welfare of the individual soldiers.

In the weeks after returning to Barracks after our tour in Afghanistan, I remember that Niall, Frank, John, and I were having a meal at the local Pizza Hut when John suddenly rushed off to the toilet to throw up his dinner. We didn't know this at the time, but John was suffering from the early symptoms of oesophageal cancer. I was thankful that I was posted back to Manchester after the tour as this allowed frequent visits to see each other without the high tempo and demands of 'Battalion life,' which often meant working weekends. It was heart-breaking to witness John slowly waste away and at his funeral in the January of 2014, I broke down and wept uncontrollably in front of all my military brethren. Since the birth of my daughter, I was no longer that emotionless machine-like harbinger of death and I was gradually regaining my connection to my mortality.

In his dying weeks, I had continuously asked John about his preferred funeral arrangements and he had informed me not to worry as he had a file prepared with everything set out for me in fine detail. He had often joked that he wanted heavy breeze blocks to be put in his coffin so that his friends who would be coffin bearers would have to work that little bit harder. John was always the joker and he would even get one over me from the grave as no such file with his funeral preferences even existed. I was at his bedside supporting his wife and daughter when he passed and this was the most emotionally charged and painful moment of my life, but I had to dig deep and suppress all of my emotions for his family and help organise the funeral.

John would have the last laugh as I liaised with his wife, his church, and the Irish Guards to organise his funeral, constantly asking about the whereabouts of this file. Then, at the wake, one of his close civilian friends thanked me for organising everything and that this had been John's plan all along. Maybe, John could not accept his own pending death despite the fact that he had witnessed so much death throughout his military career. Regardless, I hope that he had a good chuckle to himself one last time knowing that he had done me over yet again. I found it difficult to process John's death knowing of his battlefield exploits, and to be slowly taken by cancer seemed unfair and cruel. All of our lives are that little bit duller without him and I miss my brother every day.

After the funeral, I would return to the Battalion, but I wasn't the same. With the combination of the birth of my daughter Mara, then with the death of John, I was rapidly losing my love and my unquestionable loyalty towards the British Army. Besides, I had completed 18 years' service, and this meant that I had secured part of my immediate pension. I had also now queried about my eligibility for redundancy but unfortunately, as I was still not fully fit, I didn't qualify as a medical discharge was the cheaper option for the Ministry of Defence. Part of me was still chasing my next promotion and when it didn't come, I was defeated; I was done.

Later that year, I recall going to see my Commanding Officer to discuss the reasons why I hadn't been promoted to the rank of Warrant Officer and he was very direct and honest with his justification. He explained that I was his most capable and experienced Colour Sergeant, but he anticipated that I had no long-term future in the Army, therefore, he graded me lower than his less-experienced but more physically capable Colour Sergeants. On hearing this, the Adjutant's jaw dropped as this went against British Army career policy and the Adjutant was there to advise the Commanding Officer on legal matters, but I understood what the hidden message was. He had suggested that my career was over and as my promotion was my only current motivational factor to stay in the Army, maybe it was time to throw the towel in. I remember having mixed emotions after this interview and, even to this day, I am slightly conflicted. I had given everything I had and now the fight was out of my hands, especially as I was due another medical review.

The Battalion doctor was aware that my recent spinal surgery had not been successful and on my follow up appointment the next week, I was completely truthful about how I had been struggling emotionally and physically, and just like that, my career in the Irish Guards and the British Army was over. I remember making my way through the barracks to clear out my office and being inundated with the normal recruiting and welfare questions, but I was in a haze and wasn't even listening. My life in the military had ended, I was no longer a soldier and I now faced uncertainty regarding my physical wellbeing and financial future. All that was important to me now was my young family. Almost immediately, I was taken off the manning strength of the Irish Guards and placed into the Personal Recovery Unit (PRU) at Fulwood Barracks in Preston and would remain there until my medical discharge the following year.

Throughout my final year in the Battalion, the Irish Guards had Number 2 Company deployed to Afghanistan, Number 4 Company had deployed to the Falklands and the Battalion as a whole were conducting their pre-deployment training for the Op Tosca 20, the

United Nations 'peace-keeping' mission in Cyprus. (This was a six-month holiday in the sun where the soldiers patrolled on push bikes with batons). The ever-increasing commitments of the Battalion were always prioritised over the welfare of the soldiers and this was made increasingly more difficult by redundancies and the restructuring of the Regimental system where all Infantry Battalions would be slim-lined. The operational demands were still there but with lesser manning, which resulted in very little time for welfare.

One of the first to voluntarily accept redundancy was Soldier 'E'. He was a very successful and popular member of the Battalion and had reached Warrant Officer rank with five years left to complete on his service. He was destined to be commissioned and extend his career, but after returning from Op Herrick 10 in 2009, his perception of military life altered due to his own personal experiences on the battlefield. Soldier 'E' categorically believes that all military personnel who served on the ground in Helmand Province inevitably have some form of battlefield trauma. This was because of the ridiculous amount of IEDs that were hidden everywhere, and this meant that every step they took could potentially be their last. He then painfully explained how he witnessed soldiers picking up the pieces of their brethren and sometimes, unfortunate Afghan children, who were acceptable casualties at the hands of the Taliban. He states that observing such atrocities must have a detrimental effect on the human psyche. From my own personal experiences from Kosovo and Iraq, it was always the faces of the injured and dead children that haunted your dreams, the darker side of warfare that is never mentioned and is often brushed over.

Soldier 'E' recollects brave and battle-hardened men refusing to leave the safety of their armoured vehicles because they knew that the Taliban had planted IEDs in the area. Some of these grown men even pissed themselves out of fear which is not in any way a stain on their character. These were all courageous men and it was evident that they were suffering but no support was ever made available and this is part of the reason why Soldier 'E' volunteered for redundancy. Like myself, he had observed how the British Army was failing to support the aftercare of its soldiers on return from arduous operational deployments and went as far to use our self-certified assessments after the 2003 War in Iraq as an example of this. All methods of operational stress management were a formality and only in place as an umbrella. Like many career soldiers of my generation, the futility of our time in Afghanistan broke our resolve and love of soldiering and this could have been prevented with adequate aftercare, especially regarding our mental health.

For the past eighteen years, my loyalty to my regiment had been unwavering and I had given the British Army my all, but now, I was beginning to question my loyalty as it wasn't being reciprocated. However, the cost of austerity meant reducing the manning of our Armed Forces and this subsequently affected all of the injured soldiers, as a medical discharge was more cost-effective to the treasury than large redundancy pay-outs. Hence all of the perceived 'dead weights' such as myself would be shown the door in a callous calculated gesture. Personally, I felt abandoned and rejected but the methodical institutionalised soldier in me accepted that this decision was part of the greater good for the combat efficacy of the British Army. One must remember that we are trained to be selfless and putting the needs of the British Army before my own and those of my young family, was righteous, hence justified.

In reflection of my final years in the Irish Guards, one thing stands out and that is the lack of commitment towards the welfare of the soldiers. Once I had completed the Unit Welfare Officers Course, my eyes had been finally opened to how the British Army truly valued its personnel. Mission success and combat deploy ability were always the priority and this came at the expense of the soldier's individual welfare. The welfare team's only purpose was to maintain and increase combat efficiency and this was achieved by working closely with the military medical staff. Together, regardless of the long-term implication, we would do whatever it took to keep the cogs of the military machine ticking over.

During my time in the Welfare Office, I observed many failures with the most significant being the lack of Post-Operational Stress Management (POSM). All of the pre-deployment checks were completed, and the families were frequently updated whilst Number 2 Company was in Afghanistan, but the true failures occurred on return. The only mandatory check that was ever conducted was a POSM brief by the Welfare Office, a few months after their homecoming. No individual POSM files or paperwork were recorded and no follow up individual aftercare or interviews were conducted by the soldier's chain of command.[lxxi] Both Wade (who was the Welfare officer on Op Herrick 13) and I agree that as a result of the high tempo and demands of 'Battalion Life', the POSM aftercare of the individual would become a calculated sacrifice by senior commanders. POSM, in my experience, was yet another paper exercise that was paid lip service to. Even in 2021, a serving Warrant Officer in the British Army informed me that on entering a lecture theatre, he found a pile of signed POSM paperwork that another unit had just left there. It would appear that even today, the mental wellbeing of our soldiers and POSM is still an afterthought. This deeply saddens me, as I can only speculate on how many lives could have been saved (specifically veteran suicide), through proper post-operational stress management and adequate mental health support for my generation of war fighters.

Chapter 15.
There's the Door

My final day in uniform was quite surreal. For a start, I had been at a personal recovery unit for the past twelve months and had hardly worn my uniform in this period. In fact, the only time that I had worn it was when I was volunteering at the Prince's Trust. I recall that I had just finished my weekly and final physiotherapy appointment at Brookwood Barracks in Preston. I had been seeing the same physio on and off for almost five years and we had a good relationship. She had identified the deteriorating weakness in my legs and the foot drop in my left ankle (something the Ministry of Defence would later deny). My physiotherapist was also concerned that I was being medically discharged too soon. This was six months after my latest operation, my L4/5 spinal fusion, and she had insisted that the Army had a duty of care to provide 12 months of medical aftercare following all major surgery. Regardless, we said our goodbyes and I left.

On returning to my car, one of the recovery officers shouted me over. On seeing me, it had dawned on him that this was my last day and he asked if I had had a discharge interview. He was disgusted that I had not and was insistent that I had one. However, this was a typical Wednesday afternoon, a sports afternoon where soldiers take the rest of the day to play whatever sport or physical training they desire. I was ironically wearing shorts and a Manchester City football shirt, not too dissimilar to what I had worn two decades ago when I had arrived at Pirbright for my basic training. I was conscious of this and didn't want to finish my career the way it had started. Part of me felt like that seventeen-year-old boy again, unsure, and anxious about his future.

I had suggested that I return home and get changed into my suit but was informed that this wasn't necessary. This made me feel awkward as if I was going to be interviewed, my final act as a soldier, by the officer commanding the personal recovery unit, then being in 'The Guards', this was a formal occasion and my attire was not suitable. It came as no surprise that the officer commanding wasn't available as this was not a planned interview. By now, I didn't even want an interview as it was obvious to me that this process was just a tick in the box exercise, one that the personal recovery unit was bound to conduct.

Eventually, we found a newly appointed late entry Captain who was just moving into his office and he reluctantly agreed to interview me. I remember that he was more focused on unpacking his office pictures and as a result, this interview would be very brief, to say the least. He questioned me about my service, my injury and what I had planned for 'civvy street', before wishing me the best of luck in the future and that was it. It was 19 August 2015; the following morning, I would wake up a civilian, a veteran. I was recovering from spinal surgery and was battling internal demons without the protection of my military identity. These demons would continue to haunt me on a daily basis and be a reminder of my service, my sacrifices.

I am still disappointed about the way in which I was discharged from the British Army like this as I didn't receive a phone call or even a letter from my Regiment - the Irish Guards. Twenty years' service, six operational tours and not even a phone call. I remember at the time that I was even making excuses for them, justifying their lack of loyalty. As a former welfare officer for the Irish Guards, I had sat on monthly occupational health meetings where every soldier who was injured or was due to leave the Regiment was individually discussed. Due to this, I was aware that the command element of the Regiment was only too aware of my imminent discharge, yet I was still blindly loyal and justified their actions by acknowledging how busy they were. Maybe, I just didn't want to acknowledge the hard truth, that once you are no longer useful then you are simply discarded. Three years later I would be dined out by the Sergeants Mess, but this was only through the determination of Frank who was adamant that I attended, and I only really returned for him.

It's interesting as I mention loyalty here. One must remember that loyalty is one of the core values that make up the British Army's values and standards and should, in theory, work both ways. Throughout my career, I had always been indisputably loyal to the Irish Guards. Let us not forget that I had been approached by several different military units to transfer over the years, many offering rapid promotions, but I had always refused due to my loyalty to my Regiment. Even now at discharge and despite not receiving this loyalty in return, I still remained the reliable loyal soldier. This loyalty is more than a cap badge, it is loyalty amongst friends, friends who become brothers – a family. This loyalty is forged from shared experiences from both the best and the worst of times. Unfortunately, in my generation's circumstances, this was mainly the worst of times from our experiences of the hard attrition tours of Iraq and Afghanistan. Now, as a civilian, a veteran, this loyalty would be put to the test.

When you consider the mindset and identity of our veterans, loyalty becomes the most pertinent core value that they cling onto the most. The vast majority of veterans remain unconditionally loyal and proud of their Regiments and Corps, but only those on a conventional discharge. Injured veterans, however, have a different outlook as they soon realise that their loyalty is not reciprocated. The first time that I doubted or even questioned this loyalty was on my full medical board. I had previously been on less relevant medical boards that were responsible for the temporary downgrading of a soldier's ability to deploy on operations. This was different, though, as a full medical board can result in discharge from the military.

A full medical board consists of a panel of two or three military doctors who determine the soldier's ability to remain effective in service. Mine was conducted on 19 August 2014 at Catterick. On reviewing the report, I was found to 'no longer meet the mobility, functioning capability, objective test requirements' to fulfil the needs of the British Army. This was concluded after a physical assessment as I was no longer able to perform the basic battle movements of getting up from the floor. I remember putting in maximum effort in a futile attempt to keep my job, my identity. I had expected the decision to be a medical discharge but when the Colonel actually said those words out loud, I had an emotional breakdown and began to cry inconsolably. I was becoming an emotional wreck!

When I eventually composed myself, the Colonel awarded me a 'tier 2' discharge and afterwards, he pulled me to one side and warned me about the Armed Forces Compensation Scheme. I'll never forget his advice about not taking their first offer of compensation and his advice was warranted as my initial offer would be zero despite being a 'tier 2 discharge.'[lxxii]

Tier 1: for conditions that mean you are unable to do your service job, but your ability to get gainful employment is not deemed to be significantly impaired.

Tier 2: for a breakdown in health that is not considered to leave you permanently incapable of gainful employment, although your employment prospects are deemed to be significantly impaired.

Tier 3: for a breakdown in health which it is deemed leaves you permanently incapable of any further full-time employment.

Even now, I feel emotionally saddened about this experience but then the anger and disappointment kicks in and outweighs it. I was confused as to why this Colonel had said these words to me as this planted a seed of doubt which made me question my loyalty. This was something that I found emotionally difficult to process as I had sacrificed so much in my military career, so I chose to deny his advice and convinced myself that the British Army, the Ministry of Defence, the Government would return the unconditional loyalty that I had unreservedly given them. I convinced myself they would see me right and award me the compensation that my injuries warranted. Regrettably, like many servicemen who had been injured beforehand, my loyalty would not be reciprocated and along with my ongoing physical and mental health battles, I would now enter into a war against the very institution to which I had given most of my life.

Whilst attending a compulsory multi-activity course in Cyprus as part of the army's Recovery Capability Programme, I remember being part of an awkward conversation with the rest of the injured soldiers. This course was designed to provide injured service personnel with the confidence to manage or overcome their injuries. The main purpose was to return as many soldiers to service as possible, however, on my course, we were all being medically discharged within the next twelve months, so this was nothing more than a bit of a holiday for us. This particular course consisted of a dozen or so students from various backgrounds and ranks with different injuries and was run through Battle Back at Headley Court.

On this type of course, there is no rank and everyone is referred to on a first-name basis. I remember finding this somewhat awkward as there were private soldiers as well as a Colonel in attendance and my background was in 'The Guards' where everyone was referred to by rank...always! Regardless of this, it worked enormously well and after a few days, we were all relaxed in each other's company. I recall that after a day's fishing, a military photographer wanted a picture of the course to document our catch. This was not unusual, but he was insistent that all the amputees had shorts on and were front and centre to show off their injuries. It was at this point that one of the lads snapped, went into a swearing fit, and ran off in tears! Maybe he has Tourette's, I thought to myself?

The soldier in question had some burns to his arms and torso that he had managed to successfully cover up with tattoos and they were barely even noticeable. Maybe he was embarrassed about his burns? However, I would later discover that he was also suffering from PTSD, a hidden injury. When chatting with him the following day, he explained to me that throughout his recovery, all the amputees got all the attention and that the Army, the Armed Forces Compensation Scheme and now, even this photographer had all failed to acknowledge his poor mental health. He told me about his experiences, and I shared my own only to be told that 'I was more fucked up than him,' a realisation that I denied and quickly laughed off. After all, I was attending this course with a spinal injury, I didn't suffer from PTSD; I wasn't weak! I still perceived myself as a Colour

Sergeant in the Infantry, or perhaps I was ashamed of my poor and deteriorating mental health, but all things considered, I was in denial.

Later that evening, amongst the other injured servicemen, we had a very difficult conversation between ourselves regarding how the world sees and treats our injured soldiers. We concluded that the system is back to front. Yes, it was terrible that some soldiers lost limbs, yet, these injured boys and girls seem to get the best of medical treatment, quickest and best compensation and are always acknowledged by society because of their visible injuries. Like the photo the previous day, all emphasis was on the amputees with their visible injuries and due to the nature of their visible injury, they appeared to always be the priority. Some of the amputees mentioned that they had received preferential treatment within their units and were now on first name terms with some of their senior officers, post injury of course.

Next was the musculoskeletal and spinal injuries like mine. These consisted of legs, arms, back and neck injuries and were attributable for the majority of medical discharges. This is not surprising due to the heavy amount of weight that we were required to carry. Consideration must also be given to the high intensity of all physical training that was conducted at the time. There was no such thing as strength and conditioning training let alone recovery sessions. Most of us shared stories of our individual experiences but we all had one common denominator - the 'man up' culture within the British Army. As a result of poor management, every one of us had cracked on with our injuries and this had ultimately led us to this recovery course and our impending discharge.

I believe that as a subculture, The British Army throughout my generation had become fixated on amputees and that all other injuries were an afterthought. It was this attitude of refusing to accept an injury unless it was visible that had a negative impact on soldiers such as myself. In Afghanistan, I would frequently be at the hospital, whether on duty or visiting my injured friends. How could I complain about back pain when these guys were missing limbs or had bullet holes in them? Let's not forget that when I did complain, I was ridiculed, called a charlatan and a coward by my senior commanders.

My experience as a senior non-commissioned officer of the non-acceptance of my injury was nowhere near as bad as what some of the junior ranks had faced. Nevertheless, this was institutional failure by all levels of command, and I cannot help but wonder where this medical negligence originated from. At this point, I personally always carried with me an MRI scan of my bulging discs on my phone to visually justify my injury to anyone who asked about it. Even today, this is still the case as I still feel that I must provide visible evidence of my spinal injury to avoid any stigma. I still feel that I have to show visible proof to avoid being referred to as a charlatan and a fraud and this is a consequence of the poor leadership that I experienced.

On discharge, I would request my medical documents and find that my physiotherapist in Afghanistan had identified my back symptoms as being a disc problem, yet this wasn't acted on. Why? I believe that this was due to the operational needs being prioritised over the individuals. Let us not forget that the Army's needs always came before the soldiers and the medical personnel in Afghanistan were soldiers, after all. Thus, they would willingly fulfil the Army's needs.

This short-sighted medical approach has had a detrimental long-lasting impact on far too many veterans' lives as many of their life-changing injuries, like my own, could have been prevented with adequate medical care. One must also acknowledge the failure of commanders who were under impossible pressure to also maintain their operational manning. This put an immense burden on the soldiers to ignore their injuries, ignore their pain. This is what they had been taught and they are selfless, and like me, they were loyal, so this is what we did; we were indoctrinated after all. Consideration must also be given to the soldier's mindset on operations. I often felt completely numb, an empty shell, machine-like, and this was instrumental in masking my pain.

Finally, there are those with the worst type of injury that we discussed, those with poor mental health, those with demons, those suffering with PTSD. It was heart-breaking listening to the personal struggles of these soldiers and how all of them had been alienated and rejected by their units. Some were now tearful, others enraged as they shared their personal brutal stories and experiences. One thing was clear to me - even back then, mental health and PTSD were still not being taken seriously by the British Army and those who bravely came forward were often victimised by their senior commanders.

We all agreed that despite having lost their limb, or limbs in some cases, that the amputees received the best treatment in all aspects in relation to their injury. Nothing could replace that limb, but the acceptance from society, appreciation and gratitude from their colleagues, second to none medical care and an undisputed financial package certainly helped. In short, from this particular conversation, it was the immediate acceptance of their very visible injury that seemed to benefit them, especially regarding their mental health. However, when discussing this, two of the single lower leg amputees discovered that they had received very different levels of compensation for their mirroring injuries! Was this a clerical error or was the Armed Forces Compensation Scheme not fit for purpose? I would later discover the latter to be more accurate but was too loyal and naïve at the time to really question this.

We then discussed those suffering from PTSD and, even in 2014, had identified that there was a severe lack of understanding within the current military culture regarding the acceptance of poor mental health. All of those who had raised their concerns about their internal battles were initially ignored. It was only after bouts of alcohol abuse, self-harming or failed suicide attempts that they were actually taken seriously. These service personnel felt rejected by society and their units, abandoned by the very institution that had sent them to war. When finally having the courage to admit that they needed assistance, their cries for help were ignored and they were told to 'man up.' One must look at this from the indoctrinated junior ranks perspective; if they were told that they didn't have PTSD and to 'man up', then they would try to do exactly that, but at what cost?

I remember that after we discussed mental health, battlefield trauma and the lack of acceptance within military culture, the conversation quickly turned dark, with those suffering from PTSD offering a limb in return for a cure for their mental health. Strangely, the amputees were not willing to trade a miraculous full limb replacement for a life of psychological suffering. It was then that, as a collective, we understood the frustration surrounding soldiers and veterans struggling with their mental health and inner demons. Their invisible wounds were not more or less important than those with a visible injury; they simply wanted equal recognition for the hidden pain they were suffering as a direct consequence of their military service. Acceptance was vital to them and I can now understand their frustrations when managing their hidden wounds. It was due to this difficult conversation that we decided that those suffering from PTSD had the worst of the three injury groups as these unfortunate soldiers are constantly questioned about their injury, constantly scrutinised. They do not receive anywhere near the same amount of acknowledgement from society or their military units and would like the same acceptance for their sacrifice!

I believe that this is derived from the fundamental basic training point that emotions are regarded as weakness. As such, by the same definition, poor mental health is weakness, therefore, these soldiers suffering from PTSD are justifiably weak. This would explain the familiar alienation and rejection that many of these soldiers experienced from their units. Far too often, these soldiers would be compared with others who apparently 'had it much worse on operations' and they were ok, so their issues were ignored. Then there are the stories of the senior non-commissioned officers who failed to acknowledge their battlefield trauma because 'they had done more in their day' and this negative response and attitude would further exacerbate their PTSD.

I am not attempting to compare injuries or prioritise them, for that matter; this conversation was simply a reflection of what this group of injured soldiers discussed at the time. It then became apparent that all of the amputees had already received vast lump sums from the Armed Forces Compensation Scheme and had impressive pension forecasts to match, whereas the remainder of us were promised this on discharge. This was due to the fact that many, like me, were having ongoing treatment and that on discharge, a decision would be made. Looking back at this with hindsight, this should have triggered several red flags, but I was too loyal to see them or acknowledge them at the time. Maybe this denial was part of my own battle with my own rapidly deteriorating mental health, as this was something that I wanted to be kept hidden for as long as possible.

Reflecting back on my own discharge process, I believe that I was fortunate as I had an understanding wife, friends, my own house and was starting a new adventure at university the following month. More importantly, though, I had secured my pension due to serving over eighteen years. Plus, I was on the more financially favourable Armed Forces Pension Scheme 1975. This immediate monthly income from my pension would allow me to amend the mistakes of my youth and gain an education at university. It would also allow me time to recover from my latest spinal surgery and discover what career I would undertake in the future. I was still optimistically loyal and waiting for my promised Armed Forces Compensation Scheme claim. I had anticipated that this should increase my pension, or, at the very least, grant me a lump sum for my injury. Generally speaking, I was hopeful about my future civilian life.

I say that I was fortunate, but this had nothing to do with the military. This was my doing and it had nothing to do with chance. I had bought a house in Manchester long before I was married and had a very low mortgage. I had always been married unaccompanied and had segregated my family from my military life and this allowed stability for my wife and daughter. Unlike those married soldiers who had lived in military quarters close to the barracks, my family had an established support network, and this was pivotal. I was always planning for life after the military, a civilian life that was worlds apart from what I had experienced as a child. However, most soldiers who went through the medical discharge process were not as fortunate and the reasons behind this need to be discussed.

I had been a senior non-commissioned officer, I was 35 years old and had life experience and had a stable family environment to fall back onto, but what about the junior ranks, what about the private soldiers? From my experiences as a Recruiter and a Welfare Officer, it had become apparent that the majority of Infantry soldiers had come from broken homes like myself. They were, more often than not, from lower income families or those on benefits and the military had provided these kids with a way out. Furthermore, this escape route to a better life had also given them a new identity and the respect of the soldier. Now on medical discharge, where would they go and what would they do?

Let us not forget that the majority of junior soldiers were generally under 25 years old, had lived in service accommodation and did not own their own homes. Additionally, throughout the prolonged 'war on terror' in Iraq and Afghanistan, it was these junior ranks, mainly the private soldiers, who bore the brunt of the fighting. As a result of this, it comes as no surprise that the junior ranks also bore the brunt of the casualties too. So, what happened to these injured soldiers on medical discharge? Unfortunately, they generally returned to the same home and lifestyle that they had once tried to escape.

This more often than not had a negative impact on them and for many different reasons. Initially, these soldiers felt lost and abandoned as their identity was stripped away from them. We must also consider the military mindset where they are taught to cage their emotions. John, a veteran from Atherton, explained that his identity was fixated around the Army's slogan of 'Be the Best'. He had received commendations whilst serving but after a distressing rocket attack in Iraq, he began to struggle with his own battlefield trauma and had turned to alcohol as a coping mechanism. John believed that due to his deteriorating mental health and loss of identity, as a civilian, he was now by definition 'the worst.' As 'the worst', he would turn to drugs and gambling and would even contemplate suicide. I was intrigued by this notion surrounding the word association of a simple recruiting slogan and how this could define a veteran later on in civilian life.

In many cases, in the environment that these soldiers originated from (like my own), drink and drug misuse were a common normal occurrence. When these soldiers leave the military, they are seeking acceptance and more often than not rebel against the strict military disciplines associated with their previous lost identity. Bearing in mind that many veterans feel abandoned on medical discharge, it is no surprise that they reject the military values and turn to drugs and alcohol. This would more often than not lead to criminality, prison, or homelessness. Carl, a veteran from Wigan, shamefully explained how he ended up on the streets as he was too proud to seek help. Then, the unthinkable happened - Carl began to use drugs which, in turn, led to a life of criminality. Fortunately, Carl sought help and is now in a more stable place, he has a flat and a job and has turned his life around. I personally, at times, have used alcohol too as a coping mechanism for both my physical and mental pain. I understand how easy it can be to fall into a vicious cycle of substance abuse when denying the very existence of poor mental health, trauma, and PTSD.

In the months building up to my own medical discharge, I became very active within my own veterans' community. I had joined the local branch of the Royal British Legion and was also attending several injured veteran support groups. Initially, I was bemused as to why my generation were not engaging with the British Legion as I was by far the youngest member in my branch. I would later conclude that the modern veteran, who generally left the military under their own accord and were in sound mental and physical health, had become disgruntled with the treatment of our veterans, their brethren. The culmination of historic prosecutions, veteran suicides, and the poor treatment of the injured were being spread via social media and had left a bitter taste. Then, although a charity, the British Legion was associated with the military due to its formal nature, and this was an unwanted reminder of military life for some.

The injured veteran support groups were a totally different kettle of fish altogether. These were mostly organised through Help for Heroes and had a devastating impact on my own mental health. The majority of conversations at these events consisted of broken promises by the Ministry of Defence and by the Armed Forces Compensation Scheme. I was still blindly loyal, but the reality of post-military life was dawning, and I was gradually losing my confidence in the system. The common denominator was that all of these veterans would have to fight tooth and nail for a fraction of the compensation to which they were entitled.

When I was medically discharged, my Armed Forces Compensation Scheme claim was already 4 years old. I had received a lump sum award of £10,000 in 2012 as I was expected to make a full recovery after my first micro-discectomy. At the time I was quite happy with this and used the money for some laser eye surgery for Jayne and myself. This was later changed to an interim award as I didn't fully recover and was undergoing further treatments. Now, three years later and after another failed micro-discectomy, my spine had been fused. This had consisted of removing a disk, fitting two spacers in its place then bolting everything together and had been conducted six months prior to my discharge. As a result of this, my own claim would not be settled until twelve months post-surgery which I thought at the time made complete sense despite the legislation stating otherwise.

My pain levels increased post-discharge as I gradually began to let go of my military identity. Colour Sergeant Watson was slowly becoming a civilian and I was now under NHS treatment after being referred by my GP to a pain management team. I diligently updated the Armed Forces Compensation Scheme with all of my medical evidence and procedures which would only delay the outcome of my claim even further, as, under their legislation, they would not conclude a case until all medical treatment had plateaued. Unbeknown to me at the time, my treatment would never plateau and would only continue to deteriorate. I remember being excited when a brown letter came in the post six months after my discharge. This was the letter we had been waiting for. I recall that Jayne and I were very optimistic, but this sudden burst of euphoria was short-lived as the letter stated that I would be reviewed again in an additional twelve months. I remember noticing that this delayed process was also having a harmful impact on my wife's mental health. It was also affecting my family!

It is imperative that we consider my fortunate financial circumstances; due to my time served in the Army, I had already accumulated an instant pension and Jayne was also working. We lived dull lifestyles well within our financial means and had additional savings with no debts. I was in no condition to work as I was still undergoing rehabilitation, although I was attending university, but this was in a limited capacity. Overall, we were financially sound due to my nineteen years' service and instant pension. The reason that I mention this is because there are those soldiers who are discharged who are not as privileged enough to have secured their immediate pensions. What about those who may not have a source of income? What about those who, like me, couldn't work due to ongoing rehabilitation? What would these veterans do with not only being stripped of their identity, but their mobility and now finances? How would this affect their mental health?

By the time this twelve-month review came around (18 months post-discharge), I had unfortunately damaged another disc in my back. This was a direct consequence of my spinal fusion and is referred to as adjacent disc syndrome.[lxxiii] This is the result of additional stress that overloads the upper and lower vertebrae of a spinal fusion, forcing the intervertebral discs to break down. In my case, this was the disc above, the L5/S1 disc. A month after suffering this injury whilst helping my daughter wash her hands, I felt like I was back at square one and this was really exacerbating my mental health. I was suppressing two decades of battlefield trauma and the only thing keeping me together was the prospect of financial compensation for the loss of career, identity, and the seven years of physical pain that I had by this point suffered. Then came another brown letter from the Armed Forces Compensation Scheme; finally, some good news. Unfortunately, this was not to be the case.

The letter we received was in January 2017 but was dated 20 December 2016. It categorically stated that after a thorough review of all of the medical evidence, the original level 12 award of £10,000 from 2012 would now become my final award. This was the appropriate award for my spinal injury, one that I was expected to make a full recovery from. The letter stated that medical evidence was attained from the pain management team based on the premise that I was managing my pain, was attending the gym and was active. I was broken, disheartened, lost. We both were.

This evidence was subjective and only told half of the story. I had been moved on from the pain management team as they couldn't do anything for me once I had damaged another disc. Yes, I was frequently attending the gym, but conducting medical rehabilitation that kept me active and able to function. I had been open, honest, and loyal with the Armed Forces Compensation Scheme and had diligently and frequently kept them updated with my medical progression. This would be my final award and the amount I received would not change! Well, that was that, I thought. Then the rage and anger kicked in. Jayne was in tears as she couldn't comprehend how they could treat her proud husband, a twenty-year veteran like this. However, I was more concerned with the wider impact on the veterans' community. What about those junior ranks who had gone through a similar process to me? How would they cope and what would they do if they received this devastating news?

I thought back to what the Colonel had said to me on my full medical board about not accepting the first offer. 'Well, we'd be stupid to accept this,' I joked to Jayne attempting to put a smile on her devastated face. After all, we could really do a lot with £0, but she didn't laugh. Jayne was a nurse but had two degrees, one in nursing and the other in sports rehabilitation. She was aware of the impact and limitations of my injury and I was aware of the impact that it had had on my family dynamic. Rather than the focus being around my young daughter, all consideration was always prioritised towards me and my physical limitations. This is something that I still resent as my daughter's needs should always be our priority rather than my own.

From listening to other injured veterans' struggles against the Armed Forces Compensation Scheme, it was evident that this was just part of the process. The next phase would be to appeal and request a tribunal. I acknowledged this but felt utterly defeated and had little confidence in this process. I was going to a dark place; I knew that I had underlying emotional issues and thought that I was managing them, but this process was allowing my battlefield trauma to feed on my anger, my disappointment. I despised my new mindset as I was becoming bitter and regretful towards the British Army and my service and this was not who I wanted to be as a civilian. If this was the process, then where was the integrity, the respect, the loyalty? I had a loving stable family, and this process was having a destructive effect on my relationship with my wife. It was damaging my family and I was ready to call it a day and give up.

Then, I thought about all of the junior ranks again, those who had been through a similar process. I never imagined that I would be treated so badly after almost two decades of unwavering service to my country. If I was mentally and emotionally broken and had decided to give up, how would they respond to such news? If this was simply the process, how many veterans had already or would give up in the future at being told that their claims were finalised without the correct compensations that their injuries justified? This motivated me to appeal and request a tribunal. I wasn't expecting to win but to learn from the experience so that I could pass on the knowledge to other veterans to learn from.

When I composed myself, I thought back to my medical board and the tier 2 discharge that I was categorised under. This had essentially guaranteed me a claim between the tariff scales of 7-11, yet my final award was a lower award of level 12, the interim award from 2012. It was at this point that I began to do my own research, as so far, I had put my trust into a system that was designed to abuse that trust and loyalty. It wasn't long before I found Ministry of Defence guidelines that stated that a tier 2 discharge also ensured a monthly guaranteed income payment (a medical pension) as well as a lump sum. This find left me shocked and appalled at the incompetence of the bureaucrats behind the faceless Armed Forces Compensation Scheme and would further exacerbate my now noticeable deteriorating mental health. I, like many other injured veterans, now felt utterly betrayed.

It would be exactly three years and four days after I was medically discharged that I would attend a tribunal regarding my claim on 23 August 2018. I had been carrying this injury for eight years and it had gradually been getting worse. In fact, the following month, I was due to have another operation, the first of three, to have a spinal cord stimulator fitted for pain management. I had been appointed a representative from the Royal British Legion and looking back, I wish that I would have paid for a qualified solicitor as he was only a subject matter expert and was completely out of his depth.

My initial back injury in Afghanistan had developed into a spinal injury that had affected my legs. In my medical notes, there was evidence of foot drop, numbness, and weakness in my legs and this was evident as I now needed a cane to assist me when walking. My legs would uncontrollably give way, often without warning. I was a shadow of the soldier I once was, yet I still put on my regimental blazer and tie, wore my seven medals and beret, and was determined for the Ministry of Defence to acknowledge my injuries. I had constantly questioned the legitimacy of my injuries as the Ministry of Defence had effectively denied their existence. This didn't help my mental health but by now I was finally seeking therapy for my battlefield trauma. I had explained to my therapist that I often thought that I was, in fact, making up these injuries; that I was a charlatan after all. Personally, it was not about compensation anymore, as I have never been motivated by money. All I wanted was for the Ministry of Defence, the Army, my Regiment, and all those who questioned my integrity to openly acknowledge my injuries.

The tribunal itself was the most horrific experience of my life. Even now, three years later, I still get frustrated when speaking about this experience. To begin with, there is a judge who is in charge and representing the Secretary of State. She was supported by a medical doctor and a former military officer for advice. Then, there is a representative from the Armed Forces Compensation Scheme who was representing the Ministry of Defence. Normally, a decision is pre-determined, and this process takes fifteen minutes as everyone has seen all of the case files beforehand. In my case, it was over 2 hours long. I had prepared individual medical files to argue the case for a level 7 award that incorporated my foot drop and damage to my legs and handed them out. I was prepared but still somewhat loyal, obedient, and lacking any legal experience.

The judge raised the issue of my spinal fusion and that this had established 'permanent and significant functional limitations'. It was this wording that would determine a higher award under a limited category of traumatic back injuries from the rigid tariff tables within the Armed Forces Compensation Scheme legislation. Next, the representative from the Armed Forces Compensation Scheme then put an argument forward that as I was still receiving ongoing treatment for my original injury, then his award was still valid. This was due to the wording of this award that specified 'significant functional limitations beyond 13 weeks', but still under the category of traumatic back injuries. His argument was based on the lack of a cut-off period to this award and had a valid argument, especially as I was due to have further surgery the following month. However, the award was founded on an L5 nerve root compression as a result of the intervertebral disc that had been removed as part of my L4/5 spinal fusion. Thus, his argument lacked any substantial credibility as that intervertebral disc was no longer there!

I was then given the chance to speak after I had dismissed my representative from the British Legion. Within the files that I had previously distributed, I put forward an argument that I had, in fact, had a spinal injury due to my subsequent foot drop, numbness and weakness in my legs but this seemed to fall on deaf ears. This consisted of all extracts from my medical documents. The representative from the Armed Forces Compensation Scheme eventually admitted that they had wrongly assessed me on discharge and that I would be awarded a level 9 tariff which was in the tier 2 range. When he admitted this incompetence, I completely lost it and the tribunal was forced to have a 15-minute recess so that I could cool off. This should have been awarded on discharge and I had sent several letters to them stating such, yet it had taken three years and a tribunal to get this far. Where was the accountability for the trauma that this incompetence had caused to my family?!

I recall that after Jayne had managed to calm me down, we were asked back into the court. The mental health of both of us had suffered as a result of this delaying process. I now made another case for a higher award, one that would incorporate the nerve damage and lack of mobility to my legs, but yet again, the judge didn't want to listen. The judge didn't like the fact that I wasn't happy with her pre-determined award, but I didn't care. All I wanted was the acknowledgement of the damage to my legs and the impact that this had had on my wider family; acknowledgement of how, post-discharge, my injury had drastically deteriorated.

Eventually, the judge imprinted her authority and gave me a choice. I either accept the final award from the Armed Forces Compensation Scheme from 2012, or her award that was taken from the point of discharge and failed to acknowledge all of my post-service medical decline. I chose neither as this still failed to acknowledge the severity of my injury and was asked to leave the court to cool off yet again. My adviser from the British Legion then informed me that it was in my best interest to accept the judge's award as this would mean a lump sum of £30,000 and maybe a small increase in my pension. I wasn't motivated by money; I couldn't be bought. I just wanted the Ministry of Defence to acknowledge the harmful consequences of my twenty years' service and six operational tours, not just on me but also on my wider family and future civilian life. I thought about the morgue in Kosovo, the airstrike in Iraq and the futility of Afghanistan and this was making me significantly more enraged and was clouding my judgement. However, Jayne, for the second time, managed to calm me down despite also being emotionally drained and stressed.

We couldn't have done more to prepare for this day. Three years of delays, three years of rejections, only to be informed that all of our suffering had been the result of a mistake on the part of the Armed Forces Compensation Scheme. Disappointed, I admitted to myself that I was beaten, I couldn't win, so I begrudgingly accepted the judge's award. The judge then commended me on my strong argument for a higher award and informed me that she couldn't categorise me as a spinal injury as there was not enough medical evidence to support this decision. Therefore, my previous final award surrounding the nerve root damage was upscaled and categorised as a back injury. Yes, I had been partially successful and had been awarded a lump sum of £30,000, and one should not forget the generous medical pension of £7 per week. This didn't feel like a victory and I couldn't help but think to myself, 'Has this torture been worth all this?' The lump sum wasn't even a year's salary and was the equivalent to what the civil servants in the career's office had received having been made redundant several years earlier.

The following month, I was having spinal surgery despite apparently not having a spinal injury and this got me thinking; firstly, to what the Colonel at my med board had said about not accepting the first offer. I believed this was my first offer and as such would seek ways to appeal. Secondly, what the judge had said to me regarding the lack of medical evidence. All of the evidence was in my medical documents but not from a neurological or spinal specialist. I still have trouble comprehending why the diagnosis and recommendations of standard physiotherapists were not sufficient. At the time of writing this, I have appealed this decision but have added further in-depth medical information from neurological physiotherapists and a nerve conduction study. Both of these specifically highlighted the nerve damage that stemmed from the compression of my spinal canal that has resulted in my drop foot, numbness, and weak legs. I was never assessed by the Ministry of Defence once discharged and, in my experience, the Armed Forces Compensation Scheme is fundamentally biased and lacks objectivity. All I still want is the acknowledgement of the severity of my injury from the Ministry of Defence for my own mental wellbeing which is why I continue to fight this.

I would share my limited success amongst the injured veterans' community and apparently, this was, yet again, part of the process. I have no doubt that this process had exacerbated my own poor mental health and I was left, in no uncertain terms, broken by the whole ordeal. I couldn't help but think about the dark places where I had occasionally gone throughout my battle with the Ministry of Defence. I was deeply concerned about the psychological toll that this had taken on me, and, without the support of my wife and daughter, I may not have had the strength to fight it. This got me thinking yet again how lucky I was to have them, but more so about those who didn't have this support. What about the junior ranks?

What about these junior ranks who just accept their first awards? What about those junior ranks suffering with PTSD or just poor mental health in general after a medical discharge and who don't have the support or the resolve to keep pursuing their claims? What about those junior ranks who may not have an immediate pension and can't work due to ongoing medical issues; how do they survive?

I fundamentally believe, from interviewing other injured veterans and from my own experience, that the system is designed to favour the Ministry of Defence and that by putting so many barriers in place, they want injured veterans to stop pursuing their claims for compensation. It is this system that has helped forge a discord between injured veterans and society; after all, when it comes to veterans' welfare, our voices are far too often silenced by the Government through media blackouts.

I still want the Ministry of Defence to recognise the damage to my legs and it is this blatant denial of my injuries that continues to motivate me. I had lost a good friend earlier that year who had been another victim of war. He was battling internal demons and had been diagnosed with mild PTSD, but this was far from the case. Like myself, he had struggled to cope due to the Ministry of Defence's lack of acknowledgement regarding the severity of his trauma. Unfortunately, like far too many of my brethren, the bureaucrats within the Armed Forces Compensation Scheme have blood on their hands as they have had a direct influence on far too many veteran suicides. The Armed Forces Compensation Scheme favours the Ministry of Defence, and, throughout my own five years of appeals, it has caused irreparable damage to the image of the British Army. In the information age, through the use of social media, our stories are being shared and this has, and will continue to damage the British Army's ability to not only recruit but more significantly, retain its soldiers. More importantly, though, it continues to damage the mental health of our veterans and for too many, a combination of the loss of identity, abandonment and now the denial of their injuries has proved to have fatal consequences.

John, Wade, myself, and Frank. Xmas ball 2007.

Collecting my Student Ambassador Award 2018.

The 'Manchester Micks' at the Etihad Stadium for Remembrance in 2012.

Graduation with Jayne and Mara

Myself and Jayne in summer 2010.

Chapter 16.
Don't Look Back in Anger

After my full medical board, it was apparent that my military career was coming to an end. My only concern was what now, how would I be able to provide for my family and what would I do next? I had been a soldier for my whole adult life; it was all I knew. In fact, however, I had been a soldier for the majority of my life - this was who I was, it had defined me. I wasn't a Mr Watson, I was Colour Sergeant Watson, a tough robust Infantry soldier! What skills did I have to offer in the civilian world? I now had twelve months to mentally adjust, to adapt to this new deployment. I still had the mindset of a soldier and would tackle this head-on! I would succeed; I wouldn't be defeated.

Being at a personal recovery unit had given me perspective as I was living at home in Manchester for my final twelve months of service. This allowed me to gradually shed the skin of my given institutionalised military identity and evolve into my new civilian one. Normally, if I was in my unit, I would be working until my last day when my terminal leave kicked in. I had even witnessed colleagues sign waivers to enable them to deploy on operations throughout their final 12 months which was against military policy, but the operational demands of my generation were always prioritised and the soldiers obediently put the Army's needs before their own.

I have always had a 'will to win' mentality but on leaving the Army under a medical discharge, this had changed. I was struggling with rejection and abandonment issues as I felt that I was forced out, discarded, broken, and this was due to my physical injury. Soldiers would like to believe that they are in control of their destiny and their actions or they wouldn't be able to cope with the operational stresses and life-depending tough decisions whilst on deployments. This 'will to win' attitude is essential for operational success; however, I was now feeling doubtful, unsure, and afraid of the future and this changed my outlook to a more negative 'fear of failure' mindset.

I was no longer looking to the future with optimism and confidence but with concern and doubt. This was solely due to my injury as I, and only I knew the severity of it. I had been desperately hiding the true nature of my injury for the past four years in a desperate attempt to cling onto the identity of the soldier. Now, I had to accept my disappointment, my perceived failure as a soldier and being forcibly thrown out of the military haven that had defined me as a man. This was taking its toll emotionally and was engaging with and reminding me of my caged PTSD. Let us not forget that it was my identity as a soldier, my armour, that was enabling me to suppress my dormant emotional trauma. I had anxiety when thinking about the future and what would happen when I gradually let go of this armour, this identity.

As a proven coping mechanism, I decided to throw myself into work in an attempt to distract myself from my negative thoughts. I would volunteer at organisations such as the Prince's Trust as a mentor for young people. This allowed me to wear my uniform once more, my armour, and was a temporary fix. I would then complete my Career Transitions Workshop at Fulwood Barracks in Preston and I was very optimistic about this course. Personally, this course was a waste of time for me as it was basically a CV-writing exercise. It did, however, provide links to job fairs and favourable businesses that preferred to employ veterans. Unfortunately, this wasn't suitable for my personal circumstances due to my injury. Besides, I was now waiting on further surgery to have my spine fused which would add further uncertainty and doubt towards my future employment prospects.

Whilst attending this brief course, it soon became apparent that the main focus was on future employment and gaining new skills for life after the military. This is not necessarily a bad thing but, depending on how long you had served, dictated the accessibility and the level of support that was available. As a result of serving over nineteen years, luckily, I was given the maximum amount of resettlement benefits. This included an intriguing option that the Ministry of Defence would fully subsidise the cost of university fees. I had always regretted my youth and not fulfilling my potential at school. I didn't have any A levels and was fascinated at the prospect of attaining a degree, but how and in what field?

The prospect of higher educational study excited me, but I was also aware that my inner demons were beginning to surface throughout this transition to civilian life. Maybe, by throwing myself into study and keeping my mind active, I thought to myself, I would be able to contain my suppressed emotions from my battlefield experiences. I was pleasantly surprised when I was accepted on a course at the Political History Department at Salford University. This consisted of two sister courses - one in Contemporary Political and International History and the other being Contemporary

Military and International History. I applied for the latter and was successful due to the civilian accreditations that I had acquired from my command and leadership courses, but mainly through my lived experience on the subject. This new venture post-service provided me with a new purpose, one that would hopefully help keep my bubbling inner demons at bay.

Mental health was always taboo in my experiences of soldiering, so it came as no surprise that no mental health awareness training was included as part of my resettlement process. Even now, this seems negligent and would explain why so many soldiers suffer with their mental health on the return to civilian life. My generation of soldiers were exposed to brutal behavioural training methods that indoctrinated us, changed our perceptions, and pushed us to our physical and mental limits. We were drones in a hive that were relentlessly deployed on operations around the globe with little rest in between. Our core values deemed us to prioritise the greater good, the British Army's needs above our own and that is exactly what we did. The Infantry's behavioural training methods had finally been perfected and we were testament to this.

Emotionally, we were broken and in pain and we were all hurting from our experiences, whether some admitted it or not. Our training had allowed us, through 'controlled aggression', to turn from calm to killer then back again on command, without hesitation, without thought. How would this destructive mindset adapt after our service ended? Surely, there would be some form of de-escalation training to help us understand and cope with the different demands of the civilian world. Sadly not. The priority was exclusively to promote job opportunities and then, on the final day, we were informed of what charity support was available in civilian life. Charities! Where was the support from the Government? Help for Heroes, for example, didn't send me to war so why were they now responsible for my wellbeing? Where was the support from the Ministry of Defence, the Government?

After my spinal fusion in February 2015, Jayne had noticed a mood change in me. I was having trouble coping with my inner demons. My ongoing struggle with my battlefield experiences was pushing closer to the surface the nearer I was getting to becoming a civilian. I was still ashamed that I was struggling with my mental health and was determined that I was not going to admit it, that I was fine; this was weakness, after all. However, I was also struggling with my mental health regarding the loss of my military identity, plus accepting my new physical limitations. As a child, I had excelled at sports and martial arts. In the military, I had represented my Battalion playing rugby, hockey and skiing and had competed in athletics. I had always been proud of my high levels of fitness and this was part of my character, my personality, it was who I was. I was painfully losing my military identity but also struggling with the new physical limitations of being disabled and Jayne had started to take notice of this.

I remember talking to Jayne about this and she suggested that I seek help. I spoke to her in-depth about how I was struggling mentally with not being able to play sports, to run, to even acknowledge that I was now disabled. I had even begun to loathe myself due to the fact that family days out were limited by my mobility and pain needs. However, this was good as it distracted Jayne away from my true pain, my loss of identity and underlying suppressed emotions. We discussed seeking help from a sports psychiatrist, but I didn't pursue it; I didn't want to. I thought at the time that discussing part of my deteriorating mental health was a sufficient way of managing it. When I was diagnosed with PTSD, I became very open about it as I believed that it would encourage others to seek help, to break free from the perceived negative military relationship with mental health. This would not necessarily be the case; however, several veterans did open up to me about their own experiences whilst completing this book which is a good start.

Every veteran's journey is unique, but we are all fearful of the cliff edge that is civilian life. I had always laughed off the claims that we were all indoctrinated and institutionalised as I had always segregated my personal life from my military one. Some veterans found the Career Transition Workshop beneficial and it was a useful bridge, allowing us to retrain, network and find future employment. However, if you are injured and facing ongoing medical rehabilitation on discharge, your options become limited. Each journey is unique with many success stories, but, unfortunately for many, this was just a CV-writing exercise.

Kenny left the Army in December 2012, and refers to the process of the Career Transition Workshop as 'a complete waste of time' and also, like myself, he thought it was just a CV-writing exercise. The only thing that had been beneficial from his experience was to set up a 'LinkedIn' account. Kenny had already decided to retrain as a gas engineer and knew what he wanted to do as a civilian. He 'successfully' transitioned into civilian life but took up immediate employment for a military housing sub-contractor. Kenny's new role would be to repair boilers in service quarters which allowed him to still be associated with military life and as such, he was still able to retain part of his military identity by working in a familiar military environment.

When asked if he received any education prior to discharge regarding his own mental health, he replied with the expected answer of 'no.' However, he did mention that on his final medical before leaving the British Army, which was bizarrely six months after he had left, he was offered mental health support. Ironically, this offer was only for a six-month period and had now expired. Unbeknown to Kenny, or just hidden deep down, like many of my generation, Kenny was suppressing his own inner demons from his vast operational deployments and this would eventually be triggered by a life-changing event to come.

Kenny also mentioned that on arrival, all of his paperwork had previously been filled out and that he had an apparent clean bill of health. He immediately and angrily corrected this Colonel from the Army Medical Corps, due to the fact that he was no longer that obedient soldier, and insisted that his final medical was corrected to echo the truth. His hearing had deteriorated since his first deployment to Iraq and he had also been suffering with a back injury in the latter years of his military service. I found this very interesting and couldn't help but wonder how many veterans had put in failed compensation claims for injuries sustained in service, but who, like Kenny, apparently had a miraculous clean bill of health? How many of these claims were delayed or denied due to poor or complacent military administration and what was the harmful impact on the mental health of these veteran's post-service?

When discussing mental health, Kenny then courageously spoke about his own battles, how he now struggles with his own mental health due to trauma from his lived experiences as a soldier. He painfully explained that after a recent heart attack, emotionally, he has not been the same since, how, in the days afterwards, he would just burst into tears for no apparent reason whatsoever. Even now, certain triggers from TV cause him to emotionally break down. Kenny is not alone as many of my brethren have spoken about similar such experiences, but unfortunately, like Kenny, they refuse to seek professional help, and this was due to the way that we were trained. My generation of soldiers would rather struggle with poor mental health than openly admit to themselves that they are suffering with PTSD. This stems from our training and the association of emotions being weakness. Kenny, like many veterans, may have lost his uniform and military identity, but this detrimental mindset remained. With no mental health management or awareness training being offered post-service, this comes as no surprise.

Kenny then spoke of his vast experiences throughout his 25 years' service, initially as an Infantryman and then as an armourer. He had worked with many different Regiments and units but there was an obvious pattern regarding mental health. From Kenny's experiences, the command element was not interested in dealing with the issue of mental health. This was not necessarily related to PTSD from operations but all types of mental health including depression and trauma. Kenny had experience of soldiers suffering with poor mental health being segregated from their units, sent on sick leave for 12-18 months, or never to be seen or heard from again. They were quarantined; treated like they had an infectious disease that may spread to the other soldiers. I can only imagine how harmful this process would have been for those unfortunate soldiers as their brethren would have undoubtedly supported them but were never given the opportunity to do so.

Due to the fact that I was recovering from spinal surgery, I wasn't physically able enough to use the Career Transition Workshop to gain a new practical skill or qualification. Instead, I opted to attend university and make amends for my childhood mistakes. I left the Army in the August and started university in the September, studying Contemporary Military and International History. Looking back, this course and the intense study that is required for a history degree helped me in keeping my suppressed trauma hidden for a short time at least. I was completely focused on my studies and similar to what I had done to cope during my military career, I buried myself in all aspects of my studies and this allowed me to distract my subconscious and my inner demons and keep them at bay.

It was at university where I would become good friends with Chris. On our induction, I had instantly noticed that Chris was also a veteran as he was carrying a Help for Heroes backpack, the type that only injured veterans are given. We would later laugh and joke about how nervous we both were at starting university, despite both serving in Iraq and Afghanistan. Chris was very open about his ongoing struggle with PTSD and this was made obvious by his anxious demeanour. Despite not serving together, from different Regiments and the fact that he was an officer, we formed a close bond; the bond that only veterans have – built on a foundation of dark humour and childish jokes!

Chris would frequently-self-medicate with-alcohol as a primary coping mechanism when battling his own inner demons. In the final days of his life, he would also turn to illicit drugs in a deadly attempt to help him to forget about his own experiences of warfare. Chris, like the majority of my generation who served in Iraq and Afghanistan, was struggling daily with survivor's guilt. We had witnessed far too many of our friends and comrades being severely injured or fatally wounded. We had seen ethnic cleansing, first-hand, and unspeakable atrocities to civilians and our inner demons provided us with a daily reminder of this. Like many commanders from my generation, Chris would continuously re-enact his operational decisions and battlefield experiences in his mind but through the unproductive channel of hindsight. We shared some very philosophical conversations about the very nature of warfare and the naive romantic ideological notion that first attracted us to the Armed Forces compared to the cruel bitter reality that we both had endured.

We had both been commanders and had shared similar battlefield experiences and through this, our friendship was forged. I had not been diagnosed with PTSD at the time, but by sharing his own trauma, Chris was helping me realise that I too needed help and for this realisation, I will always be grateful. Personally, I had always asked myself the following questions when analysing my own survivors' guilt: Could I have done more? Did I make the right decision? Are these deaths my fault? Am I a murderer? Am I to blame? We both shared similar burdens and Chris once asked me if he had been at fault; did he make the right decisions? I had always had the outlook that you can never fairly judge another low-level commander's tactical decisions in battle as we often had to make impossible decisions on the spot. Besides, we were encouraged from our leadership training to impose our own traits and experiences onto our planning which made us all unique and difficult to predict.

Fortunately, though, I had been asked a similar question by a younger commander after the War in Iraq in 2003 and I provided Chris with a comparable reply. You can plan and train as much as you like but regrettably, you have no control over what the enemy are doing. It is inevitable that soldiers will get injured, soldiers will die and that is why the best-laid plans go to shit when the bullets and bombs start flying. The enemy, especially in counter-insurgency warfare, are sneaky bastards and quickly evolve tactically. All you can do is react to the situation and that's all that matters. There are no right or wrong decisions; it's greyer and more complex - it's just warfare!

As a commander, you have to accept that all soldiers, including your men, are expendable. Personally, like Chris, my sole responsibility was always to my men and this is why he significantly struggled with his own mental health. He was blown out of his vehicle and unable to command his men and blamed himself for the actions of the enemy and his lack of anticipation of their intent on the battlefield. Chris was not at fault, the enemy were, but regardless of how many drunken conversations we had on the subject, it was Chris's inner guilt which had manifested into PTSD that would ultimately result in his tragic and untimely death.

I was aware that Chris's self-medication with alcohol was a problem, and this wasn't for me to judge. His deteriorating mental health, continual suicide attempts and subsequent hospital admissions, alongside his inconsistent mental health care, had led to his discharge. I always thought that if he was going to get wasted, then at least if I was with him, I could keep an eye on him. Chris was financially ok, but like me, wanted the Ministry of Defence, the Government to acknowledge the depths of his injury and the devastating impact that it had had on his career, his wife, his family, his perceived identity, his whole life. He was a shadow of his former self and would question the severity of his PTSD due to the Armed

Forces Compensation Scheme denying him the compensation level that warranted his trauma. He desperately sought the validation that the Army believed him, that they would acknowledge how severe his mental health had become. That validation could only come from the compensation as it had not come from anywhere else. He was a soldier, after all, and we are trained to follow orders, to be obedient and these bureaucrats exploited this.

Chris's battle with his mental health, self-medicating and inconsistent mental health care would eventually take its toll and he would die of the physical effects of an enlarged heart, aged just 35, another victim of war. He had previously told me that after several attempts to take his own life, he now was in control of his mental health and that he was going to look after his body. I genuinely believed him when he went into the details about how he had regretted his latest suicide attempt. After the paramedics revived him, he told me that his latest brush with death had given him a real will to live and I was proud of him. This was the last time I spoke to Chris and two months later he died...another preventable victim as a consequence of the lack of post-service mental health support for our veterans. Chris was, in my opinion, an unintentional suicide due to his deteriorating mental health. He had symptoms and was treated for atrial fibrillation, but this was never explored fully by medical professionals and he wasn't able to prioritise his physical health due to his PTSD, his nightmares, his internal demons.

At the request of his family, Chris would have a full military funeral. At his service, I could not help but think, where was the support from his Regiment when he needed it? Where was this church full of uniformed soldiers in their best regalia when Chris needed them? Where was the support from the Government that sent him to war? At the wake, in a drunken emotional state, I flung my medals across the dance floor as I had become annoyed with strangers praising me for my service, my sacrifices on the basis that I had a chest full of accolades. My medals had always meant more to other people than myself and I had always believed that the medal(s) don't necessarily make the man, rather the man makes the medal(s). These were a reminder of my sacrifices, my own struggles and a system that was failing its veterans. Also, with my own inner demons becoming increasingly more difficult to suppress, I was struggling to process Chris's preventable death.

A female major eventually found my medals and attempted to give them to me, and I remember being very disrespectful and quite frankly a dick in return! I didn't want them as these were just a reminder of my guilt and the internal battles that I was having within my own mind. Thankfully, she distracted me long enough with several Jägerbombs and slipped them into my jacket pocket. When I mentioned this to Niall, he was appalled! Niall has a completely different outlook regarding our medals. I perceived these material items as nothing more than an unwanted reminder of the horrors of war, whereas Niall had a more philosophical outlook. Niall was proud of his medals, his service, and the sacrifices of our brethren, particularly those who made the ultimate sacrifice and didn't come home. Niall proudly wears his medals to honour the fallen, our brothers who gave their all. I respect his views regarding our medals, but as a result of how our veterans are disregarded by the Government, our opinions still continue to differ.

After the funeral, Chris's father described his son's death as 'unnecessary' and claimed that Britain's Armed Forces had 'discarded' their responsibilities by failing to properly help their veterans. This was 2017 and not much has changed since. Chris's first suicide attempt was in December 2011 whilst he was still serving, and the Army's mental health support was lacking and ultimately swept it under the carpet. After his mental health deteriorated to another crisis point, he was passed from one mental health practitioner to the next, totalling 13 in one single year. This lack of continuity regarding his mental health care while he was still a serving member of the British Army only further exacerbated his intense battlefield trauma. After his medical discharge, Chris was cast into the NHS system that was ill-equipped to deal with the complexity of his PTSD. Even charities such as Combat Stress could not provide a program of support to treat or help him due to a lack of resources. I unequivocally believe that it was the lack of adequate Governmental aftercare that failed Chris and I cannot help but feel that I also failed him as a friend, as a brother. Not even the trauma of Chris's death would make me acknowledge that I was also suffering with PTSD. If this ordeal wouldn't make me seek help, then what would?

Whilst I was a serving soldier, the death of former colleagues, my brothers, became an increasingly normal occurrence and was accepted but ignored. I can recall numerous accounts of Guardsmen from my former Regiment taking their own lives and, as tragic as this was, we subconsciously chose to ignore this. Whilst serving, you are in a bubble, a false economy, and this creates a world within a world, even more so in a Regiment or Battalion. When you are part of this, you inevitably become engrossed in what is referred to as 'Battalion life.'

I must point out that we were institutionalised and believed that this routine, this subculture kept us safe, but once soldiers left the Battalion, they quickly became an afterthought. As a result of this mentality, you can easily shut yourself off and segregate yourself from the outside world. I personally did this, and this helped me to ignore the struggles and dangers that the veterans' community were facing. No serving soldier would honestly like to admit to themselves that there is no sufficient aftercare on discharge. Why would they? How could they justify their sacrifices and unwavering loyalty towards the British Army's needs if this loyalty wasn't reciprocated in return?

The preventable death of my friend Chris had shaken my confidence to its very limits and, more so, my loyalty to my country. I had chosen to ignore the ongoing pandemic of veteran suicides as I was struggling to contain my own inner daemons. I was fearful that if I let the genie out of the bottle and faced the two decades of suppressed emotions, that I too could become another statistic, another veteran suicide. I loved my family; they were my only priority, so rather than seeking help, my unhealthy and irrational logic concluded that it was better to try and keep my own battlefield trauma unproductively suppressed. I subconsciously knew that I was a ticking timebomb and kept telling myself that I wasn't weak, but I was conflicted as I felt like I was about to explode!

Chapter 17.
Manchester Arena Bombing

Family has always been important to me. I enjoy nothing more than a fun-filled day out with my family, close friends, and their children. I am quite fortunate that my daughter has cousins who are the same age and I love it when they all get together and bond. However, I think most children today are spoilt; they receive far too many material gifts for birthdays and Christmas. These gifts (often crap) just accumulate around the house and often find their way to charity shops. Bearing this in mind, for the Christmas of 2016, I had decided to buy all of the kid's tickets to see the 'Marvel Live' show at the Manchester Arena early in the following New Year. The tickets were not cheap, and I could have saved myself a small fortune in buying the traditional crap, but I secretly wanted to see the show and used these gifts as a plausible excuse to do just that.

On the train to the arena, it was obvious who was going to see the show as all the kids were dressed as their favourite superheroes and even some of the adults. Since leaving the Army, I wasn't particularly fond of crowded places and avoided them where possible. I was also conscious about my limited mobility and was vain about needing the use of a cane to walk. However, this was about the kids having a fun day out, so I told myself to 'man up' and just deal with it. As we approached the Manchester Arena, I found myself becoming nauseous and anxious due to the intensity of the crowd.

This was early afternoon on a family day out, yet I headed straight for the nearest bar and downed two quick pints before the show.

This was the first time that I can recall that I had consciously realised that I used alcohol as a coping mechanism for my inner demons. The use of alcohol had enabled me to relax. I wasn't anxious any longer and was under the misconception that I was in control of my emotions, my hidden trauma. I was now able to enjoy the show and the show didn't disappoint either with both the adults and the kids thoroughly enjoying themselves. This was, of course, until the show finished, and we were herded out like cattle, or in my mind, cattle to the slaughterhouse!

None of my family or friends knew that I was suffering with emotional trauma from my battlefield experiences, although I had suspected that Jayne had her suspicions. Since leaving the Army, I hadn't felt the same as I had become more self-aware about my actions and feelings and I knew that they were not healthy. I knew that something wasn't quite right with me but was still ashamed to admit it. Now, on leaving the Manchester Arena, it immediately became apparent that I needed help. The tight concourse leading to the exits instantly became rammed, none of us could move and I felt trapped, as if I was pinned down by enemy fire! My heart began to race, and I was having flashbacks from my battlefield experiences. I needed to get out of here...NOW!

The kids were starting to get crushed and by focusing on their immediate welfare, I was able to prevent myself from being consumed by a full-on panic attack. I could feel my adrenaline kick in, I became numb, focused and driven. I was now a soldier again; I was now Colour Sergeant Watson! I was anticipating countless negative thoughts of what could occur in a potential terror attack scenario. My daughter was a toddler and in distress, so I put her on my shoulders ignoring the immense pain that this caused. 'Pain was weakness and was to be ignored,' all that was important to me now was the mission and that was the hard extraction of my team. I was taken over by my own superhero identity and was able to aggressively lead 'my men', my family, through this static crowd and out of what I had perceived as the killing zone to safety.

Once in a place of safety and away from the masses of other spectators, I tried to relax, and we discussed what had happened amongst ourselves. The kids finally stopped crying and the adults joked about how I went 'full-on Army' to get us out of there. I joined in the bravado, but my heart was still pounding, and I could hear noises, bangs and explosions, unwanted reminders of warfare. My heart was still beating rapidly, and I used my daughter's distress as an excuse to return to base - sorry, I mean to my home. I was having trouble differentiating past memories from my current reality and was now very concerned. I remembered the panic attack that I had had all those years ago and endeavoured to compare the two. The difference this time was that I now had a daughter, and as such, I didn't allow myself to be consumed by it. I was still in control; I had this. I was ok, or were these just excuses to avoid getting help, to avoid being weak?!

Once home, I was finally able to relax and became light-headed. My adrenaline had worn off as my daughter was now safe. My mission was over. Jayne knew that something had happened, and this was the first time that I spoke openly to anyone about my deteriorating mental health. In a paradoxical way, my suppressed emotions from Kosovo, Iraq and Afghanistan had manifested into further trauma as I was now traumatised by the poorly managed exiting strategy from this show. This was true inception! I explained to Jayne how I had become paranoid about a terror attack taking place as we exited. She was aware that I already hated going to shopping centres, or any built-up area with crowds, for that matter, as a result of my hyper-vigilance. I had always brushed this off as a consequence of twenty years' service and old habits, but this is also associated with a common symptom of PTSD. This was completely different though, due to my panic attack; I genuinely believed that we were going to be targeted. It felt real and I was afraid!

Jayne listened as I explained how, from a terrorist planning perspective, it would be extremely easy to exploit the flaws in the exiting strategy from the Manchester Arena. I explained that this strategy, along with the layout of the building, channelled the masses of spectators out into a designated 'killing zone' and these were perfect for a mass casualty attack; chemical, bomb or multi-weapon shoot, maybe even all three. I couldn't help but think that I was being paranoid when saying this out loud to Jayne. I certainly felt so! I now knew that I wasn't thinking straight and that I may be suffering with 'slight' PTSD. Jayne suggested that I seek professional help to which my defensive reply was 'I'm talking to you about this, and that is helping'.

This is the preferred excuse that all veterans give when questioned about seeking help for their poor mental health and this may be a short-term fix, but it is far more harmful in the long term. I thanked Jayne for listening and 'helping me' and she was pleased that I had opened up to her about my feelings. I had always struggled to be open about my emotions, even with my wife and daughter, and I categorically believe that this was a direct consequence of how we were trained. How can emotionless killing machines have feelings?

Wouldn't this compromise the needs of the Army, especially the Infantry? I was coming round to the acceptance that I may be actually suffering with PTSD. I understood that sharing my feelings and emotions had helped me cope with my new trauma, but I still felt shame, weakness. Regardless, I had a dissertation to prepare, so yet again, I buried these feelings and exclusively focused on my studies. What's the worst that could happen?

Three months after my near panic attack, the unthinkable happened; an actual terror attack occurred at the Manchester Arena! I was playing an online fantasy game with some of my friends at the time when one of them insisted that we stop to watch the news. He informed the group that a bomb had been detonated in the city centre of Manchester. I immediately thought about the Manchester bombing from 1996 by the IRA and wasn't immediately concerned. However, that morning, my wife, and daughter had travelled to London to visit the Natural History Museum and were staying with friends. As the details started to emerge, I began to have a panic attack and I needed to be with my family, I needed them to be safe.

I had studied terrorism and asymmetric warfare in an academic capacity at university. I had even highlighted the evolution of traditional regional terrorism such as the IRA to the global centric Al-Qaeda. Historically, the IRA wanted a lot of people watching through media coverage but not a lot of people hurt. The 1996 Manchester bombing was an excellent example of this due to the fact that the IRA had a long-term political agenda and even had its own political party, Sinn Fein. As a result of this, there was always the risk of political fallout and the loss of credibility and public support, which is why they generally targeted the Armed Forces and politicians for assassination. Global terrorism was different, though, especially Islamist extremists. There was no political rhetoric, just a religious crusade, a jihad where all non-believers, even children, were categorised as legitimate targets.

There was a pattern with Islamic terror attacks and follow-up secondary attacks are a frequent occurrence. Jihadists often inspired other Jihadists and my family were in London which was potentially a prime hotspot for this secondary attack to occur. I spoke to Jayne that Monday evening and urged her to come home but she was defiant that she was not going to let the terrorists win and succumb to fear. Naturally, this was not what I wanted to hear as I just wanted them home, safe! Jayne was insistent that her plans wouldn't change and that they would still be going to several public attractions in the capital, completely disregarding my rational and real concerns.

That night, I didn't sleep. I painfully watched the events unfold in real time live on the news. The following day, I felt helpless, lost, and numb. I needed my family home and was constantly checking in with their progress. The following night, again I didn't sleep. I had now been awake for two days straight, something I had not done since the War in Iraq in 2003. Now, everything was merging into one. My mind was playing tricks on me and I was experiencing flashbacks from my battlefield experiences from years earlier. I felt confused, sad, and alone but with a consuming sense of guilt. What crimes had I done? Where had this guilt manifested from? I was asking questions to which I didn't have the answers, yet I felt like a criminal and convinced myself that I deserved to be punished.

I was now in a phased state of mind. My only focus, and my priority, was seeing my family safely home. My negative and harmful thoughts were devastating me, and I felt like an empty shell. I was going to a very dark place, but it was for the love that I have for my family and their concern that kept me driven, focused. I was now facing my internal demons, my guilt. It was feeding off the Manchester Arena bombing and had almost completely overwhelmed me, but I had somehow managed to fight them off. I would have to let these demons put me on trial at a later date once I knew that my family were home safe.

That Wednesday night, Jayne informed me that they had completed their sightseeing and were finally safe at our friends' house and that they would be driving home the following morning. Finally, I could partially relax, but I didn't want to. I was conscious that I was no longer able to suppress my battlefield guilt and this was something that I was afraid to face. I was still struggling to admit to myself that I was obviously suffering with PTSD. I had never perceived myself as a failure but now this is what I convinced myself that I was. I had failed at being a soldier due to my injury, I had failed my men due to not recognising the signs of their deteriorating mental health and PTSD, I had failed the victims of this terror attack and now I had failed my family as they were not with me, safe.

That night, I don't think that I really slept, and my mind was at a war within itself but on several different fronts. I was still ashamed to admit that I had succumbed to my poor mental health as I was not weak! Therefore, in an attempt to disguise this from myself and family, I would use the trauma of the horrific Manchester bombing as a subconscious tool of misdirection. My battlefield guilt had evolved into the exclusive accountability of this unthinkable terror attack. I now fundamentally believed that I was responsible for this terror attack at the Ariana Grande concert that killed 22 civilians, mainly children. My mental health was so bad that I would rather take responsibility for the death of 22 children than admit that I was suffering with PTSD from my military service.

Even when writing this or speaking to my military brothers about my ongoing battles with my mental health, I can acknowledge how ridiculous it sounds. Then, like a paradox, part of me still feels responsible and I will always carry this guilt. In my experience, Military PTSD cannot be cured but it can be managed with the correct treatment. I had been suffering for over twenty years and for the majority of that time, alone, in silence. Then, when you analyse how little regard is allocated towards mental health awarded on discharge and the non-existent aftercare by the Ministry of Defence, one could quite easily conclude that the lack of Governmental support for our veterans is beyond negligent.

One should never play the 'what if' game through the luxury of retrospective knowledge as we always focus on the positive outcomes. After all, we like to believe that we are all heroes in our own stories. However, I am still haunted by my lack of action in raising my concerns about the exiting policy from the Manchester Arena. I tell myself that I should have had the courage to overcome my shame and PTSD. I should have spoken to someone regarding spectator safety and maybe this could have prevented the terror attack or, at the very least, reduced the number of casualties. Then, I think about what my late Grandfather said to me when discussing the death of a friend. He wisely suggested that, 'Yes, I could have helped, but then, on the other hand, I could have quite easily made things a hell of a lot worse.' Regarding my own mental health, I cannot rationalise my own thoughts and emotions and as a result, I will always carry this unwanted 'what if'.

When my family returned home, I was in a zombie-like state but finally allowed myself to rest and Jayne was naturally concerned about my mental health. On the plus side, I hadn't experienced any physical pain from my back or legs as I had become completely shut off, numb. In the following days and after several nights' restless but better sleep, Jayne asked me to open up about what was going on with me. I couldn't hide anymore but I was still ashamed at admitting that I was weak, a failure.

I still lacked the moral courage to be honest with my wife. Jayne had known me since I was a teenager and knew me better than I knew myself. It was time to come clean and be honest or as honest as my shame would allow. I explained to Jayne that I had been engulfed with guilt over the recent bombing; that I felt responsible for this terror attack. She knew about the incident (not the panic attack) a few months prior at the 'Marvel Live' show, but my mental health had deteriorated significantly since then. I secretly knew that I felt guilty for other reasons, from my experiences in Iraq and believed that somehow these actions had created a butterfly effect that had culminated with the Manchester Arena bombing. I kept this from Jayne, and, to stop her probing any further, I admitted that I needed professional help, that I was broken.

I must stress that I had now convinced myself that I didn't have PTSD and that I was simply traumatised from the Arena bombing and being separated from my family. This was the narrative that I sold to myself as even now, I was still in denial and attempting to suppress my military trauma which was showing blatant signs that are associated with PTSD. My first point of call was the charity Combat Stress. These charities are generally regionally based and as a result, they were inundated with veterans in the immediate aftermath of the Manchester Arena bombing. Consequently, it would be eight weeks before I was assessed, and I would use my studies as a welcomed distraction.

My initial assessment took place at the Royal British Legion office in the centre of Manchester and attending this was a psychological challenge in itself. It was the first time I had visited the city centre since the bombing, and this had made me even more anxious. The assessment was conducted more like an informal interview or a simple conversation, but I was very defensive from the start. Before my assessment had begun, my first words were, 'I don't have PTSD!' as I felt very defensive about sharing my feelings with a stranger, a civilian. It was easier to talk to my brethren, or, at a push, Jayne, but I was only here for the benefit of my family, so I had to make the effort. (Even if that was minimal).

As a former welfare officer, I had witnessed the damaging effects of untreated PTSD tear families apart and I was determined that this would not happen to my own family. Yet, my first words were ones of denial. I then stated that other veterans needed this charity support more than I did and that I was managing ok. After all, this is what my military therapist had said in the weeks before my discharge, so who was I to argue? I was still following orders and the more this psychiatrist probed, the more I denied or avoided the questions. I was still trying to avoid the real issues and I suspect that she saw right through me and that I was struggling. In fact, I was almost defeated; I was close to the end.

By the time that Combat Stress got back to me, I was already in my third year at university. I had drafted my dissertation that summer and this had allowed me to suppress my emotions, my ongoing battle with my PTSD, through the use of my academic study. Combat Stress had concluded that I needed treatment, but they had nothing available in the foreseeable future due to the high demand and lack of facilities and funding. They did, however, have a place at a two-week anger management course later on in the year in northern Scotland. The irony is that this offer made me angry. Due to my ongoing studies and issues surrounding childcare, I calmly gave this course a pass. Besides, other veterans would benefit from it more than I would, and I was still denying that I was even struggling with poor mental health.

Jayne was understanding about the pressures of what Combat Stress were undergoing - a charity that was established to help veterans with their hidden wounds, their demons, their battlefield trauma. Yet again, I asked the question, where was the support from the Government? Jayne wouldn't let me go untreated and as a nurse, had been made aware of the Military Veterans' Service, part of the Pennine NHS Trust. I reluctantly applied and was very pessimistic about the outcome.

Yet again, I went through another psychological assessment and was even more defensive now. From my perspective, I needed help six months ago and I was now fine. The closer I was getting to any type of help, the more I was subconsciously pushing back. I didn't want to face my demons, my fears, my regrets. I had repeatedly tried to convince myself that I was fine and that I was managing. I recall being slightly surprised when the Military Veterans' Service offered me weekly sessions with a therapist, to start immediately. This is where the toughest and most intense battle of my life would occur, the one deep within myself. I would have to face my inner demons and acknowledge my PTSD, but more so, the shame of accepting that I was weak.

My weekly sessions were conducted at a centre for drug and alcohol addicts in the centre of Wigan. This set off several red flags as this environment was not a healthy setting for those who also had poor mental health. I had never had any drug or alcohol dependency issues, yet this setting made me uncomfortable as soon as I entered as it was not suitable for those more easily swayed. I explained this to my therapist, Barry, and he agreed but unfortunately, this was the only building where he could get an office to use. Once the introductions were out of the way, my first words were yet again, 'I don't have PTSD'. Even now, I was still in denial and too ashamed to admit that I had been and was suffering with my mental health.

My first session in therapy was more like a psychological sparring match. Barry was attacking me with unwanted questions, and I was blocking and evading, giving him half-truths as answers. I didn't really want to be there and didn't feel comfortable telling anyone, let alone a stranger, my most personal and intimate feelings. Besides, Barry was a civilian - he wouldn't understand; how could he? He hadn't experienced the brutal realities of warfare. The following sessions followed this pattern. Barry would probe and I would avoid and distract. I would use our personal love of football or my studies to start conversations to take up my hour-long slot of therapy. Then one day, Barry asked me, 'Why are you here?' and it finally dawned on me that I couldn't honestly answer - I didn't know!

The following week, I thought about this question and why I was in therapy. I couldn't be honest with myself, let alone Barry. What was my aim, my endgame? At our next session, I informed Barry that I was here for the welfare of my family. My wife Jayne and daughter Mara were my whole life, and I was terrified that my deteriorating mental health would tear us apart. Hence, this was the reason why I was still in denial about its very existence. I had finally admitted to someone that I was suffering with battlefield trauma but was insistent that I was only slightly suffering, and at the lowest possible levels.

Barry would try a combination of different exercises and therapies to help me unlock my suppressed trauma. I found cognitive behavioural therapy useful in understanding my trauma and acceptance and commitment therapy in accepting my battlefield exploits. However, I still wasn't fully engaging with Barry and continued to hold back. Part of me still felt that shame, failure, and weakness at becoming overwhelmed by these emotions. Then came Chris's death and funeral and something just gave way. We had shared similar experiences from Iraq and Afghanistan and we both had survivors' guilt. I understood his mindset and had witnessed his rapid decline. If this could happen to Chris, then this could most certainly happen to me.

Chris's death had provided me with the realisation that in order to save my family, I would have to start by saving myself. This had to begin by confronting and overcoming my shame and accepting that emotions are not weakness, but in fact, for the most part, strength. This was painful and difficult to pursue but I gradually began to fully engage with my Barry. I fully opened up to him about the morgue in Kosovo and the airstrike in Iraq. I explained how I felt responsible for the sanity of my men in Iraq and that due to the notion of 'the illegal War' that I had lost my way, lost my moral compass. We discussed how I had unhealthily linked Iraq to the Ariana Grande concert bombing and my unhealthy self-imposed burden of accountability and responsibility. Personally, for me, it was more about understanding and accepting the consequences of warfare rather than pointing the finger of blame.

Now that I was making progress with my therapist, we moved onto Eye Movement Desensitisation Reprogramming (EMDR). This type of technique is designed to make you change your perception of past events and trauma. This was very weird and, if I am being completely honest, I didn't really commit to it. I don't know whether this was due to the environment as I was never relaxed or comfortable there. Every time I walked into the building, it was a reminder of how far and rapidly Chris's mental health had declined. Plus, the chairs were really uncomfortable, and my back would go into constant spasm which would break my concentration and that didn't help.

I had now accepted that all of the ethnic cleansing in Kosovo was not my fault and that I couldn't have done more to save all of those poor souls in the morgue. I had accepted that just by reporting the incoming fire from that village in Iraq and the subsequent airstrike that followed, it was not my fault. I had accepted that I was a pawn in a much larger game of combat chess where the enemy does not abide by the rules. For the most part, warfare evolves as you move forward due to the unpredictable nature of the enemy and the ever-changing tactics and strategies. As such, our training was always amended to reflect this, however, there will never be any adequate training that can prepare soldiers for the darker side of warfare and the inevitable unjust deaths and mutilations of civilians, most of whom, unfortunately, tend to be women and children. These are often referred to as 'casualties of war', 'collateral damage', a horrific acceptance by our political leaders of the consequences of war. I, however, refer to it as the darker side of warfare as no amount of behavioural training can prepare you to psychologically process it.

Therapy is painful and those who accept that they have internal issues and seek help are unmistakably brave. Initially, when therapy was suggested by Jayne, I would rather have run directly into enemy fire than seek help for my deteriorating mental health. When accumulating all of the dangerous experiences that I had encountered on the battlefield in comparison to accepting that I needed help for my emotions, there is only one winner. During my six operational tours, I had encountered many difficult situations that some may consider took immense courage to overcome. However, my most difficult and painful act was seeking out help, being honest and admitting to myself that I needed professional treatment, help for my suppressed emotions that were destroying me from the inside and overcoming my conditioned outlook that I was 'weak'.

After every session, I vividly remember that I was emotionally and physically drained and I was fortunate that my wife was supportive and understanding. I would painfully discuss my sessions with her and wouldn't hold anything back. I had never spoken about my battlefield experiences with her before, and I was quite surprised that she didn't pack up her bags and leave! It was the love and support that Jayne provided which enabled me to brave the storm. I never missed a session with Barry although I thought about it on many occasions. From a military perspective and from personal experience, therapy is like being under mortar fire in a defensive position. All you can do is take cover in your trench, sit it out and hope that a mortar bomb doesn't get lucky and kill you. Like being under mortar fire, you are unable to fight back and are under relentless attack. For me, this is how therapy felt, and it took all of my courage to continue to keep turning up for our sessions.

Although I had made progress with my therapist by partially opening up, I was never completely truthful with him. We had discussed my childhood in great detail; at the time, I couldn't comprehend why this was applicable, but I now understand the relevance. I had never really opened up about how I failed as a commander in Iraq, how I had failed as a leader, how I failed the men who had entrusted me with their lives. Over the years, within the confines of the Sergeants' Mess, crude jokes would frequently be made about these brave men. How they couldn't take it, how warfare had broken them, how they were weak. Regrettably, not once did I defend them, not once did I share the unsightly collateral damage that we had witnessed and for this I am ashamed.

Then there are the victims of the Ariana Grande Concert at the Manchester Arena bombing to consider. I still feel responsible for not raising my concerns about the exiting strategy. I do not believe that any amount of therapy will ever help me change my outlook on this. Unfortunately, I have accepted this and will always carry around this emotional weight and guilt with me.

The Ministry of Defence would later acknowledge my PTSD under the accepted conditions as between 6-14%. I still don't understand this percentage system or what this means, but the acknowledgement and accountability are what is important to me. Then I think about what it must take to be categorised at a higher level and how bad some of my brethren must be suffering. If I was at the lower end and at my darkest, close to thinking about suicide, then what about those who are considered above 14%, maybe 50%, and so on! I was once told that I lacked empathy and now all I have is excessive amounts of empathy. I now understand the emotional struggles of my brothers (and men in general) and that seeking out help is not weakness, but rather, a strength.

Overall, I was happy with the progress that I had made with therapy and I will always be thankful to Barry as he helped me understand and accept some of my demons. Jayne was pivotal as without her encouragement and support, I would have never engaged with therapy and it was Jayne who had directed me towards the Military Veterans' Service. I do still feel ashamed for not acknowledging the signs of PTSD in my men whilst in Iraq but more so on their return. The signs were right in front of me and I regret not being able to see them. Then, I acknowledge that no training was provided, and mental health awareness back then was non-existent, yet I am still conflicted by this. Likewise, with my guilt from the Manchester Arena bombing. Maybe now, with a little more acceptance of therapy, I should seek out these truths and reach out to Barry and finish what we started for the long-term sustainability of my own mental health.

Chapter 18.
Life After War

With my time at university drawing to a close, I had achieved a first-class honours degree which had surprised everyone, including myself. Whilst at university, I had encouraged and mentored (not groomed) the younger students and was presented with a school ambassador's award for my efforts. I had set up student let study groups, revision sessions and encouraged debate. We had all benefited from the shared knowledge of the group and our differing opinions and this was made evident by all of our high grades. When I started university, my studies had enabled me to suppress my PTSD. Then, through effective therapy, I was able to manage my trauma, but now the real world awaited. It was time to seek out employment, but what?

I graduated in the July, had my medical tribunal in the August and then had surgery to fit a temporary spinal cord stimulator in the September. Employment would have to wait (for now at least). Whilst recovering, I found myself frequently scrolling through social media and it was apparent that the veterans' community was not being heard, in fact, they were being silenced! There had been a media blackout surrounding the military rallies in support of our Northern Ireland Veterans, historic allegations, and their continuous trials. A historic enquiries team had been set up in 2006 and by 2013, all cases from 1968 to the Good Friday Agreement were to be reviewed.[lxxiv] Only British Soldiers were being hunted and the paramilitaries, not even the IRA were avoiding being prosecuted! These rallies would gather momentum under the banner of 'betrayal' and conclude with a series of national rallies the following May with the main focus being in support of 'Soldier F' and his part in the incident commonly known as 'Bloody Sunday'.

I was fortunate not to have been involved in any serious incidents during my two tours of Northern Ireland as these were different times. Yet, part of me was now fearful that I may get a knock on the door and that the Iraq Historic Allegations Team would come after me for my hand in that airstrike. Then again, I was now conscious that I had PTSD and unfortunately, this guilt, this paranoia, this harmful mindset was now part of my life. When reflecting on my therapy and how I had benefited from it, I was more aware of other veterans' welfare and began to acknowledge how many of my brothers were taking their own lives. That year alone (2018), there were 87 military suicides with 62 of these being veterans.[lxxv] Yet again, there was another media blackout regarding this tragedy. This sudden realisation of the lack of Governmental support for our veterans infuriated me. Many, like myself, had given their all for their country and now their cries for help were being purposely silenced and ignored.

I had always tried to be a realist and I was aware that I alone couldn't make a significant impact or influence national policy. What I could do, though, was make a small difference, save just one veteran; but how? I was already active locally within the veterans' community as I was the Vice Chairman of my local branch of the Royal British Legion. I had organised fundraisers and had the support of the local councillors and MPs. Where I live, we were fortunate that our veterans' community had the backing and support from our local politicians, but they didn't really understand us. Maybe if our voices were not being heard from the outside then it was time that someone voiced them from the inside. It was time to get involved in local politics.

I had never fully committed to the ideology of either of the main national parties. The Labour Party had sent me to war then thrown us to the mercy of the mob, and now, the Conservative Party were pursuing our Northern Ireland veterans. Locally, it was all about the impact on your local community and the major political parties were whipped, controlled, and micromanaged so I decided to run as an independent candidate in the next local election. I was fortunate that I am from a large Armed Forces community and that a sitting Councillor was a Royal Navy veteran. Stuart and another sitting Councillor, Jamie, provided me with all the necessary advice to run a winning campaign and I was successfully elected and sworn in on 2nd May 2019. Within hours of being elected, I was writing letters supporting my local veterans' community and making a difference.

In my first act, attending a Health and Social Care Scrutiny Committee meeting, I raised my concerns regarding the aftercare of our veterans, particularly their mental health, PTSD, and suicide numbers.[lxxvi] I was now able to genuinely voice the concerns of the veterans' community rather than use them as a political football, which had previously occurred all too frequently. I had two goals; to diligently represent my electorate to improve my town and to use my platform as a positive voice to improve the welfare of my own veterans' community.

The following week, I had made it into the Manchester Evening News, and as a result I was contacted by a local veteran who was at his end and was contemplating suicide. John had been a military clerk and was subject to a near-death experience in Al Amara, Iraq in 2004 on Op Telic 4. A mortar bomb landed in his place of work and had exploded close by him and this initiated a string of events, fuelled by alcohol misuse, that saw him leave the Army some years later. After this event, his life went drastically downhill as he became dependent on drugs, alcohol, gambling, and any other vice he could find as he shut himself off from the world. John felt worthless and was at the end of this tether. I never thought so, but John was adamant that I saved him when he was at his lowest and this was achieved by simply meeting once a week and listening to his concerns. I did encourage John to return to therapy and aided him with some applications for benefits, but I merely showed him the path. John should be proud of himself as he alone dug himself out of his own rut, whereas all I did was offer him moral support and guidance along the way.

There are so many other veterans whom I have helped in my initial two years as a local politician, but John was the first and deserves a mention. Besides, he has aspirations of paying my help forward and helping other veterans himself, which is easily achievable. I would later use my influence to improve all of my local GP surgeries to be more veteran-friendly through my friendship with another veteran, Simon Carr. After a full and distinguished career in the Royal Artillery, Simon was now employed as a practice manager at a local GP's surgery. Yet again, I did very little and it was Simon who did all of the leg work in ensuring that over 35 other medical practices followed his lead and therefore, all credit must go to him.[lxxvii] Furthermore, I was able to influence the local NHS trust to acknowledge that all musculoskeletal injuries post-discharge may have been caused through service. As a result, veterans in my borough would be fast-tracked to see a consultant, but regrettably, such treatment is a postcode lottery and is, more often than not, personality-led.

When I began this project, I was consumed by anger in the aftermath of yet another veteran suicide, this time a fellow Irish Guardsman. A good friend of mine asked me what I was planning to write about and who the target audience would be, and I honestly couldn't answer as this started out as just a written-down rant. My aim has always been to make a small difference and to hopefully raise some general awareness of what my generation experienced. Ultimately, my goal is to encourage open and honest conversations about mental health, and to help reduce the damaging stigma that is often associated with it. This is not just in soldiers but in the wider society in general, and hopefully, by reading this book, I may inspire and prevent just one suicide. Far too many of my brethren have taken their own lives through the stigma associated with mental health and many of these could have been prevented through open conversations such as these.

It has also been a painful journey of discovery for myself and it has made me aware that I was not fully open and honest with my therapist when I had my breakdown in 2017. As such, I have reluctantly booked myself back in for further treatment since, throughout the process of writing this book, I have found myself zoning out and reverting back to my pre-programmed military default, which is generally aggressive. As alarming as it sounds, I am not the only veteran who feels this way and once integrated back into society, this purposely trained behaviour can often lead to internal struggles which may explain why so many veterans seem to be so angry. What is disturbing, though, is the 9-month waiting list for some one-to-one therapy.

I am not bitter about my service and I am far too insignificant to implement institutional change, but I may be able to start conversations on the subject. There will always be a romantic association between susceptible young people and warfare, as nations will always require soldiers. This is despite the recent reduction in troop numbers and their current reliance on technology and autonomous vehicles. The simple fact of the matter is that there will always be a necessity for boots on the ground and close-quarter fighting. What is fascinating, though, is how the current generation of British Army soldiers are recruited and trained and only time will tell if this is a good thing. My only concern is that you cannot have an Army that is combat-effective and at the same time, one that reflects society's values and standards. This is simply due to the fact that my generation experienced the true nature of warfare over an intense twenty-year period, and consequently, are left with the unwanted psychological and emotional scars as a result.

When it comes to recruit screening, I fundamentally believe that a psychological assessment should be conducted before all trainees are allowed near any type of firearms. Maybe this should be conducted at their recruit selection or at least on their initial military medical when they begin their training as this would go a long way in preventing recruit suicide. In any other organisation or institution, this would not be tolerated, and change would have been implemented long ago. Just imagine if there was a similar trend in recruit suicides in the Police or Fire Service and how quickly policies would change to amend this. Maybe this is because the death of soldiers is institutionally accepted by the Ministry of Defence, the

Government, and by wider society in general. In 2014, the cost of training an adult entry soldier was almost £50,000 with just less than a third of trainees dropping out.[lxxviii] Surely these figures reinforce the argument of pre-psychological assessment, simply as a cost-cutting measure to the treasury? Then again, if my generation had been psychologically screened in such a way, I am certain that many, including myself, would not have been deemed suitable for service.

In recent years, it was welcome news to see that the British Army has changed its marketing strategy to recruit the current generation of soldiers. It is encouraging to see the emphasis being on feelings, but I don't necessarily agree with the mentality of 'it's ok to fail'! For my generation, failure on operations often led to death or serious injury. Training methods have become less intense both physically and mentally with the real emphasis being targeted towards sports recovery and rest. In my day, these were dirty words and every physical fitness session was high intensity and this has had a lasting impact on our bodies. If you even observe a 40 to 60-year-old in the gym, absolutely thrashing himself to within an inch of his life on a regular basis, then I will almost guarantee that he is a veteran.

James Piotrowski was finally diagnosed with PTSD in 2019, and, in a recent interview, described the way that we were trained as being similar to the way one would train a police attack dog. These dogs are kind, approachable and friendly but once the handler pulls on that lead, it instantly becomes highly aggressive. Ski is undoubtedly correct with this comparison, as, through the use of controlled aggression and particularly the very nature of bayonet fighting, my generation of Infantry soldiers were the British Army's attack dogs. The only difference is that you don't let a highly trained police dog back into society when they retire. If they are not adopted by their handler, then they are put to sleep.[lxxix]

This highlights a pertinent point about my generation and the lack of behavioural training that was provided to incorporate us back into society. When you delve into how many veterans become violent after discharge, are arrested, gain criminal records, or like Ski, become frequently imprisoned, it raises many questions. I am a responsible dog owner and I am absolutely certain that there is no such thing as a bad dog, only bad owners. Now, when considering that some of my brethren were loving caring people before they were soldiers and after discharge, they became aggressive and violent, then there has to be some form of accountability. Then, there is the taboo question; why are they like this?

Many 'boy soldiers' from underprivileged and deprived backgrounds, such as myself, had been moulded into soldiers - the very identity and concept of the soldier defined us to our very cores. A lot of effort, cost, time, and training indoctrinated us to ignore our basic predispositions of survival and to disregard our fight or flight subconscious survival instincts. We were conditioned to advance towards that danger instead and to ignore our instincts, our emotions and pain. Then, through behavioural learning such as the Skinnerian Method[lxxx], where we were rewarded for success and punished for failure, we were unknowingly reprogrammed to react, feel, and ultimately become complacent and accustomed to killing.

One must not forget the harmful lasting mental consequences of this behavioural learning that was instilled into my generation of soldiers and this was partly due to the success of the Falklands War. By default, people are not killers, and this was identified by Brigadier General S.L.A. Marshall in 1946. After conducting a series of post-combat interviews with U.S. service personnel, Marshall concluded that only 15 to 20% of the individual riflemen in the European theatre of World War II actually fired their weapons with the intent to kill.[lxxxi] As a result of this lack of combat efficacy, new training methods were introduced. Significantly, the traditional bull's eye for marksmanship training would be replaced with a cut out that resembled another soldier in an attempt to change the behavioural psychology of the soldier. This, for the British Army at least, would be replaced by a human lifelike 'figure 11' target. Then, through repetitive behavioural learning by performing a complex set of voluntary motor actions, shooting to kill became second nature, a reflex, instinctive.

These new training methods, which were reinforced with conditioning through reflexology, proved to be extremely successful in the frequently bloody 1982 Falklands War that was fought at close quarters. British soldiers were outnumbered three to one and, for the most part, were without air and artillery support and would have to rely on their military conditioning and controlled aggression to defeat the well-equipped and well-dug-in Argentine defenders. Richard Holmes, a retired Brigadier, estimates that well over 90% of the British soldiers were shooting to kill and this was a direct result of modern training techniques.[lxxxii] These techniques included reward-based success and punishment for failures, such as point scoring on shooting ranges for quickly shooting targets in the image of other soldiers, reprogramming thousands of years of instinctive human behaviour in the process. Then, as a result of this operational success, just a decade later the British Army would perfect its training methods for my generation where behavioural learning and combat conditioning were mastered.

There is no doubt in my mind that after twenty years' service and six operational tours, my own pre-set and now unfortunate default mentality is 'to kill'. I am fully aware that I was indoctrinated through generational learned battlefield conditioning and behavioural training, but what is the lasting cost to the individual? Who or what is accountable for my generation once we are released back into the civilian world? Surely, one would expect some type of reverse behavioural learning on discharge, or at least some mindful awareness training to help us understand why we feel that it is acceptable to kill another human being? This may explain why so many veterans are angry all the time and often resort to unnecessary violence. Even now, as a civilian, I have no guilt or remorse for any of the enemy soldiers or insurgents that died on the battlefield as my psychological make-up defines them as inhuman! However, no training was ever provided on accepting the true consequences of warfare and that is the darker side, the civilians, and this is where my own internal conflict lies.

Even after the introduction of Trauma Risk Management (TRiM), it was never fully implemented or used to the best effect throughout operational deployments. The high tempo of combat operations and the ongoing manning issues never allowed time for the welfare of our soldiers. Perhaps, if we were deployed for twelve-month cycles like our American cousins, then more emphasis would have been directed at welfare in general, particularly the mental wellbeing of our troops. Personally, I believe that this was partially due to the mentality of the senior commanders' attitudes towards mental health in the 2000s. These soldiers' predecessors had fought and had gained the respect of their peers in the Falklands, and my generation had borne the brunt of the fighting in Iraq and Afghanistan.

Unfortunately for them, they narrowly missed the opportunity to 'prove' themselves in battle as junior commanders and, as such, they only had experience from their own deployments as junior commanders from Northern Ireland.

Don't get me wrong; Northern Ireland was intense and extremely volatile and statistically more lethal than combat operations in the Middle East in terms of fatalities, but the operational pressures were completely different. These pressures would take their toll on all of our psychological make-up, and, as time goes on and I distance myself from my military alter ego, I am slowly regaining my humanity and becoming more in touch with my emotions. This has been harmful to my own mental health as small incidents from my battlefield experience now seem to really upset me, specifically secondary trauma. When I reflect back on all of my friends, buddies, my brethren, who were killed, injured, lost limbs and who, like myself, suffer with their own inner demons, I am consumed by guilt and regret. This is not to be confused with survivors' guilt, but rather, an overwhelming and unwanted bitterness that is directed at the institution that is the British Army. I regret this as I was once a proud and loyal soldier and I don't want to feel this way, yet, I also feel guilty in the way that I played my own part in conditioning and altering the behavioural psychology of the recruits and soldiers under my command. I had chosen the hero's path as a young naïve boy but then, after years of behavioural reprogramming, I inevitably became an unknowing villain by indoctrinating the next generation of soldiers.

Then, once I was injured and no longer combat-effective, my eyes were open to the world of welfare and the charade that it actually was. Don't get me wrong; pre-9/11, the welfare system was fantastic but as soon as the British Army committed to two prolonged counter-insurgency campaigns in Iraq and Afghanistan, the welfare of its soldiers became an afterthought. This was evident from the lack of diligence regarding the correct protocols surrounding Post Operational Stress Management (POSM). My generation experienced the non-existent POSM in the 1990s, particularly in the aftermath of Kosovo where my own mental health began to deteriorate, to the well-run 24-36 hours of decompression in Cyprus. However, I'm still not convinced that the process of relax, reflect, rest and regenerate is actually effective, though, or if this was just another umbrella for the Ministry of Defence.

Personally, I would have preferred to be compulsorily sat down with a therapist to discuss my experiences and this would have helped my own, and I'm sure other soldiers' long-term mental health. The first obvious downside to this is the financial element and second, the cost to manpower as soldiers such as myself, who, without a doubt, would have been categorically deemed unfit for service due to their battlefield trauma. Then there was the sheer neglect of POSM within individual units to consider. My personal experience was that POSM was just a paper exercise that had to be ticked off as yet another umbrella for the Ministry of Defence. The truth is that the operational demands were always prioritised above the welfare of the individual soldiers and this was evident within the individual Companies where they blatantly disregarded the welfare of their soldiers.

As a result of the high-stress working environment, operational deployments, behavioural training, and controlled aggression conditioning, I was only given a psychological assessment once in almost twenty years, where I was found to, in their words, to lack empathy. This really should have raised several red flags as, along with my indoctrination, I was showing signs of sociopathic and psychopathic traits. Yet, I was an experienced, obedient, compliant, and well-respected Infanteer...the perfect killing machine, and this is why I believe that psychological testing was not, and will never be conducted on British Army soldiers. Besides, the Ministry of Defence had spent hundreds of thousands of pounds in training and conditioning me by this point, so why would you conduct a test on a soldier's psyche when you have retrained their behaviour to go against thousands of years of human instinct to begin with? This is why I categorically believe that individual soldiers will never be screened before they join, after operational deployments or at specified stages throughout a full twenty-four-year career.

Meanwhile, there is the pertinent question of why a mandatory psychological assessment on discharge is not enforced. This would go a long way in helping our veterans understand how and why they feel the way they do, but yet again, what would be the cost - not just the financial burden, but the cost of damage to the reputation of the British Army? We are a democratic Army; we rely on volunteers to protect us, young boys and girls from all of our communities; these are our brothers, sisters, wives, husbands, daughters, and sons who join full of optimism but return broken and psychologically damaged. This is mainly due to the years of behavioural learning that unfortunately is very difficult to shake off. Imagine the lasting damage to the British Army's image as well as their recruitment and retainment policy if society were made openly aware of the long-term psychological harm to their sons and daughters as a direct result of their service. Yet again, I ask the question - where is the mental health support and accountability from the Government?

Next, there are those soldiers who are dishonourably discharged to consider. The term 'bringing the Army or Regiment into disrepute' was frequently thrown around when charging soldiers or even dishonourably discharging them. I recall walking through 10 Platoon lines with Bob in 2004, just after we had returned from South Armagh, when we both smelt something fishy! Four young soldiers who had completed two operational deployments in a year were sitting in their room smoking cannabis. Consequently, all four were dishonourably discharged and thrown out of the Army within the week. No questions were ever asked as to why these young boys had turned to drugs in the first place, nor was any consideration given towards their mental wellbeing. Perhaps, like Johno, the cannabis gave these soldiers some form of respite from themselves?

These lads were heroes from the 2003 War in Iraq, but the Army had a zero-tolerance policy regarding drugs and the clean corporate image of the Army was always prioritised. The Army, including myself and Bob, never stopped to ask why they were smoking cannabis or thought to investigate any underlying trauma. Instead, we enforced the rhetoric and fulfilled the British Army's needs like mindless drones. Then, there were the frequent troublemakers who, through drink or violence, were always being charged. One by one, these would inevitably be dishonourably discharged with no questions ever being asked as to why they were reacting in such a way. In retrospect, many of these soldiers were acting out as a coping mechanism for their battlefield experiences as well as the internal struggles that occur after being subject to repetitive behavioural conditioning. Yet again, as an institution, we failed to address the root of the problems and instead found a quick and easy solution...dishonourable discharge. When you are institutionalised, it is easier to follow the narrative and that is exactly what we did.

I used to joke with Frank that I was too mentally strong to be indoctrinated, despite, quite ironically, already being completely conditioned. Well played, Frank, well played indeed. Joking aside, my own discharge hit me immensely hard due to the fact that I was entirely indoctrinated. On my discharge, I was lost and didn't know who I was anymore. Niall describes his discharge as being stripped to his core and he has since joined the reserves, like so many others, to fill that void in his life. Identity and self-perception are important components of the soldier's psyche, and it wasn't until the Manchester Arena bombing that I stopped thinking like one. Yet again, this is where, as part of an individual soldier's resettlement programme, a psychological assessment or mental awareness training would be a valued tool to the long-term mental wellbeing on their return to civilian life. Then again, once you leave the forces, you are an afterthought and the aftercare is minimal.

The aftercare that injured veterans receive on discharge is a postcode lottery and, as such, is a disgrace. Amputees struggle with the management of their stumps and the access to decent prosthetics. Those suffering with PTSD often find themselves waiting for almost 12 months for psychological therapy and some doctors are simply not aware of how to deal with veterans. The Government has allowed my generation to become dependent on military charities for their mental and physical wellbeing which is despicable. Help for Heroes, The Royal British Legion, Combat Stress and SSAFA never sent us to war, the British Government did, so why are they not accountable for our aftercare? With the wars in Iraq and Afghanistan becoming a distant memory, the funding streams of these charities are quickly drying up leaving far too many of my brethren in dire need. This is further exacerbating the damaged relationship that the veterans' community already has with society and is reminiscent of what American society endured in the post-Vietnam era.

Once discharged, the aftercare that our veterans receive is well below par, even scarcer than one would expect for the boys and girls who have sacrificed their health protecting our country. A good example of this is Paddy's story. Paddy stood on what he believes to be a Soviet-era Butterfly Anti-personnel Mine in Afghanistan in November 2009 and was casualty-evacuated by Frank. His right leg below the knee was blown off immediately which is why he is convinced that this was a mine strike and not a conventional IED. He was subsequently medically discharged in 2014 after receiving compensation for his inarguable claim with the Armed Forces Compensation Scheme for his missing limb. However, some four years after discharge, Paddy needed to have his left leg amputated below the knee due to vascular issues that were caused by the additional pressure on that particular leg. This amputation was not a result of the mine blast he suffered in Afghanistan, but it is a direct consequence of his initial injury. Initially, Paddy had received treatment that was second-to-none from the Veterans' Prosthetic Panel and had four prosthetic limbs custom-made for different activities such as running, whereas the NHS would only provide him with one such prosthetic for that particular leg. Paddy is receiving bi-polar treatment and his recovery is shared between the NHS and the Ministry of Defence. Both departments are passing the buck in terms of accountability for these amputations as one happened in service and the other did not. Regardless, Paddy is now a double-leg amputee as a result of his sacrifice in Afghanistan and is receiving inadequate treatment. Also, there is the uphill battle that Paddy is about to face when claiming compensation for his recent amputation as I anticipate that the Armed Forces Compensation Scheme will generically deny accountability.

I have no doubt in my mind that there is a direct link to veterans' suicide and how the Armed Forces Compensation Scheme operates. Personally, I have witnessed this unproductive process destroy people's lives. The scheme is purposely designed to stall, delay, and deter claimants at every opportunity and is purposely disadvantageous towards injured soldiers/veterans. It has exacerbated PTSD in so many veterans (including myself) and has avoidably had a hand in far too many suicides. By failing to accept the depth of my friend Chris's PTSD, this led to fatal and preventable consequences. Furthermore, the process in my opinion is biased as it favours the Ministry of Defence and this is currently destroying Nathan's life and, undoubtedly, many others. The ripple effects of this inadequate scheme reach far and wide as it is never just the individual soldier who suffers; it is also their family and friends, and these are the ones who are left to pick up the pieces.

Then, there is the ongoing pandemic of veterans' suicides in general to discuss; or not, in the case of the British Government. They refused to acknowledge this, and the only people documenting the cases is the Veterans United Against Suicide group. The U.S. government has researched this and has linked military service to an increased risk of suicide in veterans, but the British Government purposely remains coy on the subject and refuses to investigate this current stain on our Armed Forces community. In 2020, suicides in the British Army were at a 15-year high and this is something that the Ministry of Defence actively monitors.[lxxxiii] What is not being recorded is the 161 veteran suicides from 2018-2020 and we need to start having conversations regarding this painful and difficult subject. It is the inadequate aftercare of our veterans that has left me with a bittersweet opinion from my two decades of service to my country. Many of these unfortunate veterans paid the ultimate price from a government and society that has, without doubt, abandoned, betrayed, and rejected them.

A study from 2016 concluded that the rate of suicide among Army males aged 16–19 has been much higher than among civilians of the same age and this cannot be as a result of combat operations due to their age. Thus, it must be correlated to how they were trained - conditioned. Furthermore, on leaving the military, those aged between 16 and 24 years old are between two and three times more likely to kill themselves. [lxxxiv] There are many contributing factors at play here but the way in which British soldiers are trained must not be ignored. This issue will not go away any time soon and the Government needs to get its head out of the sand and become accountable.

I do not blame Tony Blair for his naivety for blindly going to war with Iraq in 2003, however, to this day, I am still appalled at the successive Governments' relentless pursuit of our veterans. The combination of the ongoing pursuit of Northern Ireland veterans, and the investigations into our Iraq veterans is beyond despicable! Where is the persecution and accountability for the political elite? We, as soldiers, put our faith, our trust, our lives, blindingly and foolishly into a fractured society that was polarized by absolute party politics that toyed with our lives for small political gains. Yet, despite recent laws coming into place, such as the Overseas Operations

(Service Personnel and Veterans) Bill,[lxxxv] that should protect our veterans against historic allegations, I remain dubious. However, like many other veterans, I have lost faith in our relationship with society, particularly the Government, and we are mindful that laws and the social acceptance of veterans today can quickly change to support a future, more popular rhetoric. After all, the political elite have, quite frankly, a history of throwing individuals to the wolves at the drop of a hat to avoid any political backlash. This began with Tony Blair's political masterclass when reacting to the public outcry against the lack of weapons of mass destruction in Iraq by simply having the Army take responsibility for his actions. This political sleight of hand immediately damaged our society resulting in a severed relationship between the public and its Armed Forces that will take another generation to fully repair and this will only begin with accountability for the improved welfare of our nation's veterans.

I have so many regrets regarding my time in the British Army, but I do have vast pride in the positive impact that I made within my early career, the pinnacle being in Kosovo. The men with whom I grew into adulthood, particularly in 10 Platoon, became my family. This is much more than a brotherhood, as this was cemented through our shared experiences of warfare. Some of these men considered me like a father figure or big brother. Ironically and quite comically, Pez still refers to me as a father figure despite the fact that I am six months younger than him! I have a genuine love for these men and felt tremendous pride over the years watching many of these men successfully progress through the ranks.

Of the men of 10 Platoon who served together in Kosovo, four of them achieved late entry commissions whereas others achieved Warrant rank which is quite notable. Then there are the other men of 10 Platoon who served in Iraq. It was heart-breaking to witness some of these men being injured in Afghanistan and, even more so, the ones who have suffered with their own mental health over the years. This is a direct consequence of witnessing the true horrors that warfare has to offer, the darker side of combat that no amount of behavioural training can prepare you for. These were both excellent Platoons of equal measure and I could easily write a book about each of their exploits and battlefield experiences. Unfortunately, as a result of military restructuring, Infantry Battalion numbers have been reduced and 10 Platoon, along with Number 4 Company, are no more. This saddens me, as I continue to be immensely proud that I had the privilege of climbing through all of the ranks of 10 Platoon - from the most junior Guardsman to the most senior rank of Platoon Sergeant. I am very much a 10 Platoon soldier before I am an Irish Guardsman, and I will always have unwavering loyalty and admiration for these men that I have the pleasure to serve with.

My military career began with a bombing by the IRA in 1996 in Manchester City Centre and ended with the ISIS Arena bombing in Manchester in 2017. Although I was discharged eighteen months prior to the Ariana Grande concert bombing, I still perceived myself as a soldier and it was this traumatic event that released me from this detrimental mindset. From the outside looking in, I can clearly see the irreparable damage that has been done and is still being done by the Ministry of Defence towards our Armed Forces Community. If I had one wish and I could change just one thing, it would undoubtedly be to improve the mental health treatment of all service leavers: specifically, a psychological decompression assessment on all types of discharge. I fundamentally believe that this would save lives as well as improving the mental well-being of future veterans.

As I previously mentioned, I was initially angry when I started this project in early 2021, but after interviewing so many veterans, my anger quickly turned to sadness. In my day, the British Army was proud to refer to itself as being, 'The Best,' but when it came to the welfare of its soldiers and their aftercare post-discharge, unfortunately, this was far from the case! Sadly, my generation, my brethren, are testament to this, and we are burdened with the psychological scars of warfare every single day and that is the hidden consequence of life after war.

Poems

P.T.S.D

By John M (2020)

Pissed Tramp Stoned Disgusting,

Psychologically Tested.... Shuts Down,

Peace Time Soldiers Digging-in,

Permanent Terrors, Shadows Deluded,

Parties Together, Socially Drained,

Permanent Tears, Stifled Dreams,

Painfully Trapped, Socially Drained,

Politicians, Traitors, Spender's Denying,

Post-Traumatic Stress Disorder.

The Conflict Within

By Kenny (2019)

A soldier goes to war,

They cross that invisible line,

The person that went before is lost forevermore,

Those that return may look the same,

But a part of the brain will never look the same,

They have experienced the darker side of humanity,

Some feel guilt and shame, some feel only pain,

Suicide's dark cloak looks inviting but those left behind take on the pain,

To open up and talk is the game, take control and own the pain,

Rebuild your life and conquer all, you were a soldier, after all.

Life After Death.
By James Paul Watson (May 2021)

I was just a young boy when I was sent to war,

Now, as a grown man, I daily re-live the horrors that I saw.

We were a band of brothers, my friends, my brethren,

Many of my friends paid the ultimate price and now look down on me from heaven.

These days, I am afraid to be left alone with my mind,

As I am afraid of the horrors that I always seem to find.

The smell of death and all the destruction,

Wake me at night and I can no longer function.

Life after war has left me with so much pain,

And after 20 years of warfare, I am no longer the same!

Untiled by Chris
July 2009

The day starts to break without praise, without song.
Even nature is static, not flowing but wrong.
Friends stare through the dark with hardened fixed eyes,
Remembering a friend with whom they had no proper goodbyes.

Time has slowed, almost stopped, to remember this life,
Of someone who fought with their brothers through terror and strife.

Whose soul will live on through our memories, our tales,
Of the soldier not forgotten but immortalised and hailed,

For we carry their soul, their laughter, their voice,
So, the next generation will know their life and their choice.
We that go on will carry their name,
For that, we owe them, the soldiers, the slain.

What Makes a Man

By Dave Phillips

Once your war is over,
Once your rifle's stowed away,
Once you're home safe and alive,
To see another day.

You'll stand tall beside your comrades,
And remember those you've lost,
You'll burst with pride yet deep inside,
Your mind will count the cost.

And you'll bottle those emotions,
You'll lock away the pain,
You'll think it wrong, you're big and strong,
But let me make this plain.

That however strong you think you are,
However broad your shoulder,
First and foremost, you're a man,
And secondly a soldier.

And men are not afraid to weep,
Or make their feelings known,
And if you find it hard to sleep,
You are not alone.

So put your brave face to one side,
Your friends will understand,
It's not bravado, strength nor pride,
But truth that makes a man.

Breathe

By Ember Searson (age15)

In for four,
Hold for seven,
Out for eight,
In for four,
Hold for seven,
Out for eight.

That's what they teach us,
That's what we get taught,
When we break down,
And don't know what to do anymore.

We get told that same ritual,
We get shown that same thing that's unintelligible.

To our minds,
To our bodies,
To the lies we tell ourselves.

To our souls,
To our hearts,
To our thoughts that are kept on dusty bookshelves

In for four,
Hold for seven,
Out for eight,
In for four,
Hold for seven,
Out for eight,
In for four,
Hold for seven,
Out for eight,
In for...

It just doesn't work,
It just keeps on like an endless cycle,
Our minds constantly go berserk,
It's an endless recital.

It's a constant battle,
It's a never-ending race,
Our crooked mind lets out its sick cackle,
And then we're gone without a trace.

And just like that,
We slip into darkness,
Forever waiting for that light,
Until our hope falls flat,
But regardless,
We're stuck in a never-ending headlight.

Of doubt,
Of fear,
Of all that put us down.

In for four,
Hold for seven,
Out for eight,
Maybe just Maybe it may work today.

Generations Apart

By Matthew Greaves

As the smoke and mist began to rise and the clouds drifted apart,
All the guns fell silent, enough to hear the beating of a heart.

Soldiers stood around, amazed they had survived,
Simply staring at each other, astonished they're still alive.

Distant memories of lost friends and family, came flooding through their minds,
Emotions seized as reality, as sorrow swept across mankind.

Wives without their husbands, children to never see their dads,
Girls without their boyfriends, created a nation so angry and sad.

Finally, an end to all the fighting became a joyous thought,
4 years of living through hell, must be the story taught.

Just why had it all started, when there was nothing at all to gain,
Peace had conquered the world, let's hope war is never seen again.

I Once Knew a Boy

By Robert Worthington

A boy, no more no less.
Indifferent to the world, nothing to impress.
Tearful yet excited, treading where thousands had gone before, yearning
to make that difference, the efforts of the war.

He had that life and loved it so, those that didn't, told him not to go. But
that yearning, that loyalty and courage contained within, to do what was
right, to fight and win.

He gave his all, became a man, laid down his life so that others can. His
blood spilled, crimson as the red in the flag he defends, nothing owed
and nothing due, he did his duty because he chooses to.

I knew a boy, that became a man, I know not his name, my shame, the
hero that gave his life for mine and many others the same.

I knew a boy, a man, who was all that I could not be.
Yes, I was a soldier too, but THAT man was a hero, through and
through.

Bibliography

<u>Interviews</u>

- 26th February 2021, Interview with Niall, former Warrant Officer Class II 1st Battalion Irish Guards.

- 05th March 2021, Interview with Anton, former Lance Corporal, 1st Bn Irish Guards.

- 09th March 2021, Interview with Jono, former Ranger, 1st Bn Royal Irish Regiment.

- 20 March 2021, Interview with Tommy, former Colour Sergeant, 1st Battalion Irish Guards.

- 04th March 2021, Interview with Kenny, former Staff Sergeant, Royal Electrical and Mechanical Engineers.

- 09th March 2021, Interview with Soldier 'G', former Warrant Officer Class II, 1st Battalion Irish Guards.

- 20th March 2021, Interview with Paul, former Warrant Officer Class I, 1st Battalion Welsh Guards.

- 21st March 2021, Interview with Stevie, former Lance Corporal, 1st Bn Irish Guards.

- 21st March 2021, Interview with Pez, former Guardsman, 1st Bn Irish Guards.

- 06th April 2021, Interview with Nathan, former Lance Sergeant, 1st Bn Irish Guards.

- 09th April 2021, Interview with John, former Lance Corporal, Adjutants General Corps.

- 12th April 2021, Interview with Soldier 'E', former Warrant Officer Class II, 1st Bn Irish Guards.

- 25th April 2021, Interview with Soldier 'B', serving, Warrant Officer Class I, 1st Bn Irish Guards.

- 27th April 2021, Interview with Paddy, former Piper, 1st Battalion Irish Guards.

- 5th May 2021, Interview with Soldier 'S', serving, Warrant Officer Class II, 1st Bn Grenadier Guards.

Documents

- Personal diary of Guardsman James Paul Watson, Summer of 1999, (Kosovo).
- Op Herrick Tactical Aide Memoire, Edition 7, Sept 2009.
- Sir John Chilcot's, Chilcot Report, The Report of the Iraq Inquiry, 6 July 2016.
- Letter Rycroft to McDonald, 24 March 2003, 'Iraq: Prime Minister's telephone conversation with President Bush, 24 February.'
- Article 1227, IDF and Casualty figures, The Report of the Iraq Inquiry Report of a Committee of Privy Counsellors Volume XI Ordered by the House of Commons, 6 July 2016.
- Article 1194, Phalanx installation no later than 31st May 2007, The Report of the Iraq Inquiry Report of a Committee of Privy Counsellors Volume XI Ordered by the House of Commons, 6 July 2016.

- House of Commons Defence Committee Future Army 2020 Ninth Report of Session 2013–14 Volume II Written evidence Ordered by the House of Commons to be published 29 January 2014.
- Annexe C to Chapter 5 to Part 1 of JSP 770, JSP 770, Tri-service operational and non-operational welfare policy, October 2014.
- Article 2.2.6. Trim, JSP 770, Tri-service operational and non-operation welfare policy, October 2014.
- Overseas Operations (Service Personnel and Veterans) Act 2021, Government Bill, Originated in the House of Commons, session 2019-21.
- House of Commons, BRIEFING PAPER Number 7478, 22 January 2016 Iraq Historic Allegations Team by Arabella Lang.
- THE MANUAL OF THE LAW OF ARMED CONFLICT (JOINT SERVICES PUBLICATION 383), 17 May 2013.
- LAND FORCES STANDING ORDER NO 3209, LIEUTENANT GENERAL SIR NICHOLAS CARTER KCB CBE DSO Commander Land Forces, LAND POST-OPERATIONAL STRESS MANAGEMENT (POSM), April 2014.
- Ill-Health Benefits AFPS 05 Produced by Veterans UK, Revised March 2015

Books

- Hew Strachan, *European Armies, and the Conduct of War* (Routledge 1983).
- THE KING'S ROYAL HUSSARS, *Regimental Journal*, 1999.
- John Newsinger, *British counterinsurgency* (Basingstoke: Palgrave, 2015).
- R Holmes, *Acts of War: The Behaviour of Men in Battle.* (New York: The Free Press, 1985).

- Fergus Greer, *Kosovo: Irish Guards Battlegroup in the Balkans April – June 1999*, (Rosebud Media, Los Angeles, 2001).
- U.S. DoDIPP, *Kosovo International Security Force (KFOR) Handbook*, (DOD-2630-011-99, July 1990).

Journal Articles

- Hendricks, Kate, MD, MPH&TM Anthrax Vaccine Adsorbed (AVA) Safety Studies Since 2008, October 26, 2017.
- Smith, Simon C., 'General Templer and counter-insurgency in Malaya: Hearts and minds, intelligence and propaganda', *Intelligence and National Security*, Autumn 2001, 16/3, pp.60-78.
- Hussain, Asifa., "Careers in the British Armed Forces: A Black African Caribbean Viewpoint." Journal of Black Studies 33, no. 3 (2003).
- N Greenberg, V Langston, N Jones, JR, TRAUMA RISK MANAGEMENT (TRiM) IN THE UK ARMED FORCES Army Med Corps 154(2): 123-126.
- Marisa Cochrane, Iraq Report 12: The Fragmentation of the Sadrist Movement, 2009, the Institute for the Study of War.
- Daniel Marston, 'British Operations in Helmand Afghanistan', *Small Wars*, 2008.

Newspaper Articles

- BBC News, *Kosovo profile – Timeline*, 23 July 2019, (Kosovo profile - Timeline - BBC News).

- BBC News, *Behind the Kosovo crisis*, 12 March 2000, (BBC News | EUROPE | Behind the Kosovo crisis).

- BBC News, *Flashback to 1991 Iraq Revolt*, 2007, (BBC NEWS | World | Middle East | Flashback: the 1991 Iraqi revolt).

- BBC News, 'Higher levels of PTSD among veterans', says study, Lauren Ives, 09 Oct, 2018, 'Higher levels of PTSD among veterans', says study - BBC News.

- BBC News, *Jailed Soldier 'failed by army'*,18 April 2006 (<u>BBC NEWS | England | Jailed soldier 'failed by army'</u>.

- BBC News Online, *Combat Operations end in Iraq*, 28 April 2009, (<u>BBC NEWS | UK | UK mission in Basra: key facts and figures</u>).

- BBC News, *BBC News, Iraq lawyer Phil Shiner struck off over misconduct*, 02 February 2017, (<u>Iraq lawyer Phil Shiner struck off over misconduct - BBC News</u>).

- Birmingham Live, *Jailed thug with PTSD was a ticking timebomb after leaving the army*, 12 Feb 2017, (<u>Jailed rail thug with PTSD was 'ticking timebomb' after leaving the Army - Birmingham Live (birminghammail.co.uk)</u>.

- Daily Mail Online, *Now it's police dogs under fire: Over 84 animals been destroyed in the past three years despite families wanting to adopt them.* 21 September 2013, (<u>The police have destroyed 84 retired working dogs in the past three years | Daily Mail Online</u>).

- The Mail Online, *'David Cameron declares war on witch-hunt lawyers: PM backs Mail campaign to crack down on hounding of brave British soldiers'*, 22 January 2016, (<u>David Cameron declares war on soldier witch-hunt lawyers | Daily Mail Online</u>).

- Manchester Evening News Article, *'Former soldier turned councillor highlights urgent need for mental health support for veterans'*,5 July 2019, (<u>Former soldier turned councillor highlights urgent need for mental health support for veterans - Manchester Evening News</u>).

- Mirror online, *Army Suicides at highest level in 15 years,* (<u>Army suicides at highest level in 15 years as bosses accused of failing troops - Mirror Online</u>).

- Northern Echo, *Army embattled by claims of widespread bullying*, (Army embattled by claims of widespread bullying | The Northern Echo).

- The Guardian, , *Redundancies to civil servants*, 21 January 2012, (MoD pays out £75m to redundant civil servants | Military | The Guardian).

- The Guardian, *James Piatkowski Guardian Interview*, 11 April 2006, ('There was a little girl clinging on to her dead dad screaming her eyes out. We never had time to stop' | UK news | The Guardian).

- The Guardian database, British dead and wounded in Afghanistan. (British dead and wounded in Afghanistan, month by month | News | theguardian.com).

- The Sun, *The faces of Iraqi freedom*, Tom Newton Dunn, Defence Editor in Basra, September 04, 2007, The Sun. The faces of Iraqi freedom (Touching story of heroism, valour and sacrifice by British troops) (freerepublic.com).

- The Times, *Police arrest Iraq veteran in Birmingham*, 20 November 2004, (Police arrest Iraq veteran in Birmingham | The Times).

- The United States Army, *Brits Team with Yanks to Train Iraqi Army*, Spc. Chris McCann, August 2, 2007, Brits Team with Yanks to Train Iraqi Army | Article | The United States Army.
- US News, Troops numbers Middle East, 09 Jan 2020, (After Recent Deployments, How Many U.S. Troops Are in the Middle East? | Elections | US News).

Operational Deaths

- Bacon, Major, 11 September 2005, <u>British Officer killed in Iraq - Major Matthew Bacon - Fatality notice - GOV.UK (www.gov.uk)</u>.

- Casey, Lance Sergeant Chris; Redpath, Lance Corporal Kirk, Operations in Iraq, Armed Forces, Death notice, 10 Aug 2007, <u>Lance Sergeant Chris Casey and Lance Corporal Kirk Redpath killed in Iraq - Fatality notice - GOV.UK (www.gov.uk)</u>.

- Hickey, Sergeant Chris, 20th October 2005, <u>Sergeant Chris Hickey of 1st Battalion the Coldstream Guards killed in Iraq - Fatality notice - GOV.UK (www.gov.uk)</u>.

- Isherwood Suicide report. (<u>House of Commons - Defence - Written Evidence (parliament.uk)</u>.

- <u>Turrington, Fusilier Kelan, Fusilier Kelan Turrington killed in Iraq - Fatality notice - GOV.UK (www.gov.uk)</u>.

- Northern Ireland operational deaths, (<u>Information of servicemen and women's deaths while on operations in Northern Ireland on Op Banner, Iraq and Afghanistan (publishing.service.gov.uk)</u>.

- British Soldiers Killed in Afghanistan, <u>Afghanistan - GOV.UK (www.gov.uk)</u>.

Internet Links

- Wigan Council, Health and Social Care Scrutiny Meeting, 8 Feb 2021, (<u>Agenda for Health and Social Care Scrutiny Committee on Monday, 8th February 2021, 6.00 pm (wigan.gov.uk)</u>.

- U.S. State Department Archive, Ethnic Cleansing Accountability in Kosovo. Ethnic Cleansing in Kosovo: An Accounting (state.gov).
- 1 Sept 2004, Parliamentary debate, Colum 720W, (House of Commons Hansard Written Answers for 1 Sept 2004 (pt 10) (parliament.uk).
- Memorandum from Mrs Lynn Farr, Parliamentary Select Committee House of Commons - Defence - Written Evidence (parliament.uk).
- Suicide rates from the U.S. Army Reserve we page, (U.S. Army Reserve home).
- Coalition deaths by IED, iCasualties.org, Casualties: Iraq Coalition Casualty Count - IED Deaths (archive.org).
- The British Army Recruitment Process, (The Joining Process | British Army - British Army Jobs mod.uk).
- Accused of Murder & War Crimes following the Iraq War with Ex British Soldier Joe McCleary, The Leg It Podcast, (Accused of Murder & War Crimes following the Iraq War with Ex British Soldier Joe McCleary - YouTube).
- Adjacent Disc Syndrome definition, (Adjacent Segment Disease - Causes, Symptoms & Treatment | Bonati).
- Historic Enquiries Team, (Investigation of Former Armed Forces Personnel Who Served in Northern Ireland - House of Commons Library (parliament.uk).
- Behavioural Psychology, Kenneth R. Murray, Lt. Col. Dave Grossman, and Robert W. Kentridge, Killology research group. Behavioural Psychology | killology

Other

- Armed Forces Suicide Figures, taken from the 'Veterans United Against Suicide' group.

Endnotes

[i] Manchester Evening News Article, 'Former soldier turned councillor highlights urgent need for mental health support for veterans',5 July 2019,(Former soldier turned councillor highlights urgent need for mental health support for veterans - Manchester Evening News).

[ii] Health and Social Care Scrutiny Meeting, 8 Feb 2021, (Agenda for Health and Social Care Scrutiny Committee on Monday, 8th February, 2021, 6.00 pm (wigan.gov.uk)).

[iii] Rhianna Louise, Christina Hunter, Sally Zlotowitz, The Recruitment of Children by the UK Armed Forces, 2016, (medact_childrecruitment_17-oct_WEB.pdf).

[iv] Journal of Architectural and Planning Research Vol. 18, No. 4 (Winter, 2001), pp. 325-340.

[v] MacManus, D., Dean, K., Jones, M., et al. (2013). 'Violent offending by UK military personnel deployed to Iraq and Afghanistan: a data linkage cohort study'. The Lancet, 381, pp. 907–917; Marshall, A. D., Panuzio, J., & Taft, C. T. (2005). 'Intimate partner violence among military veterans and active duty servicemen'. Clinical Psychology Review, 25, 862-876.

[vi] Defence Committee Inquiry: Armed forces and veterans mental health Written evidence submitted by Medact, 2016, (Written-evidence-from-Medact-DSC-Mental-health-inquiry-1.pdf).

[vii] Pte Isherwood Suicide report. (House of Commons - Defence - Written Evidence (parliament.uk).

[viii] Catterick Suicides, (Army embattled by claims of widespread bullying | The Northern Echo).

[ix] Northern Ireland Operational Deaths, (Information of service men and women death while on operations in Northern Ireland on Op Banner, Iraq and Afghanistan (publishing.service.gov.uk)

[x] Hew Strachan, *European Armies and the Conduct of War (Routledge 1983), p.43.*

[xi] BBC News, Kosovo profile – Timeline, 23 July 2019, Kosovo profile - Timeline - BBC News

[xii] BBC News, Behind the Kosovo crisis, 12 March, 2000, BBC News | EUROPE | Behind the Kosovo crisis

[xiii] Diary of Guardsman James Paul Watson, Kosovo, June 1999.

[xiv] THE KING'S ROYAL HUSSARS, Regimental Journal, 1999, D Squadron, page 33, KRH COVER SPREAD

xv U.S. State Department Archive, Ethnic Cleansing Accountability in Kosovo. Ethnic Cleansing in Kosovo: An Accounting (state.gov)

xvi Halabja Massacre, 1988, Iraq: UN envoy pays tribute to victims of Halabja chemical weapons attack | | UN News

xvii James Piatkowski Guardian Interview, 11 April 2006,'There was a little girl clinging on to her dead dad screaming her eyes out. We never had time to stop' | UK news | The Guardian

xviii James Piatkowski Guardian Interview, 11 April 2006, ('There was a little girl clinging on to her dead dad screaming her eyes out. We never had time to stop' | UK news | The Guardian.

xix Letter Rycroft to McDonald, 24 March 2003, 'Iraq: Prime Minister's telephone conversation with President Bush, 24 February.'

xx Operation Deaths in Iraq, Fusilier Turrington, Fusilier Kelan Turrington killed in Iraq - Fatality notice - GOV.UK (www.gov.uk).

xxi James Piatkowski Guardian Interview, 11 April 2006, ('There was a little girl clinging on to her dead dad screaming her eyes out. We never had time to stop' | UK news | The Guardian.

xxii BBC News 2007, Flash back to 1991 Iraq Revolt, BBC NEWS | World | Middle East | Flashback: the 1991 Iraqi revolt.

xxiii Paragraph 536, The_Report_of_the_Iraq_Inquiry_-_Executive_Summary.pdf (publishing.service.gov.uk)

xxiv Veterans for Peace UK, July 4 2017,ARTICLE: ARMY AGGRAVATES PROBLEM BEHAVIOURS, ARTICLE: ARMY AGGRAVATES PROBLEM BEHAVIOURS – Veterans For Peace UK (vfpuk.org)

xxvAnthrax Vaccine Adsorbed (AVA) Safety Studies Since 2008, Kate Hendricks, MD, MPH&TM, October 26, 2017, (cdc_57597_DS1.pdf).

xxvi James Piatkowski Guardian Interview, 11 April 2006,'There was a little girl clinging on to her dead dad screaming her eyes out. We never had time to stop' | UK news | The Guardian

xxvii Police arrest Iraq veteran in Birmingham, 20 November 2004,Police arrest Iraq veteran in Birmingham | The Times

xxviii 1 Sept 2004, Parliamentary debate, Colum 720W,House of Commons Hansard Written Answers for 1 Sept 2004 (pt 10) (parliament.uk)

xxix Higher levels of PTSD among veterans', says study, Lauren Ives, 09 Oct ,2018, 'Higher levels of PTSD among veterans', says study - BBC News

xxx Memorandum from Mrs Lynn Farr , Parliamentary Select Committee House of Commons - Defence - Written Evidence (parliament.uk).

[xxxi] James Piatkowski Guardian Interview, 11 April 2006, ('There was a little girl clinging on to her dead dad screaming her eyes out. We never had time to stop' | UK news | The Guardian).

[xxxii] Birmingham Live, 12 Feb 2017, (Jailed rail thug with PTSD was 'ticking timebomb' after leaving the Army - Birmingham Live (birminghammail.co.uk).

[xxxiii] BBC News, 18 April 2006 (BBC NEWS | England | Jailed soldier 'failed by army').

[xxxiv] Death Of Major Bacon, 11 September, 2005, British Officer killed in Iraq - Major Matthew Bacon - Fatality notice - GOV.UK (www.gov.uk).

[xxxv] Death of sergeant Chris Hickey,20th October 2005, Sergeant Chris Hickey of 1st Battalion the Coldstream Guards killed in Iraq - Fatality notice - GOV.UK (www.gov.uk).

[xxxvi] Simon C. Smith, 'General Templer and counter-insurgency in Malaya: Hearts and minds, intelligence and propaganda', *Intelligence and National Security*, Autumn 2001, 16/3, pp.60-78.

[xxxvii] Article 1227, IDF and Casualty figures, The Report of the Iraq Inquiry Report of a Committee of Privy Counsellors Volume XI Ordered by the House of Commons, 6 July 2016,The_Report_of_the_Iraq_Inquiry_-_Volume_XI.pdf (publishing.service.gov.uk).

[xxxviii] Article, 1194, Phalanx instillation no later than 31st May 2007, The Report of the Iraq Inquiry Report of a Committee of Privy Counsellors Volume XI Ordered by the House of Commons, 6 July 2016, The_Report_of_the_Iraq_Inquiry_-_Volume_XI.pdf (publishing.service.gov.uk).

[xxxix] Brits Team with Yanks to Train Iraqi Army
Spc. Chris McCann, August 2, 2007,(Brits Team with Yanks to Train Iraqi Army | Article | The United States Army).

[xl] Suicide rates from the U.S. Army reserve we page, (U.S. Army Reserve home)., VA says veteran suicide rate is 17 per day after change in calculation, Starts and Stripes, 19 September 2019, (VetrVA says veteran suicide rate is 17 per day after change in calculation - U.S. - Stripes).

[xli]The faces of Iraqi freedom, TOM NEWTON DUNN, Defence Editor in Basra, September 04, 2007, The Sun. The faces of Iraqi freedom (Touching story of heroism, valour and sacrifice by British troops) (freerepublic.com).

[xlii] The faces of Iraqi freedom, TOM NEWTON DUNN, Defence Editor in Basra, September 04, 2007, The sun. The faces of Iraqi freedom (Touching story of heroism, valour and sacrifice by British troops) (freerepublic.com).

xliii Operations in Iraq, Armed Forces, Death notice, 10 Aug 2007,Lance Sergeant Chris Casey and Lance Corporal Kirk Redpath killed in Iraq - Fatality notice - GOV.UK (www.gov.uk).

xliv BBC News Online, Combat Operations end in Iraq , 28 April 2009,BBC NEWS | UK | UK mission in Basra: key facts and figures.

xlvCoalition deaths by IED, iCasualties.org, iCasualties: Iraq Coalition Casualty Count - IED Deaths (archive.org).

xlvi Article 2.2.6. Trim, JSP 770, Tri service operational and non-operation welfare policy, October 2014.

xlvii TRAUMA RISK MANAGEMENT (TRiM) IN THE UK ARMED FORCES N Greenberg , V Langston , N Jones, JR Army Med Corps 154(2): 123-126 Layout 1 (kcl.ac.uk).

xlviii TRAUMA RISK MANAGEMENT (TRiM) IN THE UK ARMED FORCES N Greenberg , V Langston , N Jones, JR Army Med Corps 154(2): 123-126 Layout 1 (kcl.ac.uk).

xlix John Newsinger, British counterinsurgency (Basingstoke: Palgrave, 2015), pp. 216-217.

l Iraq Report 12: The Fragmentation of the Sadrist Movement, Marisa Cochrane, 2009, the Institute for the Study of War, Jaysh al-Mahdi | Institute for the Study of War (understandingwar.org).

li Hussain, Asifa. "Careers in the British Armed Forces: A Black African Caribbean Viewpoint." Journal of Black Studies 33, no. 3 (2003).

lii British Soldiers killed in Afghanistan, (Afghanistan - GOV.UK (www.gov.uk).

liiiHouse of Commons Defence Committee Future Army 2020 Ninth Report of Session 2013–14 Volume II Written evidence Ordered by the House of Commons to be published 29 January 2014 Microsoft Word - FINAL Volume 2 Future Army (parliament.uk).

liv The British Army Recruitment Process, The Joining Process | British Army - British Army Jobs (mod.uk)

lv Accused of Murder & War Crimes following the Iraq War with Ex British Soldier Joe McCleary, The Leg It Podcast, (Accused of Murder & War Crimes following the Iraq War with Ex British Soldier Joe McCleary - YouTube).

lvi 02 February 2017, BBC News, Iraq lawyer Phil Shiner struck off over misconduct, Iraq lawyer Phil Shiner struck off over misconduct - BBC News.

lviiHouse of Commons, BRIEFING PAPER Number 7478, 22 January 2016 Iraq Historic Allegations Team By Arabella Lang, (CBP-7478.pdf).

lviii 22 January 2016, Mail Online article, 'David Cameron declares war on witch-hunt lawyers: PM backs Mail campaign to crack down on hounding of brave British soldiers', (David Cameron declares war on soldier witch-hunt lawyers | Daily Mail Online).

lix British Soldiers killed in Afghanistan, Afghanistan - GOV.UK (www.gov.uk).

lx House of Commons Defence Committee Future Army 2020 Ninth Report of Session 2013–14 Volume II Written evidence Ordered by the House of Commons to be published 29 January 2014 Microsoft Word - FINAL Volume 2 Future Army (parliament.uk).

lxi Daniel Marston, 'British Operations in Helmand Afghanistan', *Small Wars*, 2008.

lxii Farrell, Theo, 'Improving in war: Military adaptation and the British in Helmand Province, Afghanistan, 2006-2009', *Journal of Strategic Studies*, 2010, 33/4, pp.567-594.

lxiii John Newsinger, *British Counterinsurgency* (Basingstoke: Palgrave, 2015), pp. 231-231.

lxiv The Guardian database, British dead and wounded in Afghanistan. British dead and wounded in Afghanistan, month by month | News | theguardian.com.

lxv US News, Troops numbers Middle East, 09 Jan 2020, After Recent Deployments, How Many U.S. Troops Are in the Middle East? | Elections | US News.

lxvi British Law of Armed Conflict, JSP 383,The manual of the law of armed conflict: amendments (JSP 383) - GOV.UK (www.gov.uk).

lxvii Sept 2009 edition of the Op Herrick Tactical Aide Memoire, page 1-19.

lxviii British Soldiers killed in Afghanistan, Afghanistan - GOV.UK (www.gov.uk).

lxix Annex C to Chapter 5 to Part 1 of JSP 770, JSP 770, Tri service operational and non-operation welfare policy, October 2014.

lxx Guardian, 21 January 2012, Redundancies to civil servants, MoD pays out £75m to redundant civil servants | Military | The Guardian.

lxxi LAND FORCES STANDING ORDER NO 3209, LIEUTENANT GENERAL SIR NICHOLAS CARTER KCB CBE DSO Commander Land Forces, LAND POST-OPERATIONAL STRESS MANAGEMENT (POSM), April 2014, Land Forces Standing order (LFSO) 3209 Post operations stress management (POSM) (publishing.service.gov.uk).

lxxiiBritish Army Health Benefits 2005,(Ill health benefits - MM127 (publishing.service.gov.uk).

lxxiii Adjacent Disc Syndrome definition, (Adjacent Segment Disease - Causes, Symptoms & Treatment | Bonati).

lxxiv Historic Enquiries Team, (Investigation of Former Armed Forces Personnel Who Served in Northern Ireland - House of Commons Library (parliament.uk).

lxxv 2018 Armed Forces Suicide Figures, taken form the 'Veterans Against Suicide' group.

lxxvi Manchester Evening News, Former soldier turned councillor highlights urgent need for mental health support for veterans, 5 July 2019, (Former soldier turned councillor highlights urgent need for mental health support for veterans - Manchester Evening News).

lxxvii Leigh Journal online, Veteran helps to ensure doctors surgeries look after healthcare needs of ex-servicemen, 30 July 2019, (Veteran helps to ensure doctors surgeries look after healthcare needs of ex-servicemen | Leigh Journal).

lxxviii House of Commons Defence Committee Future Army 2020 Ninth Report of Session 2013–14 Volume II Written evidence Ordered by the House of Commons to be published 29 January 2014 Microsoft Word - FINAL Volume 2 Future Army (parliament.uk).

lxxix Daily Mail Online, Now it's police dogs under fire: Over 84 animals been destroyed in the past three years despite families wanting to adopt them21 September 2013, (The police have destroyed 84 retired working dogs in the past three years | Daily Mail Online).

lxxx Skinner, B. F. (1938). The behavior of organisms: An experimental analysis. New York: Appleton Century Crofts.

lxxxi Behavioural Psychology, Kenneth R. Murray, Lt. Col. Dave Grossman, and Robert W. Kentridge, Killology research group. (Behavioral Psychology | killology).

lxxxii Holmes, R. (1985). Acts of war: The Behaviour of Men in Battle. New York: The Free Press.

lxxxiii Mirror online, Army Suicides at highest level in 15 years, (Army suicides at highest level in 15 years as bosses accused of failing troops - Mirror Online).

lxxxiv Defence Committee Inquiry: Armed forces and veterans mental health Written evidence submitted by Medac, (Written-evidence-from-Medact-DSC-Mental-health-inquiry-1.pdf).

lxxxv Overseas Operations Bill, (Overseas Operations (Service Personnel and Veterans) Bill 2019-21 — UK Parliament).

Printed in Great Britain
by Amazon